EVERY IDLE DREAM

Every Idle Dream

By
BERNARD DARWIN

With Illustrations by
ELINOR DARWIN

COLLINS
ST JAMES'S PLACE LONDON
1948

To

URSULA, ROBIN AND NICOLA

Contents

Contents

Tin Soldiers

IT is right to put away childish things, but we need not put them away for ever. There will surely come a time when we shall love them again, either passionately for their own sake or at least with a gentle, sentimental affection because they bring back all manner of memories. In years of adolescence the game of pretending loses its charm, at any rate in its highest forms ; we so far lose the power of imagination that we need something real to stimulate it ; we can no longer be engine drivers without an engine, but with a real cricket ball we may be sending the last Australian wicket spinning like a Catherine wheel to win the match for England. It is at this betwixt and between period that we put away our tin soldiers, as no longer worthy of our attention. Years later there comes suddenly a burning desire to see them again, and then they are not.

What has become of them is the saddest and most utterly unexplained of all mysteries. Sometimes they are deliberately given away to some good cause, and that is an act of charity, not perhaps to be criticized but to be secretly regretted. Sometimes they are passed on to younger members of the family, but even so, though they may lose their spit and polish, they ought not to vanish completely, as they do, from the face of the earth. Devouring time can consume many things, but it can hardly eat up a whole tin army. Nor is it credible that there are many parents so heartless that in their lust for empty cupboards they deliberately make away with it. Even as country house libraries contain precious books of which their owners are wholly unaware, so there must be regiments of unexampled beauty mouldering in drawers that have been for years unopened. Yet who has ever been so fortunate as to light on such a treasure? When as a small boy I took to collecting stamps, I was told of an album that had belonged to an uncle and might perhaps by rare good luck some day be mine. Details of its contents were even dangled before my eyes. It must certainly be in one of two or three cupboards, and I saw myself, in imagination, pouring through my fingers the loveliest stamps of green and orange and rose, grown almost infinitely valuable with the years, even as Jim Hawkins laved his hands in moidores and pieces of eight in the cave on Treasure Island. The cupboards were unlocked and searched, rather half-heartedly as it seemed, but still searched, and there was no album. And so it must be all over the world with priceless hordes of tin soldiers. I have heard with a dreadful envy of one house in Northumberland where a large veteran army (have they fierce curling moustaches like Napoleon's veterans in *Le Conscrit*?) still survives. I have even seen a few of them, which one son of the house, now himself a veteran, claimed as his share and transplanted to Surrey. But they are the exception to prove the inexorable rule that tin soldiers are swallowed up by some malignant demon and leave never a trace behind.

It was announced not long ago that some official, perhaps a Minister of Economics, in the Russian zone of Germany, had forbidden the making of " lead toys," which must clearly have included soldiers, since such things as camps and tents encouraged in youth a false romanticism, a worship of the highwayman and the gangster. Putting on one side the use of the word " toys," an insult to all serious lovers of lead soldiery, what unimaginative folly is this? After the first war there were solemn people who thought it would be better for their children to play with tin farms and cows, lest " militarism " be encouraged in them. It would be as reasonable to suppose that those who have a taste for reading about murders are likely to commit them. I have the honour of knowing one very learned in murders who writes of them with a cheerful and inimitable relish, but not only has he palpably the kindest of hearts, but I am told the death of a mouse in real life is more than he can bear. I say advisedly " in real life." Lovers, whether of murderers or of tin soldiers, live in a snug little kingdom of their own imagination, through which there blows no cold blast of reality. The love of soldiers and uniforms has no connection with soldiering. It is a purely romantic passion, and I would even go so far as to say that in many cases it implies a quality the least well suited to a military career. I adored tin soldiers, but it never entered my head for a moment to want to be a real one. Indeed my father recorded as one of my earliest remarks—it is rather a shameful one—that I should like to be a King, " because he does not go into battle." I am glad to have been even the very humblest sort of soldier in the first war, for the obvious reasons, but it would be an abuse of language to say that I liked it. It is rash to generalise from a particular instance, but may it not be that if we all played more with tin soldiers we should be less likely to go to war? This seems to me at least as well founded a belief as that of the Economic Minister of Brandenburg.

Though tin soldiers gave me so much happiness, my earliest memory of them is a bitter one. I was taken to stay at a house where there was another little boy. Everything else about him, even his name, has faded, but not the fact that he possessed a regiment of German Cuirassiers. They were beautiful, they had white coats, shining cuirasses, and eagles on their helmets, and my whole soul longed for them. There is no reason to think that that little boy was more possessive than other little boys. If he was, he was doubtless forced to allow me to play with his soldiers, on the detested nursery principle of " Share and share alike," but that was only to intensify my feelings. I had never beheld that lovely white uniform again till many years afterwards I saw the German Emperor—or was he then the Crown Prince?—riding in a procession through the streets of London. He wore it and a fine martial figure he made, but I could only think with a renewed hatred of that other nameless little boy.

There was probably an interval after that agonised coveting of my neighbour's cavalry, but it seems in retrospect to have been as an immediate compensation that my father brought me back from Germany a present of soldiers so splendid that my mind could never have conceived it. He used to go there to work in laboratories and wrote me lovely letters, with illustrations in coloured chalks of Uhlan trumpeters. The present was one of the fruits of his sojourn, I think at Strasbourg, and consisted not merely of one regiment but of a whole division, not German but French, in camp. There were not only infantry, cavalry and artillery, with a cocked-hatted General in command and his Aides-de-Camp galloping frantically to convey his orders. There were bivouac fires with leaping flames of red and gold, stacks of piled arms and the sweetest little vivandières with bottles of wine to minister to the troops. Surely nothing could have been more perfect, and yet even here was alloy. My father rashly let fall—perhaps I was not meant to hear—that there had been a choice. He might have bought a battle on a similar grand scale, with, as I gathered, oceans of tin blood, but had thought this too horrific for me and so had decided on the more peaceful camp. There was about this something of the affront to one's manhood of being taken to Madame Tussaud's but not allowed to penetrate, the Chamber of Horrors. Still, that one poisonous ingredient was soon harmlessly dissolved in the cup of happiness.

It need scarcely be added that those soldiers were of the

elder, and I think the better, fashion. That is to say, they were small and elegant and, unlike the bloated monsters who were soon to oust them from public favour, they were thin. Had they been otherwise, no one box could have contained so great an array, and this, from a merely sordid point of view, was one of the advantages of the old soldiery, that so many more could be bought for the money ; the birthday or Christmas tip went so much further. Again, the thin cavalry were as centaurs ; they and their horses were one and indivisible. Their successors rode by means of a spike and a hole in the saddle, and fine fellows they looked as long as they were mounted ; but when they got down they had permanently bandy legs and could not stand upright on their feet.

These are my views to-day; and I believe them to be sound, but I do not say that I always thought so or that I was not carried away by the fashion for the larger and the lumpier. The new soldiers were undoubtedly imposing ; there was a specious air of reality about them ; you could look at them from any point of view, as at a statue. They dwarfed the armies of the old regime, so that there was a certain incongruity not easily to be overcome in a grand review, in which the total available forces of all kinds took part. Incidentally, it is one of the non-" militaristic " features of tin soldiers, at any rate in my remembrance, that one does not draw up two opposing forces. The enemy is purely hypothetical. There are many reviews but never a battle. I have heard indeed of other boys who slew each other's soldiers with peas or other such ammunition fired from cannons, but that was not my way.

All my later and more monstrous soldiers have grown dim compared with that French camp, save only a single regiment, or rather a platoon, of Turkish infantry. They were to be seen in the window of a toy shop in the Market Place at Cambridge, two rows of them, in fezzes, and the Commanding Officer's fez was distinguished by a gold tassel. There they lay in rows in their box of shavings, costing some immense sum of money, nearly ten shillings. I possessed ten shillings, but felt sure I should be discouraged from spending it so prodigally all at once. So, after gazing for several days, in an agony of anxiety lest I should have been anticipated, I went out alone on a secret expedition and brought them home triumphant but a little apprehensive lest my extravagance be censured. This fear was groundless, nor do I ever remember to have enjoyed buying anything so much, except, a little later, a tie of pink and white stripes without which life would have been unbearable.

There was another race of soldiers, also beautiful but which must be kept apart from the tin army, as being by comparison on a gigantic scale, and thus palpably inharmonious. These were soldiers of paper, to be bought in sheets, marching in profile and exactly in step one behind the other. Nor were they merely unilateral, for the sheet could be turned over and there they were again, still gazing straight in front of them. The paper must I think have been stiff, in the nature of cardboard, for the soldiers could be cut out one by one and mounted on blocks, so that they could march where their owner listed ; but as a rule this was too laborious a process and they remained on their sheets, like stamps on the pages of an album. There was an enchanting variety of them, and all save some of our own Sepoys in British red coats, drawn from foreign armies. Noblest of all were certain Russian infantry, of the Imperial Guard as I suppose, in green uniforms, with red plastrons after the fashion of our own Lancers, and white-plumed helmets. There was a battery of artillery, which I believe to have been Austrian, in uniforms of reddish-brown, complete with horses and guns. There was blue cavalry of Saxony, and Zouaves with baggy red trousers. I know not whence they came, but somewhere on a moraine of forgotten things " on the glacier of years gone by " I came across a few of them not long ago. Now they have vanished again, but on an emergency I believe they could still be mobilised. They are but a remnant, but to that extent paper has outlived the hardier tin.

All have so far survived in their master's brain in that all my life I have sent myself to sleep with processions of soldiers in freshly invented uniforms. I get into my travelling carriage, founded no doubt upon Napoleon's at Madame Tussaud's, for that I *was* allowed to see. Instantly, my cavalry close around me and we splash off down a miry road under darkling trees. There are secrets that few people tell, and this may be a common device. I have only known one other who confessed to something like it, and he, being of a nautical turn of mind, was borne to sleep on different lovely ships of his own inventing. Yet there is a sameness about sailors' uniforms all the world over that must make my game the more varied and full of colour. It is a game that I have never ceased to play except during wars. Then it fades away of its own accord. Only once did the image of these dream soldiers come back to me in war time. It was outside Salonica on the Monastir road ; there came a heavy shower and clattering through it a squadron of Greek Cavalry, wrapped in cloaks of horizon blue with their heads bowed against the rain. For a night or two afterwards they escorted me in my carriage, till khaki and reality drove them away.

Perhaps mine is what the Minister of Brandenburg called a false romanticism, but I take leave to think that khaki has been a sad destroyer of romance among tin soldiers. I have hardly seen any for a long time now, but once between wars I inspected a considerable army. It was gleaming with tanks and caterpillars and such contrivances, but it seemed to me a drab array. " John says these are vetrians," said the junior partner in the army, pointing to a regiment drawn up in an inconspicuous position to the rear. The poor old veterans had red coats and white pith helmets ; they were out of date but they seemed to me, in point of true beauty, worth all the rest put together. At any rate that force did not contain what I have seen with a shudder in toy shops and take to be the supreme incongruity—namely, tin knights in armour. Mr. Henry James said that he liked his murders reasonably modern but that he could " more or less swallow a couple of centuries."

15

I hold the same view of tin soldiers, but my limits would be narrower. I would not go beyond the Crimea in one direction, and I would draw the line at khaki in the other. Tin archers in Lincoln green, with Locksley at their head, might possess a certain magic of their own, but no, they would clash horribly. Let them and the knights stay in their proper place, in the pages of *Ivanhoe*. Meanwhile, I wonder whether my dear, lost, white Cuirassiers will come and see me safe to sleep to-night.

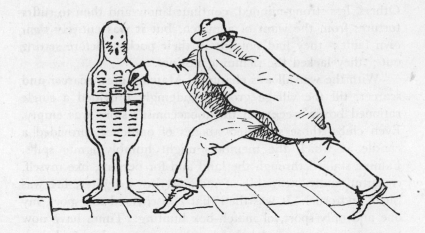

Match-Hunting

E. V. Lucas was once told of the remark of an admiring friend to the effect that he could write an article on anything, if need be on a match-box. He therefore set to work to prove himself worthy. He could not touch a match-box without adorning it, and a very delightful, amusing and on the whole comprehensive article he produced. But there was one aspect of the subject which he did not touch because the time had not yet come—namely, the sport of match-box hunting in automatic machines. In those happy days of abundance before the war, there was no scarcity of matches and we could buy them almost anywhere and at any time. Man is naturally an improvident animal and accidents will happen. It might befall a traveller to find himself in a solitary railway carriage in a non-stop train with but a single match for his pipe, a situation to try the steadiest hand and the strongest nerve. I knew one who admitted to having in his younger days unscrewed the flickering oil lamp in his carriage in order to appease his craving for a cigar. Incidentally this episode convinced him that he was becoming too confirmed a slave to tobacco, and he there and then incontinently gave it up.

Others, less strong-minded, continued now and then to suffer tortures from the want of a match, but it was entirely their own fault ; they had not felt in their pockets before setting out ; they lacked the planning instinct.

With the war all was changed. Matches grew scarcer and scarcer, till the village grocer grudgingly provided a single rationed box a week and the tobacconist's store was empty. Even clubs, those supposed abodes of opulence, provided a candle at which the members might humbly ignite spills. Famine stalked through the land and for persons, like myself, constitutionally incapable of manœuvring a lighter, life was bleak and cruel. It was then that I discovered my sport, my one and only sport, of match-box hunting. Times have now to some degree grown less hard ; there are matches, and since it is the rarity and elusiveness of the quarry which gives the hunter his supreme thrill, the sport is not what it was ; but before its triumphs and disappointments are altogether forgotten, I must try to set them down.

Let me admit at once that I am no travelled sportsman ; my preserves have been strictly limited, having been practically confined to a single large railway station. Its name I propose even now to keep to myself. In that respect I am like the man who knows one spot, perhaps a hidden fold in the downs, where there grows some rare orchis ; he repairs there in secret, taking every precaution against being followed, and refuses so much as to pass a hint to his best botanical friend. There is nothing rare about my brand of match-box and my hunting had to be done in the public eye ; but even so I cannot bring myself to any precise revelation. The mystery and romance would then be gone, and, besides, who knows that famine will not come again, when I should bitterly regret my loquacity.

The beginning was purely fortuitous, and I can claim no credit. Having bought some cigarettes from the young lady at the kiosk, I summoned up courage to say that I supposed she had no matches. The question was so absurd that she barely deigned to answer, when at that instant there appeared, heaven-sent, a gentleman who was apparently a friend of hers. " There are plenty there," he said, pointing to the automatic machine. His countenance has wholly faded from my memory.

> *Whether dark or fair*
> *His kingly brow is neither here*
> *Nor there.*

But I have never ceased to bless him. With a word of inadequate thanks I dashed to the machine. Often had I gazed at it before and at its brethren in other stations, only to find the cupboard bare behind the glass case and the little drawer permanently and hopelessly pulled out. Now it was clear that by astonishing good fortune I had chanced on it at the very moment after it had been refilled, for the drawers were pushed in again and there behind the glass, packed in serried ranks, were rows of little boxes, or rather booklets, of matches, virgin, ready to be plundered. Needless to say I put in my pennies ; not all the pennies I had, for at first the match-hunter is self-conscious, believing that every one is looking at him, and that he must restrain his greed for the sake of appearances. Still I put in as many as I then dared and the machine clicked merrily. But I did more than gain my scanty treasure. I carefully noted the day of the week and the hour of the day against future raids. Those who know Miss Dorothy Sayers's admirable story *Murder Must Advertise* will recall how Lord Peter Wimsey discovers the day on which the weekly convoy of cocaine reaches London and the elaborate system by which it is distributed in unexpected places by secret and sinister agents. I felt then like that enchanting if improbable aristocrat. From that moment I was enchained, half-sportsman and half-addict. It was agreeable to wallow in matches as I presently did ; it gave a sense of virtue to do something for the household and to be a public benefactor ; but, far beyond that, the ardour of the chase had me in its grip.

More and more regularly I found some good reason for

going to London on that particular day of the week. If there were appointments to be made that was the day for them, but the hour of refilling must, if possible, be kept vacant. The ministering angel did not always arrive at precisely the same time, and in that case I must wander aimlessly about the station, feeling as one loitering with intent to commit a felony. There were other loiterers whom I gravely suspected. They were ostensibly looking at the literature on the bookstall or feigning to consult the train time-table, but I was not to be deceived by such shallow pretences ; to my conscience-stricken eye they were match-hunters, waiting, like me, for the convoy to arrive. If it had really been cocaine, I could not at first have felt more guilty.

When the refiller, or refueller, arrived, he tried the hunter's patience almost beyond endurance. He took out his keys with intentional deliberation, checked and re-checked his precious bales of booklets and arranged them with an aggravating nicety. Fortunately this particular machine is one of many mansions ; besides those labelled chocolate cream and so in days of rationing mere hollow mockeries, it has no less than four devoted to matches, two on each side and thus hidden from one another. So the moment those on one side were filled and the official was concealed from view, the hunter could fall unabashed on his prey. Once, seeing that I was observed by him, I made some facetious apology. He was a kindly and sympathetic man and remarked : " I don't see why you shouldn't take a dozen if you want to. If you don't have them somebody else will." It seemed so sensible a view that I took him at his word.

The match-hunt has on one or two points enlarged my knowledge of human nature. For instance, I now understand why a man having made one million does not rest satisfied but toils on in order to amass another. I became rich enough in matches to have no future cares for weeks and almost for months to come ; but it was painful to see the three columns of boxes on my chimney piece dwindling below a certain point ;

I was as one driven on by a demon, longing to raise them higher than they had ever been before. Having taken my quota in the afternoon I could not resist just another penn'orth or two in the evening. The appetite for matches, as for other things, comes in the eating.

Another lesson to be learnt from this pursuit is that nobody looks at us ; we are not nearly so important or so interesting as we fancy. At first, as I said, the hunter is self-conscious. Having taken a mere two or three boxes from one compartment he feels that glaring eyes are burning a hole in the back of his head and moves hastily round to the further side. In fact, he discovers that unless it be one or two stray small boys, who have an insatiable and embarrassing curiosity, nobody pays the faintest attention to him, though the rapid clicking seems in his guilty ears to resound through the station like the fire of a machine-gun. I gained an inkling of this lesson at Cambridge. On a busy morning at the end of term, when the Great Court of Trinity was full of porters wheeling luggage, a friend of mine from another College teed up a golf ball on the grass in front of the Master's Lodge, sliced it in a masterly manner over the top of the Chapel and walked nonchalantly away without a soul having noticed him. So it is in match-hunting. I cannot for a moment claim to be unself-conscious but in this particular respect alone I have developed the virtue. There have been days on which I have stood amazed at my own brazen behaviour.

One day I was so bold as to expend some six or eight pennies under the eye of a policeman standing nearby. A young relative who was with me could not bear the strain ; she walked away, ostentatiously disclaiming any connection with any one so outrageous. I must confess to having felt a little uncomfortable under the baleful glare of the law, but I clicked doggedly on. Was I not exercising my unquestioned rights as a law-abiding citizen ? Only once on all my hunting expeditions has any one said a word to me. This was a gentleman who regarded me with a very friendly interest. " Why don't you bring a bag ? " he asked. " I think I will another day," I replied, and we laughed pleasantly together.

There is another point of a purely technical character which interests me, though the reader who has never indulged may find it less enthralling. This is the extraordinary capriciousness of individual machines. On one day they yield up their treasures with perfect meekness ; on another they are utterly obdurate, refusing either to return the penny or produce the matches. Sooner or later the hunter must expect the machine to become jammed and immovable, and so must write off that penny as a dead loss. It is sometimes very coy and hard to please as to the diet with which it is fed. In one week it presumably makes up its mind that all the pennies are too smooth or too light and so contumeliously spits them out again. Yet its next-door neighbour will tranquilly accept them and deliver the goods. In the following week the position is for no explicable reason reversed ; the easy-going machine becomes positively costive and vice versa. Among the four in my preserves some seem to me definitely more friendly than others, but one can never be sure that they will not suddenly turn nasty.

Naturally the hunter makes some preparation for the one great day in the week by hoarding his pennies. He never thinks of wasting so valuable a coin on a newspaper but insists on getting change. Here he is sometimes frustrated. There is no curse so appalling that he would not call it down on the head of him who gives him a threepenny bit and four halfpennies as change for his sixpence. He tends to love or to hate bus conductors according to the coins they return him. Indeed his economic vision becomes distorted and pennies assume for him a wholly inflated value.

And now, alas ! all these hopes and fears, hot fits and cold fits, triumphs and disasters, have almost come to an end. With the greater flow of matches the sport is losing much of its savour. Once the drawers were inevitably empty ere the day was out. The hunter having taken his fill by daylight, might cast a glance at them as he caught his after-dinner train home to find them all pulled out. Then he could give his bulging pocket a well-satisfied pat and gloat over his own foresight. Lately I have found a sufficiency of matches still left not one but two days after that particular day, the name of which no number of wild horses shall extract from me. But the worst blow fell when I found that I could buy these very same once cherished booklets in my own village shop. After that it seemed vain to go on. I might put in a casual penny or two in passing but it was not the same thing ; no true sportsman would shoot a match-box sitting. Some day perhaps after an interval I may be irresistibly drawn as by a magnet to my old friend and may experience once again that delicious fever of hurry and anxiety, the terror of being watched, the joy of getting away with my precious burden. But I remember those cruel words, " They never come back "; they are as true of this sport as of all the rest. I have had my moments, almost of greatness, and they are past. The hunter is home from the hill.

23

A Look Round the Room

" Y OU see what a domestic character I am," said Charles
Surface as he walked into his picture-room. " Here I
sit of an evening surrounded by my family." I feel a
little like Charles at this moment, as I sit by the fire and look
round the walls of my small room, almost every foot of which
is plastered with coloured prints, so that it is hard to find room
for a newcomer. Indeed he must be a highly distinguished
personage if he is now to force his way into so goodly a company.
These great men are not of my family, though I most certainly
could not be fonder of them if they were, but like Charles's
great-uncles and aunts they belong to a bygone age. They are
the mighty champions of the past—prize-fighters, runners,
walkers, a few cricketers and a single tennis player of surpassing
elegance in a frizzled white wig. They are dust " and their
good swords are rust," but the fame of many of them survives
and always will. They are a humble collection, the fruit for
the most part of fortunate glances into out-of-the-way shop
windows. I might almost call them my seven-and-sixpenny
collection, for few of them have cost more and some decidedly
less. Yet I should be very sorry to knock them down, as

Charles did his ancestors to Mr. Premium. Let me walk the reader in imagination round the room and introduce him to my illustrious friends, with one or two little stories about them, such as will not, I hope, cause them too much embarrassment.

We will begin with the wall over the chimney piece, and first of all here is Tom Sayers. He does not come first in chronological order by any means ; the ancient glory was fast passing away in his time and it expired with him. But he must come first here because this print was the nucleus of my gallery. My wife found it in the market-place in Cambridge, and brought it home in triumph. It had been used to hang, so she was told, outside boxing booths at fairs. To look at it is to say with John Gully when they met at Newmarket, " I wonder, Tom, how ever you did it." Here are his height and his lowest fighting weights, set out above his battle honours : 5 ft. 8 ins. and 10 stone 10 lbs. How ever did he hold out for those hours at Farnborough against the vast Heenan, and that with one arm useless ? He looks solid enough and very cool and confident but in no way tremendous. He has what one pictures as a typical bruiser's face, with sleek dark hair, well oiled for the occasion, and round his waist is a blue bird's-eye handkerchief, once the colours of the Game Chicken. It is pleasant to see that he is described as Champion of England. That was honour enough in those fine insular days, long before John L. Sullivan had assumed the more grandiose title of Champion of the World. Doubtless in English ears it meant the same thing, and it was good enough for Tom.

Immediately below him is a small picture, not a coloured print but an oil painting, which is, I suppose, the chief, if modest, treasure of my collection. Here is the great Tom Cribb, and the interesting point about him is that he is not delivering his one-two in professional style but posing in an attitude as an artist's model. He was found by pure luck in a curiosity shop, somewhere in the wilds of South London, where the car broke down and must be repaired. Had the shop by chance got any fighting men, it was asked. No, it had not, and then on second thoughts it produced this picture. On seeing it, my wife said that it looked very like an Etty. Some time later we took off a board at the back and there, roughly scrawled in pencil, was " Etty." That is not conclusive evidence, I know, but it was at least eminently satisfying and we have probed no further. That it is Tom Cribb there is no doubt at all, for I have also a print of him and the face is the same " wonderfully like that of a lion " as Borrow described it.

On his left, resting on the chimney piece and, as is only fitting, on a slightly lower level, is Molineaux, the American negro, whom Pierce Egan always called the Moor, the first invader seriously to shake our English complacency. The artist was determined to make him black enough. He is as black as the naughty little boys who were dipped in the big ink-pot by the tall Agrippa in *Struwwelpeter*. He also looks rather too plump. " The black was fat," said Dick Christian, who had stood up on the top of his saddle to watch his second fight with Cribb. " That licked him as much as anything." Nor is it to be wondered at, for his recorded breakfast on the morning of the fight was a whole boiled chicken, an apple pie and a tankard of stout. As for Tom, he could get as fat as he pleased in his own bar parlour after this victory, for he need fight no more and was called Champion till the day of his death, when a monumental lion was erected over his remains, with a " deep expression of sorrow expressed on its countenance."

Next to Molineaux comes Peter Crawley, the young Rump Steak, who won the Championship against the Black Diamond on what is now the cricket ground on Royston Heath. I have walked across it often and often on my way to the first tee. Next to him again—" Ah now ! " as Sherlock Holmes once remarked, " this really is something a little *recherché*." It is a china plaque, cracked and mended in two places, portraying the fight at Worcester between Tom Spring and the Irishman, Langan. On the day following it, that distinguished patron of the ring, Mr. John Thurtell, was to be hanged for the murder of Mr. William Weare, and many of his friends, having seen the fight, drove all through the night into Hertfordshire to see the end of him. Mr. Thurtell himself was exceedingly anxious to hear what had happened in the fight, and regretted that he should not be able to read his friend Pierce Egan's account of it. When told that Tom Spring had won, he said, " Thank God, he's a very old friend of mine." Mr. Thurtell's countenance, with " its blending of the bluff and the sharp," is one I would gladly make room for, but I am not so lucky as to possess him.

Now the reader can have a little rest from the ring, for on the same wall are two engaging athletes to whom he must certainly be introduced, Mr. William Spooner and Mr. George Frost, the Suffolk Stag. Both are stripped to the waist, like their prize-fighting brothers, and both are from the hand of the same artist, one John C. Anderson. Of William Spooner I know no more than the inscription tells me, that he " won the Champion's belt at Copenhagen Grounds on the 8th of December, 1851, walking ten miles in one hour, twenty-two minutes and five seconds." He is a good-looking young fellow and strides along in fine free style, with a rustic landscape and a windmill in the background. Beneath is the belt itself, coiled like a snake, a marvel of blue and silver, and within it are the words, " William Spooner, Champion of the World." He ought to have been proudly content with England.

A similar belt appears beneath the Suffolk Stag. He won it in a ten-mile race, also on the Copenhagen Ground, against J. Levett, for £50 a-side on Good Friday, 1853. In the Badminton volume on athletics it is said that copies of this lithograph were sold by the thousand, and when I first gloated over those words (in my private school days) I used to wonder sadly where they had all gone and think how happy I should be if I could ever possess such an inestimable work of art. My joy may then be imagined when my wife, trustiest of scouts with an eye for treasure-trove, reported that she had seen the Stag in a window in the Fulham Road. Heavens ! if anybody should get him before me, but nobody did, and he is by this time my very old friend, as he skims elegantly along on the tips of his toes, in bathing drawers trimmed with light blue. He has a mild, studious, even curatical air, but I am afraid it belies him. I have since found a story not wholly to his credit. He was in his dressing-room before this very race, when there appeared to him a shady person with a bottle of stout and some banknotes in his hand. If the Stag would drink the stout the notes should be his. The Stag said no, he distrusted the contents of the bottle, but if the gentleman would bring him a fresh one, with the wire on it showing it to be unopened, he would drink that. This offer was accepted in default of a better ; the Stag took the money, drank the stout, subsequently took the necessary steps to make himself sick, and went out and beat J. Levett by the length of the street. Then, knowing that those whom he had double-crossed would be after him like ravening wolves, he made a hasty escape, still in his running kit, in his backer's private cab. I can see no change on his countenance ; he looks as mild as ever and I don't think he will mind my telling that story, of course in the strictest confidence, because he fancied he had been uncommonly clever and never could quite understand why his backer would not support him again. At any rate, nothing shall ever shake my affection for him. What a romantic name he had ! The American Deer, the Lame Chicken and the North Star once ran a mile race on the Slough road, and those were stunning enough, but the Suffolk Stag touches me still more nearly.

There are some other pleasant runners and walkers, just round the corner from the Stag, on the next wall. I am particularly attached to Deerfoot, because he was running in the boyhood of my father, who dimly remembered his glory and used to tell me of it. Bennett was his real name ; he was a Canadian Indian and clearly knew the picturesque value of his Indian blood, for he is depicted in full war paint, with a headgear of red, blue and yellow feathers. He is drawn very large and is spurting away from his adversary who is drawn almost unfairly small. The spectators, as is generally the case in these prints, are the most villainous looking set of ruffians with betting books in their hands. Some of them positively frighten me, but Deerfoot is very beautiful. So, in his own way, is one of whom my ignorance is shameful—John Baker, the Rochester Pedestrian, who in 1815 walked 1000 miles in thirty successive days. He is shown finishing the last mile, where a lovely pink flag marks the winning post. He wears grey gloves —" Why do you walk through the fields in gloves ? "—and carries a walking-stick in one hand, while round his broad-brimmed hat are entwined floral decorations in green and blue, whether as pure ornament or to shade him from the sun, I know not. Close to him is George Wilson, who was fifty years old when he undertook to walk fifty miles a day for twenty successive days on Blackheath, and was stopped by the magistrates who grew frightened of the dense crowds. He does not appear nearly so old, and in fact was not so old as his neighbour Mr. Foster Powell, who looks for all the world like a Quaker, sober-suited on his way to a Friends' Meeting House. This print of him was cut out at some time from *The Wonderful Museum* (which Silas Wegg used to read to Mr. Boffin), and he was a wonderful man. He was a lawyer's clerk at the end of the eighteenth century and was always making records and breaking them, his final effort at the age of fifty-nine being the journey from London to York and back in five days and fifteen and a quarter hours. He never recovered from it, and really he was old enough to know better.

I have still one more very famous pedestrian, but I shall come to him in his turn. Now back to the fighting men, and to a narrow strip of wall on the other side of the fire, which is a place of great honour. Here—I must beg my reader not to be too reverently overcome—here are Hen Pearce, the immortal Game Chicken, and John Gully, sometime M.P. for Pontefract. It is right that they should hang together, for they fought each other at Hailsham a fortnight before Trafalgar. Byron had come down the night before in a barouche and four with his friend and teacher, Mr. John Jackson, who hangs, by the way, on another wall, very demure and genteel, worthy to be called Gentleman Jackson, with his neck imprisoned by an immense white neckcloth. All the Corinthians were there in their tall white hats, and the Duke of Clarence, afterwards King William IV., rode over the downs from Brighton and stood up in his stirrups to see the fight. He got back very late for dinner to tell Lord Thurlow and Mr. Creevey all about it, and talked of it till the day of his death. And well he might for it was a terrific battle. The Chicken won—nobody could ever beat him—but it was not till the fifty-ninth round, and he could barely drag himself across the ring to shake hands. " He must be a sharp chap," he told his friends afterwards, " and get up very early in the morning as beats John Gully."

They should hang together for another reason, that Gully owed the start of his career to the Chicken. The two had been friends at Bristol ; Gully was in the King's Bench Prison for debt, with no prospect of getting out, when the Chicken came to see him and they had a set-to with the gloves. It was done deliberately in order that Gully might find a backer to pay his debts and that the Chicken, when Champion with no more worlds to conquer, might find an opponent. And John Gully never forgot it. Many years afterwards, when he was a rich man and the poor drunken, debauched Chicken was long since dead, he chanced to look at the school list of one of his grandsons. Seeing there the name of Pearce he insisted on discovering whether this was a relation of the Chicken's. What a noble tip that boy would have had, but alas ! he could not claim the honour. It is a pleasant story and a true one, for I had it from the grandson himself.

Well, here they are, one above the other, not perhaps in the highest style of art but vast and formidable, especially the Chicken, whose arms are almost too huge and muscular to be true. He was " quite an uncultivated man " (I quote Dick Christian again), and has a rustic air, but a kindly and rather handsome face. Gully, with his tip-tilted nose, is guileless and innocent enough, but look at the little print above. Here he is as an old man, with benevolent white hair, but shrewd and resolute and perhaps a little hard. He has passed through many stages since that earlier picture. He has held his own with Crockford and the other " legs," and made and lost great sums of money on the Turf. He has, either in his own name or that of one of his " confederates " as they were called—the word has a sinister sound—won three Derbys. He has survived some ugly rumours in a time when the Turf was full of ugly rumours, and is now something of a Grand Old Man of racing. He has begotten twenty-four children, has become an owner of coal mines, and a member of the first reformed parliament, and has made his bow to the King at Court. He has lived up to the Chicken's estimate. He looks a very sharp old chap indeed.

After that overpowering honour the reader will not care to be introduced to too many others of the bruisers of England ; so, though there are plenty more, I must pass over them swiftly. I have got Shelton, " grim savage Shelton, who has a civil word for nobody and a hard blow for anybody." And here are David Hudson and Johnnie Walker, the Champion of the Light Weights in 1819. Then of a later date are Bendigo and Deaf Burke. Bendigo has a fine, lurid background, portending a storm ; just such a storm as came up out of a clear sky, when Borrow and Jasper watched John Thurtell splashing triumphantly through the rain gushes, and the gipsy foretold for him a bloody dukkeripen. The print next door of the scene at the Fives Courts (it is quite a common one) was found of all odd places in a shop at Pau.

Now back to my last and greatest pedestrian. Here is Captain Barclay walking his thousand miles in a thousand hours on Newmarket Heath. He is dressed all in white, except for the yellow neckerchief which I like to think is the Bristol " yellowman " once made famous by Jem Belcher. On his head is a black tall hat. He is standing by one of the lamps which lighted his way as he walked through the night hours, and a powerful lamp it seems to be, for the landscape in the background is almost as bright as day. He was a kind present from Lord Simon, who once lived at Fritwell Manor in Oxfordshire, which had been Barclay's home. There is so much to say about him that I must keep an iron hand on myself. He was, I am glad to say, a kinsman of a kinsman of mine, Francis Galton, who saw him as an old man. It would be pleasant to call him " Cousin Robert ; " cousinship can stretch a long way, but not as far as that.

He was the best amateur boxer of his day and the best runner over long distances, amateur or professional, having run the leading professional " off his legs." He could go on almost for ever, partridge-driving all day and dancing all night. He could drive a coach from London to his native Aberdeen and be so fresh at the end of it that, when he backed himself to turn round and drive straight back, there were no takers. He had one good long sleep after his great walk at Newmarket, and then set off to join the ill-fated military expedition to Walcheren. He had a ferocious system of training, full of purges and sweats under feather beds, and nearly killed poor Tom Cribb by taking him away to his house at Ury before his second fight with Molineaux, and making him climb the Aberdeenshire hills, while the Captain ran in front of him pelting him with pebbles like a malignant Puck. Nimrod once went to stay at Ury and found all the chairs as hard as a rock and their backs as straight as a tree. The only thing he admired was the picture of the Game Chicken over the sideboard. I should like to think it was a copy of my picture, but I am sadly afraid it wasn't.

Of my one tennis player I know nothing save that his portrait was published in Soho. He is called simply " Monsieur Masson, the Tennis Player ; " he wears, as I said, a white wig and stands racket in hand leaning against a pillar. I think he must have flourished in the days before the Revolution and given lessons in the game to no one under the rank of Monseigneur. The four cricketers framed in a row are much more familiar. " Me a-bowlin', Pilch a-battin', and Box behind the wicket, that's cricket," said William Lillywhite, the Non-pareil, and here are all three of them playing their various parts, in top hats. The fourth, worthy of his fellows, is James Cobbett. But where is Alfred Mynn?

And where, it may be asked, are the golfers? There are none, save a Dutch gentleman, hidden behind a turn-about bookcase and playing on the ice, in a print called " Les amusements de l'hiver." The print is agreeable enough, but the game is emphatically not golf. I have the gravest doubts whether it ought to be admitted to this great company. The only suggestion of golf in the room is to be found in two rather attractive views of old St. Andrews. Mr. William Innes of Blackheath in his red coat hangs elsewhere.

Now the reader has completed his personally conducted tour of the walls, but there remains one picture, lying on the table. It has lately come back from the framers and the problem is to find a place for it of sufficient honour, for it represents the greatest all-rounder of his own or any other age, who could do almost everything as well or better than any one else. Reader, let me present you to Mr. George Osbaldeston, The Squire of England. You had only to tell him there was something he could not do, and he would have a wonderfully good try ; he was an ill man with whom to make a match. Famous Master of Foxhounds, unbeaten rider of steeplechases, the best game shot in England and the second best pigeon shot, fast bowler, oarsman, billiard player, tennis player and " heaven knows what besides." I do not add Member of Parliament because he was so busy with hunting, shooting and athletic feats, and, as he ingenuously added, " ladies, etcetera," that he really could not find time to attend the House. I do, however, add " writer," because in his old age he wrote a most entertaining autobiography in good, racy, spirited English, such as many a more practised author might envy. He did it to please his wife and it was rather an odd book for the purpose, but Mrs. Osbaldeston was a sensible, broad-minded lady.

In my print he would seem to have been spending a

convivial evening, perhaps after a long day with his hounds. There is a bottle on the table, and he has a glass in one hand, while in the other he waves a fox's brush over his head. He kept himself wonderfully hard and fit, but on this occasion I think he has allowed himself a little relaxation from training.

I must find a place for The Squire where he can see as many as possible of his old friends, for he knew a number of them well. Spring and Langan he certainly cannot have forgotten. He had a good run with the Quorn, then posted through the night to Worcester and got there in time for the fight. Several of the stands broke down under the weight of spectators, including that on which he stood. He was not much hurt, because he fell on the top of a rascally betting man and was much amused to hear such a blackguard fervently thanking heaven for his escape. He was still more amused on his way home. The horse he was driving in a gig—it had been a hunter —jumped over a hedge into a ploughed field. He was thrown out and lay helplessly entangled in his cloak, but could not help roaring with laughter because, as he said, " the horse's antics were so extraordinary."

Then he will remember John Gully very well, for Gully helped to shoulder a way for him through the crowd after his famous ride of 200 miles at Newmarket, and they kept it up till daybreak at the Rutland Arms. Later they had a quarrel over some queer doings in the St. Leger, a race in which queer things were always happening. Gully's daughter remembered to have seen her father and The Squire, "a little man in a green coat " according to the family legend, laughing together over this imaginary duel, but I think they had been on the verge of fighting for all that. Tom Cribb he certainly knew, for he came near to standing in the dock with him over a fight in which a man was killed ; and Bendigo too, for he was the referee in one of his fights with Caunt and gave a highly unpopular decision. The cricketers were after the time when he had devastated England with his tremendous underhand bowling. He may have seen them, but before their great days he had scratched his name off the list of members at Lord's in a temper. However, that is enough, and perhaps more than enough, about The Squire. As he hardly seems in a condition to hear what I say, Reader, let me whisper to you that there never was such a gallant, vain, peppery, reckless, lovable little old gentleman. And with that the reader will be doubtless much relieved to end his tour ; he must be yawning already for there is nothing like looking at pictures to make the legs ache and the eyes water. Not that I should ever tire of my heroes. " Gentlemen," as Charles Surface said with a bow to his ancestors, " your most obedient and very grateful servant."

Giving Up the Game

SOMETIMES man gives up the game and sometimes the game gives him up. Very often the desertion is mutual. However it happens it is a sad wrench and its sadness does not depend on the distinction to which the player has attained, but rather on his love for the game and all the fun he has got out of it. Fortunately there is, as a rule, a merciful gradation and few of us realise when we have played our last round. We may suspect and, as time goes on, feel almost sure, but we shut our eyes and always have a hope either that Nature will vouchsafe some miraculous restoration or even, failing a miracle, that, on some particular occasion, and with a particularly kind and forgiving partner, we may yet take the field. It is true that for the more illustrious who formally retire there does come a definite break, a last race, a last championship, a last innings in first-class company. The batsman as he walks back to the pavilion, cheered all the way whether he has made a duck or a century, gives a sorrowful little flick of the head to take one last lingering look back before the chapter is ended. But it is only one chapter, if the brightest, and he still hopes to play many more innings in less exacting cricket and perhaps with a lighter heart. The abhorred shears have not made too clean and ruthless a cut.

" Vell, gov'ner, ve must all come to it, one day or another," as Sam Weller said to his father, and the golfer ought to take a long time coming to it. He has perhaps less cause to complain than any one else. One evening, a good long while ago now, I arrived at Aberdovey, walked into the well-known room to find the expected company of friends and asked cheerfully, " Who's going to play me to-morrow morning ? " The answer came in a chilling chorus, " Oh, we none of us play golf." It came as a sudden and depressing shock, a *memento mori*. I ought to have felt, and I hope I did feel sorry for them, but there was, I am afraid, in my sorrow something of rejoicing in my own still comparatively unimpaired powers. There still seemed so many years of golf left, and in fact there were a good many, if not quite such an unending vista as I then saw. The golfer ought to have plenty of sympathy to spare for other people whose pastimes make greater demands, for his is, in one sense at any rate, worthy of that blessed reproach, " an old man's game." He is first of all sorry for the runner whose time is terribly short, very seldom more than the span of two Olympiads, and not always that. Then he is sorry for the oarsman. His fame may be enduring and his time on the bank long, with his blue blazer growing tighter and tighter and more and more gloriously faded. But *exceptis excipiendis* his active days are cruelly brief. The Latin tag may be freely translated, " Schoolmasters don't count." They are well known to go on for ever, and this perennial quality of theirs is noteworthy in another pursuit in which the ordinary man's time is short, football. It is an historical fact that one Eton master used to play the Wall Game at the mature age of fifty-six. If some of his energies were employed in haranguing the bully rather than joining in its mysterious rites, still he did play and that at a game by no means deficient in a certain static vigour. All men cannot be schoolmasters, and for the rest of the world a thirtieth birthday is as the bell which announces the

37

last lap. After that, at least in the higher walks of life, selectors shake their heads over them. The cricketer has a much longer life, though his place in the field grows ever nearer the wicket, and so has the player of tennis. The famous Barre went on to some fabulous age even though he must lean panting against the dedans exclaiming of the then youthful Heathcote, " Mon dieu, mon dieu, il est si jeune." And now Heathcote in his turn—but the subject lends itself too easily to sentimental, Thackerayan moralising. Let it be enough then that, compared with all these players of other games, the golfer comes nearest to attaining a practical immortality and has much to be thankful for accordingly.

Whatever the game, many give it up when the decline of their powers is still a slow and gentle movement. I once asked the late Stanley Jackson whether he played much cricket nowadays, and with that perfect candour and the quality of taking himself for granted which made one of his great charms, he replied that he did not ; " the fact is I don't play so well as I used to and I don't like it." Then he added something like these words : " I play once a year at Harrow and I generally go in and make fifty or sixty runs and then when I go on to bowl they won't take me off because they know I shall be so stiff that I could never go on again." I can see the spot where he said it, on a golf course in Cheshire, and it struck me as so simple and engaging that the words there and then burnt themselves into my memory and I can almost guarantee their accuracy.

Nobody can like it, when he finds himself not so good as he was, but some dislike it much more acutely than others. Presumably the ideal is to dislike it so little, or to like the game so much more, that even an eighteen handicap or a series of ducks and missed catches make " a sundown splendid and serene ; " but that is a great deal to ask. A little allowance must be made for the vanity of poor frail human nature, and in golf at any rate I have observed that those who go on the longest have had, as a rule, no very high standard of achievement from which to fall. The octogenarian foursomes, of which we sometimes hear, are seldom composed of old internationals. It is not, I hope, unbearably sentimental to say that there is something sad in watching a once fine player beginning to slip. I remember a conversation with Harold Hilton at Hoylake, on the evening when the side to play for England against Scotland was being chosen. He remarked that in a year or two people would be saying, " Hilton—h'm—is he good enough ? " It sounded in my worshipping ears a kind of blasphemy uttered by a deity against himself. Could such a time ever come ? And yet it did, as it now appears, almost in a flash. But that very great golfer continued to play the game when the little jump on to the toes and the follow-through seemed the same as before ; only the remorseless, realistic ball refused to go.

That is the braver course and surely the happier, but this " menace of the years " affects different people in different ways and sometimes in, to me at any rate, unexpected ways. Those whom I imagined going on for ever make a sudden break, and those who, as it seemed, could hardly bear the descent, go philosophically topping and slicing down the hill. I can recall one whom I should have thought as nearly as might be untouched by vain regrets, and yet he gave up early and utterly. He never tired of looking on, with a club under his arm, but only in the far distance, when he believed nobody by, could he be seen now and then to play a shot with it, nor, I think, would it have been tactful to admit that one had played the spy on his privacy. More enviable was another, a great player in his day and one of perennial keenness, who went on playing in a green old age, hardly realising what had befallen him. He still experimented with clubs of vast weight, because some lusty young driver used them ; still walked on and on expecting to find his ball, long after he had passed it. He must have been puzzled now and then, but I doubt if he ever clearly drew the painful deduction from the obvious facts. Dickens once wrote a story called *A Child's Dream of a Star.*

I think that old friend was happily dreaming it till the day of his death.

There was one golfer whom in this regard I admired more than any other, and since I have nothing but praise to give, why should I not name him? This was the late Mr. Mure Fergusson. In his prime he had not suffered bad players very gladly, but when he was old and stiff and full of rheumatism, and had to receive many strokes from those to whom he had once given them, he went on his way round the links with a dour cheerfulness. He recounted with grim enjoyment how his small caddie had declared that he might yet become a player if he could learn not to drop his shoulder. He even adopted the mental attitude of the poor and lowly so far as to murmur at the unfairness of certain bunkers into which his best shots found their way. I could not help reflecting how tersely he would once have received such complaints, but I expressed the deepest sympathy and felt it.

It is sometimes said that every officer should serve some time in the ranks in order to know and understand what the private soldier is thinking. It might be similarly argued that the good golfer should graduate through the ranks of the long handicapped to learn the fiery but often unspoken indignations of the humble. As a rule he has begun too young for such knowledge and has forgotten the time when the bunkers seemed hopelessly far away. It was pathetic to find Mure of all men attaining to it in his old age.

For myself, if I may for a moment be wholly egotistical, I incline to think that the game gave me up in what seemed a hard way and yet may in reality have been a merciful one. I could still play not too outrageously ill when arthritis made so sudden and rapid an attack that the descent from two rounds to one, one round to nine holes and then to just a few practice shots was rapid too. Vanity had little to endure and no excuses were needed for that which was obvious. The practice shots can still be played now and then and give pleasure even though a rather painful one, and if vanity dies so hard that it prefers them in solitude, that is an innocent and forgivable weakness. Even as I write, I am looking forward to a few of them within sound of the sea.

And so " avay vith melincolly " and let me count the blessings of giving up. They are not to be despised and are reasonably free from the reproach of sour grapes. At least some of the fun, much of the companionship and all the friendliness remain. There is great pleasure in watching, though it must be owned that golf drives a harder bargain with the retired than does any other game. He cannot sit at his ease in the pavilion or on a stand, but must pursue the players over a broken and difficult country. He comes to watch more and more on inner lines of communication. He resigns himself to the knowledge that the holes at the far end of the course are not for him ; he must be content with ghoulish hopes of an agonising finish about the sixteenth and seventeenth greens. If he inclines to be censorious in his comments he cannot be put to the proof ; no one can say to him in effect, " Go and do better yourself." I do not think, however, that he does grow fiercer but rather milder. His judgment is apt to err on the side of admiring very ordinary strokes, since it is tinged by his knowledge that he can no longer make any strokes at all. It is so hard to maintain a wholly impersonal standard of criticism. He falls unconsciously into a second childhood of making pyrotechnic noises at any normal drive. The fact that he could once make such a drive himself may be obvious to him from well-known landmarks on the course but he does not believe it for all that. It is an excess of humility and not of arrogance that makes him a less and less trustworthy judge of others. He is so humble as to mistake anything that glitters, however faintly, for gold. I would put little faith in him now as a chooser of teams.

There is no great comfort in that to be sure, but in some other compensations there is very real comfort. For the retired warrior there are no anxieties, no agonies, no thwarted ambitions, no wretched little jealousies, no bitter regrets.

Never again will he toss and tumble, thinking of the match that is before him on the morrow. No black demon of a missed putt from the match that is past will crouch beside his pillow to arouse him at midnight. He will not watch his conqueror going on gaily from round to round and murmur to himself that that is where he ought to be. There will be no penitence for having been cross, for as far as the game is concerned he need never be cross any more ; no miserable pretence of being a good loser, for there is nothing to lose.

On the morning of the match the course had always a hard, unsympathetic look. The greens so beautifully trim and smooth seemed like places of public execution made ready, on to which the criminal must step out with a show of bravery at the appointed hour. The very flags blowing out straight from their sticks spoke to him of the wind as a personal enemy. Fate still hangs brooding heartless over the course but him she cannot touch. The voice of the starter is no longer the voice of doom. There will be heaps of slain ere the bloody day is out, but he will still be alive in inglorious security.

Gone too are those frantic inquisitions into wrongdoing, that last minute searching for a remedy. The retired, like the King, can do no wrong and so does not want to find out what he had been doing wrong. Once upon a time he could scarcely bear the thought of the morrow, to say nothing of the intervening night, unless he had exorcised the devil of error. He must light on a new device before darkness inexorably fell. The gathering dusk still found him hunting feverishly while the lights began to twinkle in the clubhouse, and all the sane people had long since gone home. It was so essential to peace of mind to finish with a good one ; the risk of just one more was so terrible and yet something stronger than himself drove him on.

The wear and tear of those researches was great, alike for body and mind, and yet I incline to think that they are what he misses most. Practice shots are now but a pleasant recreation; they have no serious object in view and so can have no ending of triumphant relief. He can still say to himself that he now knows what he was doing, that he has got it at last, but all too soon comes the thought, "After all what's the use?" The instinct to end with a good one is not to be eradicated (good is a relative term) but it is only an instinct, unsupported by reason. There is this consolation; it is now possible to study a new work of instruction on the game without seizing the fire-irons to test the author's doctrines. Let AB be the intended line of flight and let CD be anything it pleases! He can read the stuff, not without a certain detached interest, but as tranquilly as he would the *Pons Asinorum* itself.

I have made the best case I can for giving up, and there really does seem something, not much perhaps but something, to be said for it.

Superfluous lags the vet'ran on the stage,

but people are wonderfully kind in not telling him so, and he is happily stupid enough not to find it out for himself.

In the Cotswolds

Ille terrarum mihi præter omnes Angulus ridet

To every one of us that pleasant little Horatian tag has its own meaning : I have applied it impartially and unhesitatingly for most of my life to my own small corners of Kent and Merioneth. Now in my old age I am not sure that I have not turned traitor to both, dreaming of the Cotswolds and of one particular nook there. Certainly it has an entrancing smile that can put any allegiance in jeopardy.

It seems odd to reflect that till a comparatively short time ago I had never even seen the Cotswolds. Chipping Camden was a Cotswold name, because I had read and re-read the eternally fascinating puzzle of the Camden Wonder ; I knew that the luckless Joan Perry and her two sons had been hanged on the top of Broadway Hill ; but I never expected to see Camden or imagined that that hill would become one of the landmarks of an annual and eager expedition. Still less did I think that for hard on two years I should stay almost immovable in the Cotswolds. I had only the most shadowy notion where they were to be found on the map.

My original introduction to them I owe to one particular

friend. He regularly made the journey to Merioneth in his car and I as regularly stuck to the train, which I knew to be comfortable and believed to be romantic. Among the attractions that he offered me, for some time in vain, was that we should go through the heart of the Cotswolds. At last one year I gave way to his kind persuasion and was instantly filled with the intemperate zeal of the convert. The journey was often repeated but I remember the first with extraordinary clearness ; how we set out on a morning of unutterable rain, which bore out my worst forebodings ; how we stopped for petrol on the crest of the hill above Benson, where the rain miraculously ceased and the rest of the day was all blue and gold ; how after passing Oxford and drawing near to Woodstock he uttered the memorable words, which we whispered to one another on so many occasions afterwards, " Soon we shall be in the Cotswolds." Sure enough, once through Woodstock, there came a long low grey wall on the left, shaded by tall trees, and after that the whole world became an enchanted one of grey stone.

Chipping Norton was thoroughly engaging, for we had not then discovered the alternative way past the Rollright Stones, that tiny little stonehenge bowered in trees, with its most distinguished member, the King of the Stones, standing in lonely grandeur over a hedge on the other side of the road, keeping himself to himself. My enthusiasm was now rising higher every moment, so that I even remember—I admit nothing could apparently be duller—the man in the brown coat in the car in front of us, who turned off the main road to Cornwell. Even he was exciting and would have been still more so had I then known that Cornwell is near Warren Hastings's Daylesford. Next was Moreton-in-the-Marsh, and then suddenly, with a real passion of pleasure, I came to Bourton-on-the-Hill. I have seen many lovely places in the Cotswolds since that day, but the first vision of Bourton with the Manor House at the foot of the hill and the cottages clambering up it, each with its bright garden of flowers, remains unmatched. Let others praise Bourton-on-the-Water with its succession of dear little bridges, that give a feeling of the Backs at Cambridge in miniature. I shall always be faithful to the one on the hill. Then after the signposts had cried and cried to us to go to Blockley—there surely never was a village so persistent in calling attention to its charms—came the steep, winding hill (with a thought for those unfortunate Perrys) down into Broadway. Broadway is wonderfully beautiful, and its beauties are disclosed gradually and with perfect art by the curve of the road. Yet there is something about it too trim and self-conscious as if it were dressed for a party. It pays the penalty of its fame and makes us feel as if we were mere sightseers instead of honest travellers. On a drive through English country I like to picture myself as Tom Smart in his clay-coloured gig with the red wheels and the vixenish mare, not as a tripper with a guide-book. However that may be, and perhaps I am unjust, Broadway marks, as far as that road is concerned, the end of the true Cotswolds,. for the lovely curving grey street ends lamentably in a suburb of red brick. I must confess that in the Cotswolds the over-zealous convert becomes priggish and tiresome about anything but grey stone, and shudders away from as much as a brick chimney-stack in a highly affected manner. Still those red houses at the end of Broadway do come as a shock. Soon after them we are among the plum and apple orchards on the way to Evesham, with all sorts of attractive things still before us—Worcester Cathedral, a dim vision of Stokesay, the glorious Castle at Ludlow, and the tree that puts forth perennial shoots of Union Jacks and red and white ensigns at Aston-on-Clun. Nevertheless, on leaving Broadway we heave a sad little sigh, for the best is over and the Cotswolds are behind us.

My appetite for that magical country had now been fairly whetted. No more trains took me to Wales as long as the friendly car was available, and its owner and I even made a pilgrimage of the inside of a week to the Cotswolds and saw all manner of new and delightful places. We were frankly trippers this time and did the Slaughters and Bibury and the Gatehouse at Stanway, Burford, Fairford, Stow-on-the-Wold and Chipping Camden, the Roman Villa at Chedworth (which I was to know so well later) and in short made a " merry-go-rounder " of it. It is a fine country for such explorations, for, apart from the actual sights, the views are on so grand a scale. The roads for the most part run high, as it were on the roof of the world, and we can see far on either side of us. The drives, apart from their objects, are delightful for their own sake.

However, I must not become a guide-book, considerable as is the temptation, but will come to the war-time when our dear little village—the possessive pronoun must be forgiven—became for our family a blessed haven of refuge. It is on the banks of the Coln, a river well known to fishermen, of whom, sad to say, I am not one, with Ablington and Bibury on one side, Coln Rogers and Coln St. Dennis on the other, and the metropolis of Cirencester a few miles away. We had stayed there before the war and been enthralled by everything to do with it, even the mooing of early cows that woke us as they passed along the road to their meadows ; but we only came to know it well when, on a sudden impulse and through the lucky chance of a house, we took ourselves there, bag and baggage, out of poor battered Kent.

It was when we settled down that we really came to know and love it, and our love was reinforced by gratitude. There is little of it to know, for it is the tiniest of villages, with no shop, and no public house, and no parsonage, nothing indeed in the way of public institutions but a church, under the shadow of which our house nestled, and a post office. The great and only adventure was an occasional expedition into Ciren—it is too rarely called Cisseter nowadays—to shop. For that town I had had almost from the dawn of life a romantic feeling. A house-maid at my grandfather's house had come from there and on going away to get married had in the kindness of her heart given me as a farewell offering a little picture of her native church under a glass case, something in the form of a child's snowstorm. I am afraid I had not thought of Jane for years until in driving on our pilgrimage through Gloucestershire and having but the haziest notion as to where we were, I caught a glimpse of a tower in the distance. Then she and her present came back in a flash and I exclaimed with absolute certainty, " Cisseter Church ! " A most noble church it is, not of the typical Cotswold grey, but of a golden colour, such as is often to be seen at Bath. It was an enchantingly restful place to wander in, while the family went on their virtuous errands to the butcher and the baker, and I shall never so ungratefully forget poor Jane again. At the risk of writing myself down an irretrievably sentimental idiot I must add that I still treasure a tie that I bought in Cirencester. I could find my way to the shop blindfold. It is a tie of no conspicuous qualities—blue with white spots, and the white is now becoming as the Cotswold grey ; but we all have our private fancies in the way of keepsakes and no ruthless domestic tidying shall ever wrest my tie from me.

Our refuge would have seemed peaceful in any case, in contrast to Kent. The nearest siren was in Cirencester, and since it was inaudible, the air-raid warden used to blow a whistle when now and again the enemy squadron poured over our heads to attack places that they thought more important. The village itself was not so sure of its unimportance. As the warden remarked, some people liked to hear the whistle and others did not : so he blew it softly, a very discreet compromise.

Leaving the war out of the question, the village was wonderfully peaceful. If ever there was real country this was it. It made me feel sadly urban, I confess, to stand gaping at a threshing machine, throwing up its cloud of misty gold into the air or following another mysterious machine, said to have come at vast cost from America, which reaped and bound the corn all at once, as it went purring round the big field. I was not as good as I could have wished at talking to the ploughman, ever ready to desist from his labours for a little conversation. I could not acquire the real knack of leaning over a stile or a gate, gazing into vacancy in a pleasing vacancy of mind. If I had only been a fisherman ! But the best I could do was to look on at the catching of some form of crayfish to be found in the Coln—a picturesque amusement indulged in after dark by the light of lanterns, and thus reminiscent of the salmon-spearing by torchlight in *Guy Mannering*.

The real and rather humiliating truth is that too many of us, though we may live away from the town, have no right at all to call ourselves countrymen, and know next to nothing of our own countryside. We are seldom at home for long enough at a time, and are for ever flitting elsewhere, save when we are comatose in our own gardens. In reading the early chapters of *Tom Brown's Schooldays*, one of my most faithful bedside books, I had always felt the author's lash on my own back when, in upholding his beloved Berkshire, he breaks out against the gadabouts who do not know their own fields and woods and lanes. Certainly I had never " stayed put " anywhere for so long till we took refuge in Gloucestershire. A very occasional dash to London, reluctantly undertaken, was the only break in that placid monotony. So all our mild walks became extremely familiar, though never tiresome, and all sorts of things, quite dull and prosaic in themselves, such as the great clamp of potatoes on the road to Ablington, were soon our oldest friends and as if we had known them all our lives. I have only to shut my eyes to see with astonishing clearness the little secret path where we must brush our way through a tangle of wild roses. It was there that we once encountered a small pig, apparently detached from his family, who fled before us, ever and anon turning at bay and then, finding at the last instant that he could not bear us, scuttling away again with infantile squeaks. Doubtless there are many small pigs in the world but there is an eternal Cotswold glamour about that one.

All the fields became my intimate friends, since in my capacity of hedge golfer, if I may so call myself, I used to wander off with a club and ball on voyages of exploration. I could still, I think, enumerate nearly all of them ; the field with the stone wall to carry, and the one so near the river that every shot was a fearful joy. There was the large and splendid one that had here and there tiny mysterious patches of sand, as if some golfing promoters had " salted " it, as they are said to do with gold to entrap the unwary. And at the cost of a climb there were the heights of Ablington Downs, where the wind blew freshly and one looked down on the village and the river in the valley, as if on a large-scale map. Some of my lost balls are doubtless mouldering there to this day and may in future ages give rise to curious geological speculations. I came to love those fields and the very trees in the hedges by which I tried to mark the ball. Some of them, as the war went on, were ripped from me by the remorseless plough. So it was with the noblest of them all, fifty-five acres of short, kindly turf. It was there that I used to talk to the friendly ploughman, engaged on his task of gradually reducing my playground strip by strip. He had been, he said, a sailor, and so had seen other lands far from our valley, but he was redolent of his own soil and I doubt if he had ploughed any other. At any rate, I liked to think of him saying with Cuddie Hedrig, " I am not clear if I can pleugh ony place but the Mains and Mucklewhame, at least I never tried ony other ground, and it wadna come natural to me."

The ploughing was pleasant to see, even though it destroyed that peerless field. There was always some game to play by oneself, whether in watching the exquisite curve as the furrow turned the corner, or in timing the tractor on its way to the far end of the field, or in backing one furrow against another, as we do with the waves when looking idly at the sea. Before that there had been the exciting moment in which the tractor had made a beginning of its deadly work by cutting the first brown stripe across the green, as it were a sudden bleeding gash in the meadow's flesh. Stolid men in leggings and mackintoshes stood gazing at it with unwinking eyes, and it was easy to catch the infection and as hard to tear oneself away as it is from watching a cricket match. And when the green field had all changed to brown there was in the newly-turned earth a wonderful susceptibility to all manner of colours. The wet furrows seemed, in imagination at least, to reflect a pale-blue glint from the sky, and at sunset they were stained red and gold and purple. So there was compensation for the loss of the field, even if one could have grudged it to the plough, and besides there were always pastures new to be explored.

As to the greyness of the houses and the instinctively lovely slopes of the stone roofs, familiarity with them bred only a greater affection. Those who belong to the soil and have lived on it all their lives grow so accustomed to these beauties that they take them for granted and sometimes tire of them, thinking of themselves as dwelling in a grey twilight and longing now and then for a change, even to that staring red brick. I remember one day that two of us stood watching a man building, or rather re-building, a stone wall with an evidently skilful and practised hand. In answer to one or two questions he explained his art in a very friendly way but could not wholly conceal his surprise, almost his contempt, for our interest. Strangers, he admitted, often seemed to be interested, but " we don't think nothing of it ourselves." No doubt it is surprising to find others admiring what to you is simply the commonplace of everyday life. It is very likely tiresome to be asked questions, but the politeness in answering them never fails. Indeed politeness is not the right word ; for it is a natural courtesy born of genuine friendliness. It is one of the most delightful things about the Cotswolds, where every one is ready to talk and the smallest child passes the time of day to a stranger on the road as a matter of course.

It can be cold in the Cotswolds ; they generally have an honourable place in the weather reports in times of snowfall, and I solemnly assert that nobody knows how little feeling there can be in the toes and how much comfort in fluffy boots till he has spent a winter in a Cotswold house with stone floors. So it was only part of the appropriate romance that we should

be more or less snowed up there. To say so much is perhaps
to plume ourselves unduly, but there were at least one or two
days when only the heroic baker from Ablington got through
to us, and he was regarded as might be one who had wriggled
through the enemy lines to a beleaguered town. The walk
down the icy slope to the post office took on the character of
an arctic expedition, and the cheerful plump, plump of the
snow shovelled off the roof still rings in my ears. Sounds, like
scents, can on the instant recall a whole picture, and that is
one which will always bring back our village. That and the
early-mooing cows and the tripple of the farmer's pony and
the hammering in the carpenter's shop on the tiny village green
over the way. They all go to swell the " live murmur " of our
Cotswold day.

A Day in Bed

No one would wish to be ill. The mere suggestion demands much touching of wood. It is in itself a thanksgiving for being well. " Yet surely a little trifling indisposition —isn't there something unkind in this violent, robust, unfeeling health ? " There are moments when those words of Faulkland's seem almost sensible, when the thought of a day or two in bed make a strong appeal. Especially on a bitter winter's day the common cold presents itself in seductive colours. Nothing serious of course, but just a gentle snuffle which might grow worse if we did not take it in time. That is the limit of our modest ambition. It is to that that we draw attention outwardly with a fine bravado, inwardly with the hope that we may be encouraged to cosset ourselves.

It may be said that there is nothing simpler than to take a rest in bed if we have a mind to it, but that would be altogether too shameful. Especially in these days, when there is a shortage of domestic help, we should feel intolerably guilty. Meals in bed demand a good conscience if we are to taste their full piquancy. Trays and bed tables and the whole apparatus of illness cannot be too lightly invoked, but a cold in the head, which makes us only a very little sorry for ourselves, will also make conscience amenable to reason.

I have a recollection that when at school we " stayed out " for some trifling or even imaginary ailment, our first act was to put on a " change coat," which had a certain foundation in sense since it was loose and comfortable, and also an elaborate collar and tie, such as we should normally wear only at home. That now sounds wholly absurd and yet it enhanced the pleasures of idleness. It was a symbolical act, signifying that for the time being we were not as others but were pampered and fortunate persons. There are many such pieces of symbolism which, though tiresome in themselves, such as packing before a holiday, are a hundred times worth while, because they rub in our felicity. Here was one, costing no trouble at all, which by proclaiming us enviable, heightened the luxury of our feelings. So it is with the act of going to bed with a cold, and I say " going to " rather than " staying in " bed. The absolute of enjoyment is to be attained by getting up for breakfast, not without some little affectation of martyr-dom, and then being over-persuaded into going back to bed again. It is tiresome to undress so soon after dressing, but it is worth it, for the resumed pyjamas become the garb of a holy and beautiful sacrifice.

Neither, within certain limits, is the cold itself without its charms. We do not think much of other people's colds, but there is hardly any one who does not detect a peculiar quality in his own. We boast that we do not often catch one, but when we do, it really is a cold ; it is " certain to eventuate a spanker." That preliminary sensation at the back of the throat is not in itself comfortable but we can bear it for its presage of great things to come. When in due course it melts and resolves itself, we surrender to the ensuing state of liquefac-tion with an utter abandonment. We let our sneezes rever-berate unrestrained through the house and enumerate the handkerchiefs we have used as a conqueror counts his captured standards after a battle.

54

A Day in Bed

Clearly our cold must not be too bad, or there will be no fun. Let us have no nonsense about a temperature, or at most let it rise half a degree or so at night. We have given our proofs with our sneezes and snuffles and so need not be afraid lest the thermometer should pronounce us impostors. We must be essentially well and yet objects of pity. Charles Lamb in his essay called *The Convalescent* enlarged on the " regal " character of the sick bed. It is the perfect epithet, but he had been too ill. He had tossed and tumbled and had " nothing to think of but how to get well." That will never do. The ideal is rather to have nothing to think of but how to wring from authority one more day, or, if not a whole day, then just one more breakfast in bed. By all means let us " enjoy monarchal prerogatives " but we must be well enough consciously to revel in their exercise. Granted so much, they are delicious. Ministering angels come tiptoeing into the room in a manner most gratifying to the feelings ; they shut doors with infinite delicacy inch by inch, as if we had just fallen into a light, sweet sleep on which our life depends. The dog gives but one sharp bark and then has obviously been smothered in a cushion. The daily routine of the household is but a faint and distant murmur. For our sake a beautiful tranquillity reigns. The telephone bell cannot indeed be restrained, but we would not have it stifled if we could. It only emphasises our bliss. In the ordinary way, having given everybody else a chance of answering it, we should have to go and answer it ourselves. Now we are absolutely forbidden to do so. If after repeated attempts it dies away into a reproachful silence, we can think without a pang of some frustrated person who has been told that there is no reply. Possibly he had something very important with which to trouble us, but we are not to be troubled. It will brace him up to have to try again. Let him ring !

The first hour or two of our seclusion are so fully taken up with contemplating our own bliss that there is no need for any other occupation. The patient, especially if he be a golfer and so given to the inventing of new styles, may pass his time very pleasantly in experimenting with his own arms and legs. Even as he has constantly discovered the vast importance of fresh attitudes in putting, so now he lights on some slight deviation from the ordinary, a mere matter of an inch or two, productive of eternal comfort. Another golfing game deals with problems of design. The eiderdown is a flat, open expanse of links to be moulded into a noble course, full of fascinating undulations. The patient has but to raise his knees and there springs up a mountain range over which he must drive to an unseen green beyond. Another dexterous turn and behold there is a narrow valley winding between sand hills on either hand. Banks and braes and hollows, uphill lies and downhill lies—never were such kaleidoscopic changes, such magical architecture.

When he grows tired of this childishness there is always the resource of sleep. In workaday life anybody can go to sleep after lunch but hardly before it. That is neither decent nor possible. Yet on a day in bed we can glide away into a snooze at any time. Moreover, it is accounted to us for virtue. We are told that there is nothing so good for a cold as to sleep it off. Even so there will be moments to be filled up, and then comes the question of reading. Newspapers are not to be encouraged, for they bring the outer world too near, and it is part of our happy pose to shut it out. If we are conscious of it at all it should be as the shrill of a railway engine miles and miles away which comes faintly to us on the breeze. " Confound their politics " is the motto for a day in bed.

Books are the thing, and it is essential that they should be old books. Here again it is one of the beauties of our situation that we can do openly that which might otherwise provoke some sense of shame. He who constantly reads *Pickwick* to the exclusion of more modern literature does so for the most part in secret ; he may not deny the charge but he is a little confused if caught red-handed. Now there need be no pretence ; he can enjoy a sick man's fancies. It is at such moments that the most brilliant inspiration sometimes comes to him in a flash. Just as Mr. Pitt when *in extremis* wished for one of Bellamy's pork pies, so the patient feels a sudden conviction that a little *Treasure Island* would do him all the good in the world. Or there is Sherlock Holmes. Undoubtedly *The Six Napoleons* is the very thing, and with the invalid's licensed caprice he sends people hunting all over the house for it. No, *Boscombe Valley* or *The Speckled Band* will *not* do ; at any other time they would be capital but now it must be that one story or nothing, and the search is renewed. Above all, we desire on a day in bed to be happy and comfortable, and how can we be sure of that if we read a new book ? We may be miserably disappointed, whereas in an old one we know exactly what to expect and the anticipation heightens the pleasure. So do our recollections of some of the many times we have read it before. If I pitch on *Middlemarch* I am instantly transported to the year 1918 and a truck on a Decauville line through Bulgaria, in which I am being sent back sick to the base. *Middlemarch* is a great comfort but an even greater one is the hope that I shall be sent home. It is a vision that cannot even now be thought of calmly. Again, if I choose one of the earlier Holmes stories, I see myself at school making privateering expeditions across Weston's Yard to intercept the paper boy and so grab the first look at the *Strand*. With luck the new adventure might be read before Chapel. Holmes was new then, but he is better still now that he is old, a monument hung about with memories.

Fully as important as the question of what to read is that of what to eat. A normal diet would too palpably demonstrate us to be humbugs, and is opposed to all proper notions of playing the game. It is an integral part of the pomp and circumstance of a cold that we should submit to reasonable restrictions. The only proper diet for a convalescent is whiting followed by rice pudding, with a hope of chicken on the second day, if indeed there be a second day. The whiting is the mildest and most innocent of fishes, only saved from positive dullness by his amusing parlour trick of eating his

57

own tail ; but who will deny him a certain glamour in bed ? Rice pudding is for the moment a thing of the past, but let us forget that and look forward to happier days ! Here there arises a question of some nicety. To attain perfection rice pudding demands jam, preferably strawberry jam. If we have jam with it now, will it be an artistic mistake ? Will it too crudely expose our pretence of illness ? It is a question that each patient must decide for himself, but for my part I think the risk may be taken.

Such being the manifest charms of a mild cold, it is odd that more people do not appreciate them. I read the other day of a hospital in the West of England where experiments were being made as to the source of the common cold. To that scientific end a flow of volunteers was necessary and the stream showed signs of running dry. Apart from the sense of virtue in aiding the cause of research the patients would have a holiday in warm and comfortable quarters and a modest sum of daily pocket money into the bargain. They were assured that the treatment did not always produce a cold and that, if it did, it would not be a bad one. And yet they hesitated to answer this modern Mrs. Bond who cried, " Dilly, dilly, dilly, dilly, come and be inoculated."

It seemed singular, and yet there was one possible defect in the plan. Not only must these self-sacrificing persons be strictly isolated but they must be isolated in couples, and voluntarily to shut yourself up for ten days or so with a perfect stranger is to take an almost heroic risk. It is well known that Arctic explorers, imprisoned for months amid the snow and ice, sometimes come near to hating one another, and even in ten days seclusion there loom hideous possibilities of boredom and irritation. For a day or two the pair might compare symptoms with a cheerful interest but after that the subject would surely pall. " I don't care about other people's dinners," once remarked a very honest small boy, and is not the same true about other people's sneezes ? And then, suppose one prisoner caught a cold and the other resisted all the well-meant germs, an odious jealousy might spring up, though on which side it is hard to determine. The regrettable fact is that this enjoyment of a cold is a selfish one. The sick bed may be regal but what if there are two kings?

In Macedonia I once wrote some lyrics for a divisional pantomime. They have wholly vanished from my mind, save two lines, for which I claim no merit whatever, but they now come pat to my purpose:

Dear Miss Anopheles
Do come and bite my knees.

I need scarcely add that the female anopheles was the carrier of malaria, and malaria, though an unpleasant ailment, yet might mean some days of peace and quiet with perhaps a convalescent camp to follow, and even—a wild and frantic dream—the chance of being sent home. The lady never bit me, or at least not to any effect, for which I am now profoundly thankful, but at the time there was a genuine home-sick ring about those two doggerel lines. They ought not to have been written but they came from the heart. We ought not to wish for a cold, especially as we never know that Providence may not respond with embarrassing generosity. And yet sometimes when the rain is beating on the window—Avaunt! thou black, shameful, impious desire. Get thee behind me!

Watching Cricket

I T is doubtful whether in real life it occurs to any one to
take a distinguished foreigner to see a cricket match, on
the ground that it is a typical British institution without
which his impressions of our national life would be incomplete.
In print, however, it happens regularly, and the foreign gentleman as regularly and politely wonders why so many people
go to watch anything so solemn and so dull. There are even
Britons, blind to the glory of their birthright who wonder too,
and that less politely. They are, it is to be feared, irredeemable,
beyond the reach of our prayers, lost sheep who will never find
their way back to the fold ; we sorrow over them as men
without hope. We wonder when we go to a cricket match, but
to a very different effect. The marvel to us is that on the day
when we chance to have a free afternoon, there should be so
many thousands presumably with the same unimpeachable
excuse for idleness as ourselves. Moreover, we gather from
their talk that this is for them no rare treat, no snatching of
an hour or two. On the contrary, they have been there since
the first ball was bowled and will remain till stumps are drawn,
not as we shall, from a despicable infirmity of will, but of

deliberate purpose ; they were there yesterday and mean to be there to-morrow. They are one of the standing mysteries of existence.

They are clearly addicts, and we who visit a cricket match but seldom and then on some sudden impulse, begin to feel after a while that we too, are under the influence of a drug. It must be a dreadfully potent one, for it soon becomes apparent that we shall never tear ourselves away. We may vow over and over again that we will see just one more over. It is but the shallowest pretence. Once the watcher has settled down in his seat with his packet of sandwiches, appointments to keep or trains to catch yield up their power before the infinitely more compelling magic that now has him in its grip. " Malice domestic, foreign levy, nothing can touch him further." Only when stumps are pulled up and he rises and stretches himself and rubs his eyes, does he awake from his beautiful, drug-sodden dream.

Doubtless the game possesses great and intrinsic qualities which promote these sensations in the onlooker. Beauty there is beyond question. It is not always necessarily in the setting, as it were in the frame of the picture ; but there is always enchanting beauty in the picture itself, in the field of play with its white figures, and here and there a touch of brighter colour. Constable, I have been told, would often cunningly add a tiny splash of scarlet to the quieter colours of his landscape, and in the panorama of a cricket field one Harlequin cap can play a similar part. And there is the beauty of movement. It is not the violent movement of the football field wherein at every instant the whole scene changes like a kaleidoscope. At cricket most of the figures remain relatively tranquil and the gaze is concentrated on a single one chasing the ball to cut it off in its flight, while in the middle :

The run-stealers flicker to and fro, to and fro.

There is about this game a kind of restful excitement which

no other can quite afford. To watch it is like reading a book
in which at the moment nothing very particular is going on,
but the reader feels in his bones that in a few pages something
unknown and overpowering will happen. The stage may be
occupied by secondary characters, talking their superficially
dull little talk, but its very dullness intensifies the thrill of
waiting for the sudden face at the window or the sound of
wheels that announces the coming of who knows what
tremendous event into our lives. In cricket the two stolid
batsmen scoring an occasional single are as the solitary Life
Guardsman who tells us that the procession is coming. In
themselves they are not enthralling, but there is always the
hope, often long deferred but never dying, that something
will happen at last and that it will have been a thousand times
worth waiting for.

Only rain can extinguish that ever springing hope, and then
indeed, it must be owned, cricket compares unfavourably with
some other rivals, or let us rather say presumptuous competitors. Other games can be watched in mackintoshes, but on
a cricket ground rain means blank despair. The saddest words
of tongue or pen are surely, " No play." They are sad enough
when we are robbed of our earliest morning's reading in the
newspaper, but how far worse for those actually on the ground
who wait on and on buoyed up by a false optimism ! There is
a dreadful difference between the walk of the umpires at the
beginning of an innings and as they come out to inspect the
wicket. In the one case they are cheerful and jaunty ; they
may even bowl a ball down to one another as if to proclaim
" Et militavi." In the other they are too clearly fulfilling a
formal duty. Back they go and the world becomes again a
dreary, sodden blank. Far wiser to go away, but that is what
we cannot do. We stay on, not quietly or resignedly, but filled
with a horrid restlessness. We read our programme with the
same desperation with which we look at the illustrated papers
of the week before last in the dentist's waiting-room. Ever and
anon we think we see a rift in the clouds, but should our neigh-

bour, however mildly, assert that he sees one, we could do anything to him that is malignant and revengeful. We are at once
hoping against hope and determined to be hopeless. But will
that bitter experience deter us when next we have the chance ?
A hundred times no. Cricket has too fast a hold. In this grip
on our affections, cricket has one great advantage, that we
play and know it before all the other games worthy of the
name. Its metaphors are much more generally used and more
widely understood than those drawn from any other. Its roots
are so deep that we cannot trace them. I began to play golf
when I was eight, a very early start for an English small boy in
those days, but I was by that time a veteran, though not a skilful
cricketer. Already for some years past a devoted housemaid
had bowled to me with a lawn tennis ball down a dark passage
with a portable vermilion fire engine for wicket. Already my
one consuming ambition, which remained alas ! ungratified,
was for real white flannels and a blazer. I can remember the
time before golf was, but not the time before cricket. And so
it is with thousands of others. They may have transferred their
active allegiance but the original loyalty survives.

The sounds of cricket are as old as the other country sounds
that are coeval with earliest consciousness—the whetting of a
scythe, the creak of the well wheel, the clink of a pail in the
stable yard and the thunderous approach of a traction engine
down the lane. Whether it be the rapid tap-tapping of French
cricket or the boom of a boundary hit, it is unmistakable and
eternal. It happened to me not long ago to be sitting alone in
a Hampshire garden when there smote upon my ear, deep-
mouthed and solemn, that sacred sound. Somewhere, someone
had, in the words of W. G., put the bat against the ball. It was
not repeated and my hosts told me that I must have dreamed
it since there was no village match that day. I remained un-
convinced and later we heard that there had been in fact a
knock-up or practice game ; the music of one glorious stroke
had penetrated to me. How triumphant a vindication both for
me and for cricket !

Other games have sounds both pleasant and essentially their own. There is the thud of an unseen football, late on a winter's afternoon, when perhaps the players are veiled in mist. That too, gives an unmistakable thrill. The click of a golf ball, struck perfectly clean, especially with an iron, is eminently satisfying, and there are doubless others which mean as much to the lovers of their particular games. A little while after the war had ended there was a charming little account in *The Times* of revisiting the tennis court in Paris. The writer approached full of doubts and fears, but before he had opened the door there came to him the sound of the ball rattling on the pent house, and with an overpowering relief he knew that all was well. *Laudabunt alii ;* I shall cling to the sound of the ball on the bat as the most beautiful, the most characteristic of them all, and the one most deeply rooted in the memory.

There are other memorable sounds that belong to cricket at a later stage of our existence, in particular those of the different brands of applause. When we have not been to see a big match for some time, they come back to us with a delightful freshness. Sometimes a burst of clapping takes us wholly by surprise. A commonplace single produces a sudden storm and we wonder why, till a kind neighbour—neighbours are always very friendly at a cricket match—takes pity on our ignorance. By that one run the batsman had achieved a recondite record ; the whole ground had been panting for it and we had no presentiment. Then there is the little scattered volley that greets the end of a maiden over, a piece of almost formal politeness, but one never omitted. That too, is apt to surprise the visitor if he has grown so out of practice as to be rather a visitant. Not so the burst of clapping all round the ground that hails a century. The telegraph board is here a great help ; it is like the official cheer-leader at an American football match. Indeed it is better, for it not only tells us when to clap, but when to get ready to clap, so that we wait poised and expectant. The applause for a century differs slightly but perceptibly in quality from that which salutes the maker of a great score on his way back to the pavilion. The one breaks out immediately in full chorus ; the other hesitates for a moment, as if in decent regret, and then gradually swells and swells till he vanishes from sight. Incidentally, I always want to know, and no one can tell me, how many runs justify (*a*) the batsman in running rather than walking up the pavilion steps, and (*b*) the pavilion in standing up as one man to greet him.

I am afraid I have become rather a rare and lazy watcher nowadays, and it is the more shame to me, for I was well brought up and early broken in. Since my home was at Cambridge, I was taken now and then to Fenner's and remember a time, now almost prehistoric, when the notices of the University matches in the shop windows were signed " M. B. Hawke." There was a glorious day, perhaps my very first, when Cambridge made a great score against Mr. A. J. Webbe's team—J. A. Turner 109 not out, and I need not look it up. There was another sad one the next year when many of the same heroes were unaccountably bowled out by Crossland (of course he threw) for a miserable total. And then there was one day of combined splendours, which must have been in the May week. In the afternoon I went to Fenner's to see the Australians and in the evening down the river in a boat to see the May Races. And there on the tow path— this was the culminating moment—was Mr. H. W. Bainbridge, the Cambridge Captain, taking some of the Australians to look at the rowing. It was such an overwhelming event to see those heroes not in white flannels, " mystic, wonderful," but clad as ordinary persons. It was as if the gods had come down to earth—with walking sticks. It was exciting but somehow a little shocking, and I am not sure that they ever appeared quite such thoroughbred divinities again. There was something a little terrestrial about them ever afterwards.

Later on, the watching of School Matches on a half-holiday afternoon—in Upper Club, for Agar's Plough was then a plough—was a pleasant, easy-going amusement, but it lacked something of the old hero-worship. Perhaps this was because,

as it so happened, the Titans in those days were too palpably
on the other side. To know that A. C. MacLaren was at Harrow
and J. R. Mason at Winchester was reluctantly to admit that
we at Eton had only dwarfs. Still, on a fine day, with a rug
to lie on, it was agreeble enough. There were some who took
books with them, and others bags of cherries, and, apropos,
there comes suddenly back to me a W. G. story, once told me
by a kind correspondent. He was a schoolboy at Clifton, and
was duly watching a match with his bag of cherries, when there
suddenly loomed up before him that famous figure. The
Doctor, with his usual kindness to the young, began to talk
to him and condescended to share his cherries. Presently there
was another match and the same delightful thing happened
again. In fact, it happened so often that at last hero-worship
became tempered with apprehension, so quickly did the
cherries disappear. I do not know whether the Doctor said,
like the waiter in *David Copperfield*, " Come on, little 'un, and
let's see who'll get most," but there were moments when the
worshipper was almost tempted to hide from his divinity's all-
seeing eye. To-day, however, there remains no bitterness and
only a proud and happy memory.

To think of W. G. is to think of Gloucestershire and of the
village cricket that in my years as a war-refugee I watched in
the Cotswolds. I am conscious of having written of it before,
but I must pay it another brief tribute. The ground was perched
high, as it were on the roof of the world ; below was the valley
of the Coln ; and beyond it the hills rose steeply again, and,
as I sit in imagination sheltered from the wind under a stone
wall, I see the cloud shadows passing swiftly across them. How
beautiful were the caps of our side, red and white in quarters !
How still more beautiful their official braces, bearing a pattern
of roses and green leaves intertwined ! How pleasant to know
that there was one smiling corner of the earth where men still
batted in braces, as did Fuller Pilch !

One of my regrets, not indeed a bitter regret but rather a
gentle sadness, is that I have never beheld cricket on a northern

ground. I have seen Sheffield Wednesday play football at now departed Olive Grove, but never watched cricket at Bramall Lane. Old Trafford is but a name to me, though a heart-stirring one. Would any northerner feel thus about southern cricket, dreaming of the unknown beauties of Canterbury or Worcester ; I doubt it ; he would be confident that he had nothing to learn. There is about the north " a gloom, a glamour " for which the south can offer no counterpart. It is black and terrible ; it means to win and makes no pretence of doing anything else. I know not whether it is because they have had their *vates sacer* in Mr. Neville Cardus, but the north seems to have produced at once the raciest and the most formidable characters among cricketers. Whether it will continue to do so in such rich abundance, it is hard to say. I mistrust those admirable lighthouses, the Board Schools. Are there still such great huntsmen as we read of in the Druid's pages, or were they great only because a writer of genius described them ?

Ulyett and Hall, Grimshaw and Lee, Emmett and Saul Wade—these were my unseen heroes when I first mangled the family *Times* by cutting out the cricket and storing it in a box, and something of a similar halo hangs round their successors. I am Kent, born and bred, and I want with all my heart Kent to beat Yorkshire—but I hate Yorkshire being beaten. Perhaps, after all, Bramall Lane unvisited is best. It could not be more murkily romantic than is my picture of it.

Portrait of an Old Friend

THERE are some people who are such deep-rooted and familiar institutions in the lives of a particular circle that it is hard for its members to believe that they are not known to all the world. One of these was Mr. C. H. Allcock —everybody called him C. H.—who died last year at Bryntegwel, his house at Aberdovey, at the age of ninety-two. For those who had stayed with him there every year almost from time immemorial, his death meant the end of a pleasant and unique chapter in their lives. C. H. and his house had a taste and character entirely their own, and, though I fear that the task of conveying it intelligibly to other people is something too much for me, yet, for old sake's sake and in gratitude for much kindness, for many happy days and old-grouse-in-the-gun-room jokes, I think the attempt ought to be made. To the friends who shared with me the joys of those esoteric festivals, I can have nothing new to say. We have always been conscious of being a small and elect body as that of " the brethren assembling in Lantern Yard " in *Silas Marner*. We were partakers of the Bryntegwel mysteries ; we told each other C. H. stories whenever we met elsewhere, and were, possibly a great nuisance to the uninitiated. Yet even that now diminished band may, I hope, like to breathe again for a moment the airs of Merioneth and their comparative youth.

Sometime a Fellow of Emmanuel, first a master at Wellington, and then at Eton, where he was for a while a housemaster and for a number of years senior mathematical master, in his day a good cricketer—that was the summing up of his life in *The Times* when he died, and it was perfectly true, but how very far from suggesting anything out of the rut of an ordinary schoolmaster's career, anything of the odd, most kindly, lovable and, if the word may be ever so tenderly used, laughable personality? That, if it appears at all, is most likely to do so from some picture of our annual pilgrimages to the shrine.

C. H. was a very accurate man, with an accuracy always to be reinforced by books of reference (he knew the place of every one in the shelf) and not easily to be vanquished in argument. He was, likewise, if I may so describe him, a very traditional man. He had long since made up his mind whom he liked and what he liked them to do, and so the visit and the visitors must follow an exact tradition. So clearly was this recognised by us all that the annual invitation might be expected almost to a post at a particular date in early December. If ever it was a day late, we began to be afraid that we had committed some crime and were not to be asked, but the fear was groundless, the faithful letter always came. One friend of mine, who was regularly bidden, had once the ideal setting out. His porter at Paddington, about to label his luggage, said, " The same old place, I suppose." Nothing quite so beautiful ever happened to me, but there was an ineffable and immutable thrill about the starting on that journey. I look back particularly to the time when I was of the first batch of guests, some three or four days after Christmas, and we met C. H. and his brother, A. E., at Shrewsbury, and packed ourselves and our clubs into a fresh carriage for the last lap, a somewhat prolonged one with twenty-two stoppages

69

and one change, to Aberdovey. That was as unchanging as were all the other rites. Beyond the little station of Talerddig, where the train, after a painful climb, begins to rush down towards the sea, there is a certain natural arch in the rock. Several of us always thought we knew where to look for it, and C. H. always knew that we were all wrong. It was invariably too dark to see it, but that did not impair the argument, which was still raging at Cemmes Road and had barely ceased by Machynlleth, where we changed and had tea. There followed in due sequence the arrival at Aberdovey, where we were mobbed by small, competing caddies, the walk through the village street, with the Borth lights twinkling across the estuary, the climb up the hill and then one of the great events in every visitor's life, the greeting by Marshall.

Marshall was a dour old Scottish soldier, the perfect custodian and minister for such a temple. C. H. was accurate but Marshall was, if possible, more relentlessly accurate still. One by one he led us slightly apart, as if about to communicate something of private and peculiar importance, and asked at what time we should like to be called. Eight o'clock, each one replied, and—this was one of our oldest jokes—then came the invariable answer in a tone of palpably reasonable remonstrance, that he could not call everybody at the same time but would call one at two minutes to eight and another at two minutes past, an undertaking scrupulously carried out.

There followed in due course the first dinner, plain, honest and admirable, and if the sweets did not consist of rice pudding, apple tart and cheese cakes, my memory is sadly at fault. I wish I could do justice to the noble vintages, especially to the port wine, but I am too ignorant and it would be an insult to their memory. Enough that they were superlatively good, and one of the most familiar pictures in my mind is that of C. H. decanting them with loving care and providing a minute account of their respective years and shippers as he did so.

" Coffee in about twenty minutes, sir," Marshall said to C. H. at a precise moment and in a confidential whisper. He said it every night in exactly the same tone, as if originating an entirely novel suggestion, and after the coffee came the bridge. I have written to little purpose if I have not suggested that we always did much the same thing and that we did as we were told, and it was now, after dinner, that our discipline was seen at its rigorous best. There were very occasionally some so brave, even foolhardy, that they openly declared their preference for reading a book. Now and again they may be said to have got away with it. As a rule, however, four were set down to bridge, after a due process of cutting out, and the others were sent into the billiard-room next door. I imagine, indeed I am sure, that the standard of our bridge was on a par with the stakes, which were extremely low. It was too conversational a game for the more serious, and C. H. in particular, when he had two hands to play, did so to the accompaniment of a running soliloquy. The chief feature of the game was that it was forever Auction. Contract would have entered the house only across our host's dead body. Not that he had ever played it ; I doubt if he had ever seen it played, but he knew it was a bad game. So, even as whist lingered for years in some common-rooms or combination-rooms at Oxford or Cambridge, so Auction remained the last enchantment of the middle ages at Bryntegwel. As for the refugees in the billiard-room, it might be thought that they would enjoy a certain liberty, but there too, a beneficent despotism reigned. If the click of the balls was not heard, C. H., when he was dummy, might pay a domiciliary visit and it was better not to be caught without the cue in hand. As years went on there was, it must be confessed, a certain relaxation. In earlier days, bridge began after tea, but, gradually and imperceptibly, as people grew older and more tired after the day's golf, a period of surcease between tea and dinner was first allowed and then encouraged.

However, when I was first initiated there was no such

leniency. Marshall duly called us at eight, breakfast was, I think, at eight forty-five, and after breakfast we clattered down the hill to the links. By half-past twelve we were lunching in the club-house, with benedictine to follow. Soon after one we were at it once more, nor was that all, for after the second round we were mobilised yet again for a nine-hole foursome. If Satan found any mischief for our idle hands to do it will be admitted that he had but limited opportunities. There were occasional wet days, of course, when we might possibly stand easy for a little, but they were few, since Aberdovey is rightly called by the guide book the Madeira of North Wales. As for cold days or windy days or frosty days, these were never permitted to interfere.

Shame on the false Etruscan
Who lingers in his home.

Our Lars Porsena led his army marching down the hill, and it knew better than to hang back.

And who, it may be asked, composed this docile array? Nearly all were schoolmasters, or, as time went on, retired schoolmasters, who had doubtless learnt, as they enforced, the lesson of obedience. I was very nearly the only one of another profession. There are those who entertain a fear of pedagogues, especially when, as is their habit, they descend in herds. " Going away ? " somebody once said to a golfer at Bembridge. "Why ? " " Eton masters coming down next week," was the answer. May I say, with all humility and respect, and in gratitude for many friendships, that it was a grossly unjust one. It may be that, as with any other class of men, the outsider will take a little time to adjust himself, to acquire the tone of his company, but I will hardly admit even so much. I suppose there was a certain knack of the talk to be caught, as according to Stevenson, men catch the knack of talking schooners in the South Seas. What did we talk about, besides our own rounds of golf? I know so well, and yet I can hardly say. If I sat

at that cheerful board again, I could fall into the way of it
as easily as if I had never left it, and yet it eludes me. Cricket?
Yes, sometimes. We most of us liked cricket, and C. H. was
full of cricketing lore. Every now and again at suitable
intervals we would get him to tell us of the crowning glory of
his career, of the wickets he had taken for Cambridge Past and
Present, when they had beaten the Australians. There was
one year, so long ago as to be before the days of wireless, when
the Test Matches had reached a crucial point in Australia, and
heroic volunteers went down that steep hill in the dark after
dinner to buy an evening paper that we might gloat over the
triumphs of Barnes and Fielder.

Cricket was undoubtedly a topic, and so were vintages, on
which there was much learning displayed. So were stocks
and shares, for the schoolmaster is, in my experience, far from
being the unworldly innocent that he is supposed to be in
this regard. There were likewise the apples and pears at
dessert, but this was a rather dangerous topic. It was apt to
produce an almost too detailed flood of information. C. H.
knew every fruit tree in the orchard, as a shepherd does his
sheep, and was not easily deterred from pursuing any subject
to the very end. Books? Not to any great extent, I think, and
yet one year we suddenly discovered that C. H. had shut
himself up in a little room upstairs and read the Elizabethan
dramatists straight through with the same thoroughness that
he did everything else.

The discovery only came by chance, through his providing
a quotation for a cross-word puzzle. The house possessed a
large library, and its owner's knowledge of where any book in
it was to be found was extensive and peculiar, as also was his
knowledge of the wretch who, some years before, had failed to
restore a volume to its right place in the shelf. If he had not
read them all, he had read a great many of them, but he
seldom discussed or quoted them and would, I think, have
regarded any display of enthusiasm on the subject as being a
little indecent. There was deep down in him some shyness

73

which forbade and distrusted any such expression of the emotions.

This shyness or reserve was as fundamental a part of C. H. as was his abounding kindliness of heart. In some ways he reminded me of Mr. Grewgious, a comparison that may not convey as much as it ought, because too few people know *Edwin Drood* as well as they ought. Mr. Grewgious described himself as " a particularly angular man," and so C. H. might have done, if he had deemed it becoming to analyse his own qualities. There was a marked angularity about his golf, which he played quite well ; he was so rigid as to resemble a pair of compasses attired in coat and trousers. He looked very uncomfortable, and he was similarly angular and uncomfortable when confronted with strangers. He loved to give but it made him uneasy to receive, so that he laid down for himself the rigid rule to entertain his friends and neighbours at Aberdovey in his own house but on no account whatever to enter theirs. With this angularity went a certain quality that it would be misleading to call inhuman, and yet it is hard to express otherwise. He was sometimes curiously insensitive to other people's feelings, if they were sufficiently far removed from his own. He was most anxious not to hurt them ; he simply did not realise that they existed. Some quite ordinary human weaknesses had never touched him, and so they left him a little puzzled and unbelieving. The fact that he was one of eight brothers and sisters, no one of whom married, in itself suggests a strain of something out of the common run. He would have done anything to help a friend out of a hole, but why in the world the friend had fallen into that particular kind of hole he never would have understood. So, at least, I think, and yet as I write the words I am conscious that I may be utterly wrong and [that it is I who could not understand.

If C. H. had had in his life any ambition unfulfilled or any disappointment, I doubt if any of our party knew what it was, unless it was a Blue missed at Cambridge. He was very im-

personal in his talk about himself, or, for that matter, about
other people. There were, to be sure, plenty of stories and
jokes about friends, but they did not penetrate very far below
the surface. Our jokes were like our wine, fine, old and crusted.
There was a whole saga about one D, long since dead, and it
trembles on the tip of my pen, but I refrain, knowing that such
things are delicate plants which will not bear transplanting from
their native soil. The late Mr. Edward Austen-Leigh, sitting
on some barbed wire on the edge of a boarded bunker, was
another favourite, but its reproduction calls for mimicry
capable, as I understand, of reaching the upper G. Then there
was the singular adventure of the tooth at Shrewsbury station.
The station was, for some reason, perhaps a strike, lapped in
darkness, and C. H., sitting waiting on a seat, became aware
of a dim figure prowling round him as if in a reconnaisance
before an attack. He was growing anxious when the figure
suddenly said, " Are you Mr. Allcock ? " C. H. admitted that
he was. " Do you remember playing for Staffordshire when
someone knocked one of your teeth out ? " Yes, he remembered.
" Well," said the figure, pointing to his tie, " here it is "—
and there, sure enough, it was, handsomely mounted as
a pin.

I have already drawn one comparison from *Silas Marner*
and now for another ; C. H. told us his stories as did Mr.
Macey to the village worthies in the Rainbow at Raveloe.
He would pause at intervals in order to be set going again
according to precedent by the appropriate question. There
was no pretence that we had not heard the narrative before,
for if anybody asked, perhaps of malice aforethought, a wrong
question, C. H. would turn on him, as on a stupid boy over
his Euclid, with, " God bless my soul and body, how often
have I told you ? " and then continue wholly unabashed. We
delighted in those stories, and so did he, for tears of enjoyment
would pour from his eyes, and he had sometimes to make more
than one false start, helpless with laughter, before arriving at
the culminating point.

Life at Bryntegwel was wonderfully pleasant, but it was hard work. Enough of it was perhaps as good as a feast, and yet with what sad steps we walked down the hill, while the rest of the house was still sleeping, to catch the early train ! Like a schoolboy returning to school, we envied those who were staying on and would presently be going down as usual to the links, with us " far away on the billow." It was a strenuous existence but C. H. himself went through three weeks of it every holidays, with a succession of guests filling the house and himself not turning a hair. As the years passed, there came changes of routine. The car largely superseded the train on the way there, and also helped ageing legs to the links and back. For years I went there in one particular friend's car, a journey which became for us fully as traditional and as full of small private jokes as all the rest of the visit. Oxford, Woodstock, Bourton-on-the-hill, Broadway, Worcester, Bromyard, Leominster, Craven Arms, and Newtown (with the sign-posts proclaiming twenty-eight miles to Machynlleth)—how nostalgic a sound their names have in my ears ! The drill of the house became insensibly less fierce. Two rounds shrank into one, and there were more and more visitors who no longer played golf at all. C. H. himself had hurt his arm and gave up golf and shaving simultaneously. Yet the atmosphere remained the same.

As I read what I have written, I feel that I have miserably failed to suggest the true essence of that atmosphere. It is so easy to describe little oddnesses, so impossible to convey what boyishly, poignantly good fun it all was. We liked meeting each other, we enjoyed the games, we were fond of Aberdovey, but above all we were fond of C. H. He was the link that bound us together ; he was the mainspring of the machine and the founder of the feast. It was he that gave to all those good things their peculiar, nay, their unique, flavour. If mankind is made up of hosts and guests, then he was all host. Hospitality sparkled out of him. It was as " the positive light " which we are told " appeared to issue from Fezziwig's calves " at the dance on Christmas Eve. It illumined the whole house. The popping of corks was as a music that for ever accompanied him. His " Good morn, good morn," at breakfast was a perpetually recurrent invitation to everybody to enjoy himself. He had gusto and the gift of imparting it. I like to think that something of it remains, though he has gone.

The two wars naturally curtailed the activities of Bryntegwel. As to the first, I cannot speak, since I was of necessity absent, but I well remember that I was promised that the last bottle of a very special Madeira should greet me on my return, and there it was faithfully awaiting me in December of 1918. With the second war there came almost an end of the old life. I was there in the early months of 1940, when there was still petrol for the old magical drive through the Cotswolds, and again in 1942, when we must revert to the earlier rites, now somewhat maimed, of Talerddig and the natural arch. That was the last time I ever saw C. H. It was beginning to be apparent that visitors would soon be too much for him, but he was still full of talk and cheerfulness. He could no longer prune his beloved fruit trees, but could occasionally go his little scrambles up and down hill. He had filled a considerable part of the house with refugees from Birkenhead, and bought all the children gorgeous new waterproofs against the winter rains. Every evening, with the revived instinct of a housemaster going round his house, he would pay them a visit and, having done his duty by a brief and rather embarrassed conversation, would return to his own room with obvious relief. He was growing a little anxious about his dwindling cellar, but it is pleasant to know that it lasted his time. He wrote now and then, saying, gratefully, that he had no pain and only murmuring a little sadly that it took him so long to do anything nowadays. He had always fought an obstinately good fight against any form of ailment ; in all his time at Eton he had only once missed a school, and now he continued to resist doctors to the end. He was looked after by two devoted servants, and the last account I had of him was that he could still take his glass of port after dinner. Only at the very last did he fail a little, and then the end came swiftly. I think he would have said, if he could have brought himself to say it, that he had had a happy life. He had given a great deal of happiness to other people.

The Cure

CURE is, I am afraid, too flattering a word. There is sometimes a temptation to put it in ironically inverted commas. It is a palliative, a rest, an agreeable routine, not without a certain monotony, which far from being tiresome is one of its chief charms. The patient at first inclines to receive with a politely concealed cynicism the assurance that he will only feel the benefit of his treatment after he has gone away. Yet this is one of the unlikely prophecies that really come to pass. When he was a small boy, rebelling against a clean collar and a children's party, he was told he would enjoy it when he got there. However grudgingly, he had in the end to admit that it was true, and so with the grown-up rebel. After he has resumed ordinary life for a week or so he becomes conscious of a renewed sprightliness, a modified stiffness, which he is bound to assign to the right cause.

I have no knowledge of the wonders of foreign spas. I have never tried the waters of Jordan. I am a true blue, unadventurous Damascus patriot and my own Abana and Pharpar make up the sum of my experience. Once, and only once, my timid nose savoured for an instant the waters of

79

another famous resort, on which, lest any one has the law of me, I refrain from expressing an opinion. Within these narrow limits I have now been taking the cure for hard on a dozen years. On the banks of Abana I was very nearly bombed out of my seven senses, and thereupon turned to Pharpar, where, once and sometimes twice a year, I have been placidly bathing ever since.

Any plunge into an entirely fresh and unknown world is alarming, and certainly not the least alarming is a first visit to a cure. The visitor feels like the new boy in the Harrow song, " so strange and shy." He is painfully conscious of not knowing the ropes. He cringes visibly as, with his doctor's prescription in his hand, he goes to buy his tickets from the young lady in the office, and, having got half-way down the long passage to his bath, he is almost inclined to run away. Yet once the first step is taken he becomes wonderfully bold. In a very few days he will be greeting the kind gentleman in the white coat who puts him into his bath, almost with familiarity. And it is one of the beauties of a cure that there will soon be still newer boys. The population is always changing ; at the end of every week those who have dreed their weird and served their sentence pass away into the outer world and are succeeded by a new generation. These can be treated with the patronising airs of the boy who has spent one whole term at school. At the end of the three appointed weeks he who began in the lowest has attained to the sixth form ; he is numbered among the oldest inhabitants of his hotel ; let him stay but one more week and he will be the Father of the Marshalsea.

Moreover, that dreadful sense of newness never comes back. The second arrival is by comparison a triumphal home-coming. The lounge may be populated in the main by a different race, but there will generally be one or two veterans, warriors of previous campaigns, wearing their metaphorical medal ribbons, to be greeted as such. And those that really matter, the eternal deities, from the welcoming hall porter

upwards, these will be the same. The visitor may even be told
that he is to have his old room, number so and so, which sends
a glow to his heart. And the meeting next morning with George
in his white coat is as a reunion with a long lost friend. There
are few things in the world better than coming back, however
faintly we may be remembered.

I recall vividly my first coming to Pharpar, as I will continue
to call it, in war time, and my walking along the rather
commonplace little red brick street (the whole of the local
cabs were engaged at a wedding), and speculating as to where
the baths were. It was a day of drowsy, murmurous heat, and
the war seemed blessedly far away. Here at least I should not
be killed, like Marat, in a bath. There were few people
stirring and they for the most part hobbled and limped even
as I did and crossed the road with leisurely precaution. It
looked an odd, quiet, out of the way sort of place, and I confess
that I wondered a little how I should bear three whole weeks
of it.

Now I know that it is this very quietness and the doing of
very nearly the same thing every day that makes the time go
like a flash. It is true that this wild rushing of the minutes
does not begin at once. The first day, and this holds true of
every visit, appears one of the longest that man ever spent.
When the doctor has given his orders and the bath tickets been
bought and times appointed and the newspapers have been
bespoken (everything is very near everything else at Pharpar)
the hours seem to stretch away into infinity ; the visitor feels
as did Charles Lamb on his retirement, that he " wants some
steward or judicious bailiff to manage his estates in time for
him." That happy, unaccustomed holiday feeling of having
nothing to do after breakfast evaporates and leaves life a little
blank. But let him be worthy of his name of patient ; he will
soon acquire the knack of this strange, new, passive existence
in which he does nothing and other people do things to him.

It is, for instance, quite wonderful how a bath can pass
away a morning. A deliberate reading of the newspaper and

the reluctant answering of a letter, and it is eleven o'clock, the appointed time. The bath itself deserves a word of description, for the waters of Pharpar are many times—I think it is six— as salt as the sea. So when we have climbed into our bath we do not rest on its floor but have a pleasant sensation of floating. We are so buoyant that we must be clamped down with a baton of wood across our chest and another to restrain our feet that would otherwise be constantly rising in rebellion. There is another peculiarly pleasant feature which panders to that innate indolence of every human bather. In his ordinary domestic bath he has often longed after a certain time to turn on the hot tap again and so gain a new lease of lethargic happiness. But in order to do so (unless indeed he lie with his head at the wrong end, and taps make an uncomfortable head rest) he must get up, and as sure as he does so the spell of enchantment is broken ; he may as well obey the voice of conscience, which has for some time been nagging at him, and get out. Here, however, the beautiful passivity of the place reaches its ultimate point. He has been ordered perhaps ten minutes at one temperature and then five more at a degree higher. He is, therefore, given an hour-glass, or rather a minute-glass. Lazily, for he has nothing else to do, and yet with a certain concentrated intensity, as of a condemned criminal whose time is running out, he watches the sand inexorably seeping away. When the last grain is gone, he has but to ring a bell, and in comes his friend in white, thermometer in hand, to turn the tap for him, let in a rush of hot water (his toes soon learn to beat a temporary retreat) and grant him a blessed reprieve of five whole minutes. Then, when a second glass proclaims that time is up, he allows himself a few illicit moments of indulgence and at last rings the bell, even as the condemned man drops a handkerchief as a signal to the firing squad.

The supreme felicity is over for the day, but there remains something but little inferior ; he is wrapped in a " hot pack " of towels, and reclines on a couch in delicious lassitude. After

a time, he slowly uncoils the towels, allowing a little breeze
to play upon him through the window. He dresses very gently
lest he grow too hot again, for a recalcitrant collar stud can
bring out the perspiration like rain. And so home.

That is not all, however, by any manner of means ; his
pleasant persecution has not yet come to an end ; the doctors
of Pharpar are, like their prototype in *Pickwick*, " wery
fierce," and fiercest of all in the matter of resting after the bath.
And this must be a real rest ; no mere lounging in idleness.
The patient must lie on his bed for the prescribed time, and, as
surely as he does so, he goes to sleep, which leads me down a
by-path to the whole agreeable subject of diurnal slumber in
ordinary life. In this matter there are two schools of thought.
There are those who make a solemn parade of a snooze which
they dignify by the name of rest. They insinuate, if they do not
actually say, that they are acting under medical advice, and
retire in ostentatious procession to their bedrooms. Those of
the opposite school hate this disguise of virtue. For them, if
they are to get the full relish from their slumbers, there must
be something furtive about it. They choose an arm-chair and
a book—a very old one—not that they make any shallow
pretence of not sleeping, but in order that they may taste the
very quintessence of joy, the reading until the book drops from
their nerveless grasp in the middle of a paragraph.

I confess myself a member of this school. I prefer the
comparatively light repose in a chair from which the sleeper
can awake almost as bright as a button and, after a reviving
cigarette, can fall to work. Formally to lie down on a bed
produces, in me at any rate, a deplorable swinishness, for
which tea provides the only restorative. In work-a-day
existence man cannot afford this long drawn-out paralysis
of all his faculties, but in a cure it is another matter ; the
interval between lunch and dinner is painlessly, and indeed
agreeably, obliterated.

It cannot be denied that now and then some desperate
expedients have to be adopted for spending the evenings until

that early bedtime which is universal. I have even been induced to play bridge, though I prefer the less exacting rôle of looker-on and critic. I have always declared that a surfeit of bridge in a troop train through Italy after the first war had destroyed my appetite for ever, and that I played only in a single holiday home where it was part of the tradition, one of the few fastnesses in which Auction still survived. At Pharpar, however, I have succumbed under strong persuasion to the new-fangled game of Contract. I suppose it is impossible to teach an old dog new tricks, for on each visit I find that I have to learn all over again from the beginning ; but my partners are very long-suffering, and when I say that I have on occasion won or lost as much as three and sixpence it will be realised that the pastime is not without its thrills.

Such is our normal day, with an occasional cinema thrown in or a tea at an engaging little tea-shop. I must admit that I have pined now and then for some cricket to watch. It would fit to admiration into the pattern of this somnolent and contemplative life. No hours go by with a lovelier swiftness than those during which the watcher vows that he will see just one more over. But we cannot have everything.

If Pharpar itself possesses no conspicuous beauties, it has lovely places near it within reach of a kind friend's car. Worcester, Stratford, Malvern, Bewdley, with its riverside houses as in a Dutch picture, and, above all, noble Tewkesbury, make each an afternoon's jaunt. Beyond Evesham lies the gateway into the enchanted country of the Cotswolds and the road to Wales, Broadway and Bourton and Moreton and Blockley, that calls so insistently in our ears with its siren sign-posts. If it is the time of the fruit blossom, the whole country-side is a dream of snowy beauty. And each break in the routine, since in the days of petrol scarcity it cannot come too often, has the rare and romantic quality of a treat. We are conscious of creating a little flutter of interest in society as we set out, and when we get home again we have something to talk about.

The Cure

It may be thought that normally we talk about our various ailments—nobody comes to this haunt of peace purely for fun —but we do not do so overmuch. There is no such tacit compact as there was in wartime as to listening to the other fellow's bomb if he would listen to ours. Still, I suppose we have our mild shop. We ask each other if we are reclining or being aerated this morning or only going swimming, and we compare our respective doctors' little ways, and the exact temperatures and length of rest they prescribe, and the hateful exercises they urge on us. We are all very faithful partisans, and stick up for our own doctor, and hint at the besotted infirmities of somebody else's. It is not perhaps superficially exciting, but the tone of it is soon caught.

We are, as I said, a fluid and perpetually changing population. There are none of those permanent and formidable residents who establish vested rights to tables or corners. Nobody looks at us with a baleful glare if, in perfect innocence, we take his accustomed chair. No doubt we gradually sort ourselves into little loosely knit societies, but they are not worthy of the name of cliques and do not produce those brushes to which hotel cliques are prone. Flora Finching remarked of her life with Mr. F., " It was not ecstasy but it was comfort," and much the same may be said of our placid, comfortable, unexacting lounge.

And yet it has, as indeed have all lounges, a dangerous lure. Three weeks of it are nearly enough for many reasons, and not least because if we stayed much longer we might never go away. As it is we always feel a little sorry for those departing, whose luggage we see piled in the hall. We do not envy them their liberty, but rather count with a mild gloating the days or even weeks that still remain to us. It would be dreadfully easy, out of pure futility, to stay for ever and ever, lotus-eaters with our own table in the window and our own ministering angel, with our little daily stump to the baths and back, and our visit every three days to the cinema when the programme changes.

All too soon our time is up, and after genuinely affecting farewells, we must tear ourselves away. But before we go we never fail to engage our rooms provisionally for next year. As the appointed date approaches, we come near to counting the days when once more we shall go

> *Dreaming through the twilight*
> *That doth not rise nor set.*

Let others praise, if they will, brighter and more dashing resorts of which, I make no doubt, there are plenty. I am entirely of Naaman's mind. Pharpar, river of Damascus, is good enough for me.

Sherlockiana
The Faith of a Fundamentalist

I AM a Fundamentalist. A number of learned persons have
written books on Sherlock Holmes, proving from the dates
that the events recorded in the sacred text of Dr. Watson
did not happen and could not have happened at the time and
in the order in which we have been led to believe ; that
Professor Moriarty, for instance, could not have been plotting
devilry at Birlstone Manor in 1899 if he had tumbled over the
Reichenbach Falls in 1891. Some of them even push profanity
so far as to allege that the Doctor, at a time when we sympathised with him as mourning the first Mrs. Watson (née
Morstan) must in fact have married a second wife, possibly
Miss Violet de Merville. I have read these authors, or some
of them, with interest, and even with a certain reluctant
admiration for their diabolical cleverness, to say nothing of
their industry. It is the same sort of admiration as that with
which one watches a conjurer, conscious of one's own incapacity
either to emulate him or to understand how he does it. They
have, thank heaven, written no wrinkle on my innocent brow,

nor affected my orthodoxy in the slightest degree. I still believe that the various adventures occurred exactly in the order in which they were told to us—the *Study in Scarlet* first, the *Sign of Four* second, the *Scandal in Bohemia* third, and so on down to *The Retired Colourman*. The evidence of the dates troubles me no more than the incontestable evidence of the rocks troubles those who believe that the world was created in a precise order in the course of six days. If there is some little confusion or disagreement between them it is not for me and others of the true faith to try to reconcile or explain them. I continue to read the stories over and over again with an undisturbed mind. I do not wish to be uncharitable and so to condemn the commentators as very wicked people ; I regard them merely as misguided, and all their daring and brilliancy slip off me as easily as water off a duck's back.

At the same time, in so far as it is possible to study the stories without doubting any fundamental truths or too grossly emending a possibly faulty text, it seems to me licit to do so, and there are one or two points on which I have views, and even theories, however humble. I have not read all the commentators, and it may be that I am like poor Mr. Casaubon, " groping about in woods with a pocket compass while they have made good roads." Nevertheless, I will venture on one or two remarks. I have always been interested in the question of Holmes's University career and have lately re-read once again Miss Dorothy Sayers's essay on the subject. It is an erudite, almost a monumental work, giving proof of the most scrupulous research ; and yet it seems to me that she has founded her views too exclusively on the vital passages in *The Gloria Scott* and *The Musgrave Ritual* and not paid sufficient attention to the other stories dealing with University life.

With her conclusion that Holmes was at Cambridge I respectfully agree, and the more gladly because it is my own University. Even as the " curious incident of the dog in the night-time " was of vast importance in the case of Silver Blaze, so the incident of the bull terrier is here decisive, as Miss Sayers following Father Ronald Knox, points out. The argument runs briefly thus. Victor Trevor's bull terrier " froze on to " Holmes's ankle one morning as he " went down to Chapel." The dog would not be allowed in College, therefore the incident happened outside, while Holmes was on his way from his lodgings. Holmes was up for only two years. If he had been at Oxford he would have spent his first two years in College. If he had been at Cambridge he would have begun in lodgings and only come into College in his third year. Q.E.D.

It is when Miss Sayers tentatively suggests that Holmes's College was Sidney that she is on much less sure ground. In fact, I do not believe any Cambridge man will agree with her. The question hinges on Reginald Musgrave, who was undoubtedly at the same College as Holmes. Musgrave was " of an exceedingly aristocratic type " and " a scion of one of the very oldest families in the Kingdom." Holmes could never look at him without thinking of grey archways and mullioned windows. He was a considerable landowner and " always a bit of a dandy." With all possible respect for every one concerned, Sidney would not have been his college. Granted Miss Sayers's assumption that the college was a small one, then there is an obvious choice, Magdalene, " that horsy home of revel " as it is called in *Horace at the University of Athens.* That is to be sure only a guess, but it is a much better guess than Sidney.

Now to turn back for a moment to the general question of which was Holmes's University, is there anything to be gleaned from *The Creeping Man, The Missing Three-Quarter,* and *The Three Students* ? From the first, I think nothing, for the University is disguised as Camford, and the fact that Holmes remembered the inn there and that " the port used to be above mediocrity " gets us no further, though the words " used to be " point to recollections of undergraduate days. In *The Missing Three-Quarter* the University is definitely named as

Cambridge, and that being so it is a little odd that when Holmes goes there, as he does, to prosecute his researches, he does not mention it as his *Alma Mater* and shows no emotion or interest in revisiting it. It is true that he says to Watson, " You are not familiar with Cambridgeshire scenery, are you ? " and that might be held to imply his own familiarity with it ; but as he had just returned from some hours of bicycling through the county it is not conclusive.

It is when we come to *The Three Students* that difficulties thicken. The University is not named and the College is St. Luke's. The tutor's room, as Watson specifically states, looked on to " the ancient lichen-tinted Court." That points to Cambridge, and yet a little later Holmes remarks, " We will take a walk in the Quadrangle," which as definitely points to Oxford. Watson would not know the difference between the two languages, but Holmes unquestionably would. Yet it might be that, although St. Luke's was at Cambridge, Holmes used the word " Quadrangle," which came natural to him as an Oxford man. It makes me a little uneasy, but not nearly so uneasy as the fact that Holmes talked about " the three students." Moreover, in *The Musgrave Ritual* he had referred to his " old fellow students " at the University. Now this is a really serious matter. Would any one who had been at either Oxford or Cambridge talk of students in that connection ? To me that is not to be thought of. He might have called them men or undergraduates or anything but students. It is so incredible that at one time I almost came to think that Holmes's University career was a figment of his imagination.

Mr. A. G. Macdonnell declared that Holmes had invented Moriarty, or rather had " selected a perfectly ordinary ex-professor and fastened on to the unfortunate man the fearful reputation which has dogged him ever since." My supposition is not nearly so blasphemous as that, but luckily there is for the faithful a reasonable way out. Watson himself was at London University and might well use the word " students."

Furthermore, though he knew it was not the correct term to put in the mouth of Holmes, he might think it permissible to do so because the word would be more intelligible to his myriad readers who had not had Holmes's advantages. That will have to do, and I think it suffices. So Holmes was a Cambridge man, and all is well with the world.

Apropos of Colleges and youthful pursuits, I have always wished to know more of Dr. Watson's career as a football player, but there is so very little material. All we know (from *The Sussex Vampire*) is that he played for Blackheath when Big Bob Ferguson played three-quarter for Richmond, and once threw Watson over the ropes at the Old Deer Park. Where did Watson play? Not three-quarter or he would have mentioned it. Neither was he fast enough, for though he once declared that he had been " reckoned fleet of foot," Holmes completely outpaced him in that wild chase after the Hound across Dartmoor. Full back perhaps, a post for which his " admirable tenacity " might have fitten him, but I doubt it. He was a good, solid, hard-working forward who put his head down and pushed without too much thought. Apparently he had ceased to follow the game after his playing days were over ; otherwise when the Captain of the Cambridge fifteen asked despairingly what to do in the absence of his crack three-quarter, Godfrey Staunton, Watson would have had some suggestion to make. As it was he showed remarkable modesty in not referring to his feats on the Rectory Field ; but what I want to know is what he was doing at Blackheath at all, when he ought to have been playing for Bart's or the United Hospitals. The hospital must have had first call on his services. This lack of loyalty is disturbing. However, we know that after his student days he was either a house surgeon or house physician at Bart's, and it was then presumably when no longer qualified to play for his hospital that Blackheath claimed him.

Now I have a word to say about a little social peculiarity of Holmes. We always think of him as a man of a highly democratic turn of mind, who almost too consciously spurned personages of high rank. He turned brusquely away when the King of Bohemia extended his hand to him ; he appeared to be bored with the long list of a Duke's titles ; he refused a knighthood. When Watson was much impressed by the crest on a letter, Holmes remarked, " I assure you without affectation that the status of my client is a matter of less moment to me than the interest of his case." And yet I have always had a notion that this was to some extent a pose. In his secret heart I believe that he had social aspirations, and that when in looking at Reginald Musgrave he thought of mullioned windows and feudal keeps, he longed for some more exalted lineage than the country squires whom he claimed as his ancestors. Probably this longing increased as his practice took him into higher spheres.

This is only a guess, but it is certainly curious that in his earlier days he was ignorant of some simple social usages. When Lord Robert St. Simon came to consult him, he said genially, " Good day, Lord St. Simon. Pray take the basket chair," and continued thus to refer to him. But somebody must have told him of this little solecism, and it was not Watson, who was himself guilty of it. Perhaps he privately looked up the point in a book of etiquette, which told him how to address letters to the nobility. At any rate, he found out and was later inclined to go too far in the opposite direction. In the case of Charles Augustus Milverton, that blackmailer in high life, Holmes laboriously alluded to his client as " *The* Lady Eva Brackwell." It was the same in the case of the unfortunate Lady Frances Carfax, who was so nearly buried alive. " Ah, what has happened to the Lady Frances ? " he exclaimed passionately, and kept it up throughout. He was not to be caught napping again and called the Duke of Holdernesse " Your Grace " with the utmost punctilio and almost wearisome iteration. That is the trouble about converts ; they will overdo it.

But the subject is perhaps too painful and embarrassing.

Sherlockiana : The Faith of a Fundamentalist

Let me turn to another redounding almost wholly to Holmes's glory. Has full credit ever been given him for his constant and successful antagonism to the Germans ? At the beginning of the last war Dr. Goebbels and his associates prayed English literature in aid for a violent attack on Mr. Churchill. They made a not notably apt comparison between him and Quilp. They overlooked the fact that their real enemy in literature was beyond question Sherlock Holmes. They cannot possibly have forgotten *His Last Bow*. Only a sense of humiliation must here have kept them silent, for, as is well known, Holmes, in the disguise of an American with a chin beard, utterly bamboozled their master spy, Von Bork, palmed off on him a mass of false information as to the Fleet, trussed him up with the help of the faithful Watson and added insult to injury first by drinking his best Tokay and then cashing a cheque for £500 handed to Holmes for his supposed treachery.

That was the most conspicuous example, but it is really remarkable on how many other occasions he opposed some German villain or villainess, as a rule to their disadvantage. In his first encounter he was not wholly successful : Irene Adler, though born in New Jersey, presumably had German blood in her veins, and she got rather the best of him, even if his client, the King of Bohemia, was entirely satisfied. Next came Colonel Lysander Stark, who cut off Mr. Hatherley's thumb. That was obviously not his real name, for he spoke " with something of a German accent." Incidentally, the alias must have appealed to Holmes, for some time later, in *The Three Garridebs*, he himself invented an imaginary person with a very similar name, Dr. Lysander Starr. Holmes was not deceived by the Colonel's wiles and easily discovered the hiding place where he had been counterfeiting coin ; but it must be admitted that after that he failed. How several people in a heavily loaded cart, one of them with a German accent, entirely vanished in the middle of Berkshire is a discreditable mystery.

93

Holmes was far more successful in the realm of high politics. In the matter of *The Second Stain* there can be no question as to the foreign potentate who wrote the indiscreet letter, the publication of which was calculated to plunge the country into war. Of course it was the Kaiser. Holmes wrote down a name on a piece of paper and the Prime Minister replied, " Exactly." Holmes got the letter back and no harm was done.

He was equally triumphant in the case of the plans of the Bruce-Partington submarine. Can anybody doubt that it was the German navy to whom they were to be sold ? The very name of the agent involved, Oberstein, is almost conclusive. Holmes made a complete fool of Mr. Oberstein, who came obediently, bringing in his sheaves with him, to the smoking-room of the Charing Cross Hotel, where doubtless Lestrade, that trusty bulldog, awaited him.

Then at the bidding of that *Illustrious Client*, at whose identity we can only make a reverent guess, Holmes outwitted the unspeakable Baron Gruner, robbed him of his infamous brown book and saved Miss de Merville. He was not equally successful in the case of another book, the novel which Douglas Maberley had written about Isadora Klein, but at least he blackmailed her to the tune of £5,000 for his client's benefit (*The Three Gables*). True, Isadora was Spanish, " the real blood of the masterful Conquistadors," as Holmes observed in a sudden gush of romantic language, but she had married an aged German Sugar King, and so may fairly be added to Holmes's German bag. The Russians are now trying to ban him on the ground of his capitalistic tendencies, but he never did them any harm. The rascal who pretended to be a Russian nobleman in *The Resident Patient* was neither the one nor the other. It is the poor, ponderous Germans who were consistently outwitted by him. True, I had almost forgotten one item on the other side of the account. Holmes alleged that he had saved from murder at the hands of the Nihilist, Klopman, Count Von und Zu Grafenstein, a relative of Von

Bork's. We take his word for it since that story is one with those of the Paradol Chamber and the Giant Rat of Sumatra. They were used to tantalise his Boswell but were never told.

I have set down a few of the thoughts, " elementary, my dear Watson," as I am too well aware, that have occurred to me in some fifty-five years of persistent reading. Even a Fundamentalist may have his preferences among the sacred writings, and as to the short stories at any rate I have no doubt that the spring time was best. In his preface to the collected edition Sir Arthur Conan Doyle expressed the hope that the reader, being able to take the stories in any order, would " not find that the end shows any conspicuous falling off from the modest merits of the beginning." It would be pleasant but it is impossible to agree. In one respect there is something to be said for this view. The clash of temperaments between Watson and Holmes becomes more noticeable in the later stories and Watson's character shows a marked development. In early days he muttered " Brag and bounce " to himself when he was annoyed by Holmes's vanity, but he knew better than to speak his thoughts aloud. Later he developed, as Holmes himself noted, " a certain unexpected vein of pawky humour " at the Master's expense. This in its turn produced such pleasing retaliations as (on two occasions), " You are scintillating this morning." " Perhaps there are points which have escaped your Machiavellian intellect." " Watson, I have always done you an injustice. There are others "—and so on. These little bouts of thrust and parry are more frequent as the stories go on, and add a zest to life, though it must be owned that Holmes's weapon was more often the bludgeon than the rapier. Yet they do not wholly make up for something of lost freshness. That freshness may have been not in the early stories but in the reader himself. It may belong to a time when his love was purer and less critical, when perhaps he had not even begun to smile, however tenderly, at the two great creatures. It is so hard to recall the sensation of that first breath-taking plunge into delights, grown long since familiar. The Fundamentalist always goes back to the Book of Genesis, and I always return to the stories enshrined in the earliest volumes of the *Strand*. They are the impregnable rock on which my faith is founded.

Some Writers on Sport

THOSE who to-day try at all regularly to write about any form of game or sport must always feel a passionate admiration of their predecessors in this field and sometimes a little envy. They admire them for reasons that are simple and obvious enough, because they produced pieces of prose which are acknowledged masterpieces. Hazlitt's Fight and his account of Cavanagh the fives-player, Borrow's outburst on the bruisers of England, Nyren's praises of the Hambledon cricketers and the ale that they drank—these are in all the anthologies, they are known to all lovers of good writing ; they will never be forgotten and are out of reach of all competition.

So much for admiration, and to that I will return. As to the envy, the minnow does not envy the Triton ; it would be indeed foolish to be jealous of Hazlitt because he could write such noble stuff. Yet there is a little envy on other grounds. The earlier writers who touched and adorned sport had, however greatly they used it, the greater chance. For one thing, they came first, while the subject was still fresh. True, writers of the quality of Hazlitt and Borrow would have triumphed whenever they came, but not so conspicuously perhaps in that particular direction ; they might not have thought it worth while to essay a subject on which columns were being turned out every week. We may leave such giants on one side and take the instance of a lesser but still an admirable writer, Tom Hughes, the author of *Tom Brown's Schooldays*. He had never thought of himself as a writer and only wrote his book because, as he said, he wanted to preach to boys. Then he discovered in himself, or others discovered in him, a power of depicting simple pleasures and outdoor life with raciness and vigour and an infectious zest. His winter coach drive on the Tallyho to Rugby is worthy to be classed with that of the Muggleton Telegraph on the way to Dingley Dell. But that which I have in mind in this particular connection is his School-house match, which remains after some ninety years the classical description of Rugby football. The game has changed almost out of knowledge since that was written, but there it still stands, an unique thing. Thousands and thousands of words have been written about football since, but they are forgotten, almost before their ink is dry, and the School-house match remains. There Hughes had an immense advantage in coming first. Rugby football was in his day something of an esoteric mystery. He was writing about a game wholly new to most of his readers. There was no need to be technical, and too much technicality does not make for moving and exciting literature. He could paint a broad, general picture. He did it as few other people could have done it, but he was fortunate in having a brand-new, clean canvas.

The point need not be laboured, and this priority is not the chief reason for envying those illustrious pioneers. It is rather that they were not, as concerned writing on games or sports, professionals ; they were splendid amateurs. They were writers on other topics, who turned to sport only once in a while, when it pleased them. Samuel Butler in his notebooks, writing of painters, says, " There is no excuse for amateur work being bad. Amateurs often excuse their shortcomings on the ground that they are not professional : the professional could plead with greater justice that he is not an amateur." Whether or not that is generally true, it has, I think, some application here. Hazlitt having made his excursion to Newbury to see his first fight and written his immortal account of it could leave well alone. As far as I know he never again touched the subject. It is interesting to reflect that, had he written that essay to-day, he would probably have been overwhelmed with fabulous offers from editors to report the next big fight. That he would have accepted them seems unlikely, but he might have been tempted. That his other fights would have been good reading no one can doubt, but would he have ever risen to quite such heights again ? He would almost inevitably have been cramped by the fear that he was repeating himself. No matter how tremendous the conflict, he could never again have equalled, because he could not bear to reproduce it, his picture of the Gas-man's face before he fell— " a human skull, a death's head, spouting blood." Other and fine phrases would have come to his pen's tip, but there might have been, ever and anon, some inhibition. The history of fights or matches must repeat itself, and so much the harder is the task of those who describe them. They may not be found out by their readers, who have fortunately short memories, but writers have long ones for their own words, and so are apt to be stricken in their artistic consciences. No doubt this fear of having said it all before must occasionally attack writers, however wide their scope, but it must be more constant where the field is essentially narrow.

Such agonies were the less likely when the total number of pages devoted to any form of sport, and in particular to games, were very few. In sport, in a more restricted sense, there was Nimrod, a very solemn personage, whose shining virtues I have never been able to detect, and there was another Rugbeian, the Druid, who seems to me to have had some qualities approaching greatness in his line of country. There was also Pierce Egan, in his day most famous of them all, though heaven alone knows why. If one can feel any affection for him, it is for something of the same reason that one is fond, ever so much fonder, of Dr. Watson, because he is so ridiculous. The other day, by repeated charges, pulling myself together for yet one more desperate assault, I fought my way through *Life in London*, and wondered why that mixture of solemnity and slang and excruciating puns, that dreadful delicacy in skirting the indelicate, once sent his sales soaring to heaven. To-day, only the enchanting pictures can redeem the book.

In the realm of games there has really been very little writing till quite modern times, or at least there has been very little reporting that could be called writing. I have now been " doing " the golf in *The Times* for forty years. A very short time before I began, practically all the games in that great journal were dealt with by one presumably omniscient person who was called " Sporting Ward," to distinguish him from Humphry Ward. To-day, games are no longer treated with so niggardly a hand. Every paper in the kingdom has a team that pour out their unceasing columns, and for their short-comings they could, in Sam Butler's phrase, " plead that they are not amateurs." They are overdriven, over-written professionals, and as the season of their game, whatever it is, goes on and on and they feel themselves getting ever more stale, they might say, as did a once overworked bowler to his too exigent Captain, " What, sir, a Yorker ! In August ! "

That it is possible to defy this weariness, we know from one distinguished example. In his intensely interesting auto-biography, Mr. Neville Cardus says that in every summer between 1920 and 1939 he wrote roughly speaking, 8,000 words a week on cricket for the *Manchester Guardian*. That is a record to " strike awe and terror." It is truly wonderful that through it all he retained his freshness and his fire, and that his enthusiasm, not only for cricket but for life in general, never ceased to get into his ink. Perhaps in those words " for life in general " may be found something of the secret. If the day's cricket did not interest him over much, he had other resources at his command. Cricket was his bread and butter, but he constantly spread it with all manner of engaging jam. He never let himself grow stale. " It is possible," he says, " that towards the end I was apt to repeat myself ; " but if he ever did it would have needed a close student and an ungenerous one to notice it, and indeed in the phrases of an admired author it is pleasant now and then to recognise an old friend. Of course, Mr. Cardus was primarily a writer who found cricket a vehicle well suited to his imagination, so that in a sense he kept his amateur status blessedly untarnished. There are others who are cricketers making a living by writing about the one thing they understand, cricket. That makes all the difference in the world, but it does not diminish the wonder of Mr. Cardus's achievement.

In praising one modern writer who thus overcame the difficulties of so continuously exacting a craft, I must not forget a much earlier one. I come back to Henry Hall Dixon, the Druid. He wrote and wrote to support a large and ever-increasing family. He refused the Editorship of *Bell's Life*, which was then the unquestioned prize of his profession, because he loved writing and freedom so much, and, I suppose, hated the thought of performing solemn editorial functions cooped up in an office. He wrote too much and too fast, and so his work was necessarily unequal, but at its best it reached the heights ; it is not only racy and full of fire, but sensitive and touching, with something of real poetry. Writing on sport must have been in his blood, for as a schoolboy at Rugby he had already contributed regularly to *Bell's Life*. That was, I imagine, under the rose, for Dr. Arnold, who had some hopes of him as a classical scholar, would hardly have approved. Everything conspired to fan the flame ; Rugby was set in a hunting country, and the boy would rush off after second lesson " in the generally visionary hope " of seeing Lord Chesterfield's hounds draw Hillmorton Gorse. When he went to Cambridge, where incidentally he was Wooden Spoon, Newmarket was a permanent temptation, and finally he was articled to a Solicitor at, of all places in the world, Doncaster. Perhaps there would in any case have been no holding him. As things turned out there certainly was not. He liked the law as little as he had those odious mathematics. He became a hand-to-mouth, day-to-day journalist, and it had been justly said that all sporting writers who succeeded him in his own line " have lit their torches at the Druid's flame."

Thousands of people—I am emphatically one of them—who know nothing of horses, and to whom many of his allusions are obscure and unintelligible, have yet enjoyed the Druid. And with that let me try to see what are the qualities that make for our passionate admiration of these great writers on the sport of the past. First of all, I would unhesitatingly put that quality which we call gusto. They had greatly varying degrees of skill in writing, but they all had gusto, an intense relish for their subject, and on that account, I suppose, a wonderful power of bringing scenes and persons to life before their readers' eyes. It would be easy, and doubtless tiresome, to pile up instance. Nyren was full of gusto, and not only for the ale, " genuine boniface," on which he grew so lyrical. Mrs. Cowden Clarke told how the old gentleman came and recounted to her husband his stories of Hambledon " with chuckling reminiscence," and we can positively hear him chuckle as he tells of the discomfiture of Lumpy by the yokel " with an arm as long as a hop pole." As a boy he had been made happy and important by going to Windmill Down early in the morning with David Harris, to see the famous bowler choose his wicket, and we can still feel the fresh morning breeze blowing in our faces. As far as I know I have never breakfasted on coffee and kidney and pigeon pie, but I have done so in imagination many times since I first read Tom Brown's coach drive. There hangs about it a quite divine quality of splendour and repletion. Tom Hughes must once have eaten that gorgeous breakfast himself.

Then, how Hazlitt enjoyed hearing Cavanagh's balls resounding against the chimney when " the joints trembled on the spit " ! How carried away with excitement was the Druid when he saw Voltigeur win the Leger, and how near he came to tears when he heard the trainer exclaim, " Oh, ma horse ! ma horse ! "

This immense zest brought with it, as I fancy, two other qualities without which no writer on sport or games is really worth a rap. First of all, they were not afraid to let themselves go. They were treading a narrow, dangerous, slippery path, for their subject was one that will not stand emotion and heroics beyond its natural capacity. The epithets that suit the winner of a Victoria Cross must not be applied to the man who catches a difficult catch. Now and again perhaps some of them went too far, as did Nyren's reviewer, the Rev. John Mitford, in telling how he put Silver Billy's bat to his lips and " returned it to his sanctuary." But if he did, it was an amiable weakness at which to laugh, if at all, very tenderly. And the very best of them never made ever so slight a slip. Cavanagh, says Hazlitt, " did not throw away the game to show off an attitude, or try an experiment. He was a fine, sensible, manly player, who did what he could, but that was more than any one else could even affect to do." That seems to me the perfect description of a great game-player. It says everything ; it makes him supremely great and yet there is not a word more than the subject can bear. And apropos, may I put in a word here for a companion picture, admittedly by a lesser artist, the account of William Gray playing rackets by Alfred Lyttelton. It is full of perfectly restrained emotion, inspired alike by the splendour of rackets in general and the exquisite grace of a master's strokes.

There is another thing ; these writers did not merely enjoy the match or the race or the fight they described ; they had just as great a relish for everything that led up to it, and let themselves go on that. For them to travel was at least as good as to arrive. Here, to be sure, they had a great advantage over the reporter of to-day, for if he were to embroider too much the blue pencil would come down on him like a hundred of bricks. Yet, if those elders had a better chance and could, as the saying goes, " spread themselves," how they used that chance ! To return yet again to Hazlitt, who must be in the nature of a King Charles's head, his fight is vastly enhanced by details of the journey there and back, and even the preparations for the journey. We love to read how he waited outside The Hole in the Wall for news of the battlefield, how he cursed his folly for missing the right coach, and was saved after all, how he talked to John Thurtell on the way and finally how he sat by the kitchen fire at Newbury with the yeoman who kept it up all night with good cheer and good talk. " Confound it, man, don't be insipid," said the yeoman to one " shuffling fellow " in the company and Hazlitt thought that here was a good phrase. I suppose all this wealth of preliminaries might have been insipid if someone else had written the essay, but as it is they add as much to our happiness as they clearly did to his. What fun, what tremendous fun, they made it all seem ! Yes, even when the most desperate and blood-curdling things are happening and we are conscious of the onlookers holding their breath, this pungent sense of happiness remains. They were hero-worshippers and a proper measure of hero-worship is another indispensable quality in writers on sport, but they never let their heroes become too solemn figures. They did justice to technical skill, but they spent themselves most freely on character. And here a futile jealousy is apt to creep in again, for they had rare characters to describe. The thing can still be done, as witness Mr. Cardus's gallery of Attewell and Ted Wainwright, Tyldesley and, above all, Emmott Robinson. Yet I wonder if even he could find quite such a mine in the north to-day. I have a notion that the world has been bitten, in Jasper Petulengro's phrase, " by the mad puppy they call gentility," or perhaps it is only education, so that there will never be such vintage characters again. At any rate, the older generation of writers had here no cause of complaint and their heroes gave them much good, rollicking talk, redolent of the soil, to set down.

And here it is worth noting how much of the old writing on sport consists in this setting down of good and sometimes superlative talk. There can surely be no real doubt as to the shares of the two partners who produced *The Cricketers of My Time*. Nyren talked his great talk and Cowden Clarke, with immense literary skill, wrote it down. Nor must Mr. Pycroft be forgotten. With Nyren's book in hand and his " ink horn at his button," he made a pilgrimage into Hampshire to seek out the few survivors of the Hambledon epoch and came back richly laden. Old Beldham's talk was that of a great rustic, as full of individuality and spirit as it was of memories that would otherwise have been lost to history. There was in it one really immortal sentence which I know I have quoted over and over again and shall never cease to quote for the sensual pleasure it gives me ; I have almost come to believe that I wrote it myself : " There was no mistaking the Kent boys, as they came staring into the Green Man." It is not only in itself a complete picture of those " anointed clod-stumpers " ; it tells us how small and far removed from each other were the cricketing communities of those days, strangers from neighbouring and yet foreign counties, with their own strange customs and strange tongues. It suggests too, one of the reasons why Nyren had talked so well ; he had known his men so intimately in his own little Hampshire world.

There is this same sense of intimacy and of a small community, beyond the boundaries of which all was dark and unknown, in the talk of Dick Christian, the old rough-rider of the Quorn, and in that of Will Goodall, Tom Sebright and the other famous huntsmen whom the Druid so lovingly recorded. For them, we may imagine, Leicestershire and Northamptonshire constituted the world, and hunting was its sole pursuit. Hunting keeps breaking into the account of the fight between Cribb and Molineaux at Thistleton Gap, which Dick Christian had watched on " a mare of my own, I gave Mr. Harper eighty pounds for her." He enjoyed the fight and remembered the great Captain Barclay in his carriage, and the place under Cribb's eye " as big as a goose's egg," but perhaps he remembered still better that Captain White's Jupiter had been killed on the place where the stage had stood.

I cannot think that the Druid ever did anything better than that, another man's story of something that he had not himself seen, and it shows what rare skill and what power of selection is needed to make the very best of the spoken word. It would have been a temptation to someone less skilful to keep the old man to the point and ask him more questions about the fight itself. Instead, he let him wander away over that " bit of stiffish land, a good deal of plough," and talk about the farmer who would not take a cheque for the use of his field—" he knew nothing about them things." And in the result we have in one short page a picture of the fight that leaps into life, so that we too can hear the sound of the blows " as plain as a drum."

To make scenes and people come alive, so flamingly alive that they live for evermore. I come back to that in the end. That was the secret they all knew.

The Yule-Tide Spirit

" ' **D**OES one desire the Yule-tide spirit, sir ? ' asked Jeeves frigidly. ' Certainly one does,' replied Mr. Wooster, for once not to be cowed, ' I am all for it.' " There are probably a good many people, myself among them, who are in theory all for Mr. Wooster and yet every now and then feel a horrible, cold, unworthy shiver of Jeeves creeping over them. This is a strange admission from one who annually and joyfully reads Dingley Dell to his family. Perhaps it is not really true or perhaps it is a survival from the time when every year immediately after Christmas there came a journey, as good as the drive on the Muggleton Telegraph, to a week of seaside golf. Now the kind of Christmas that Dickens described and Caldecott drew demands for its perfection a good hard frost and a fall of snow. There was always the thought that if once the snow came it might never go away again, for snow is like a shy undergraduate at a dinner-party : it never knows when to say good-bye. True there was one Christmas time when the snow lay thick all the way to the very last hill top, and then magically vanished so that the train slid down into a green and open country. So there was always hope, but there was also the dreadful haunting fear. That journey belongs now to a closed chapter but something of the old feeling remains, and that is one excuse. Another and perhaps a better one is that I was badly brought up.

He never had a Christmas stocking of his own. It sounds like the title of a picture to appeal to the charitable for poor little boys in mean streets. In fact, it is a statement of one of my own very mild grievances, not against any one in particular but against life in general. I have enjoyed other people's stockings, but never to have had one's own is to have lost one of the exquisite excitements of Christmas for which there is no substitute. It so happened that my early years were spent as a lonely little boy in a house full of uncles and aunts who had naturally enough outgrown the more dramatic celebrations of that festival. Once upon a time, according to a family legend, Parslow the butler had come into the dining-room on Christmas morning and said in a ceremonial form of words, always exactly repeated, " Ladies and gentlemen, I wish you all a very happy Christmas." But by my time Parslow had become for me Mr. Parslow, a friendly old gentleman with white whiskers living in retirement in his cottage, and his successor never attempted to revive the tradition. No doubt there were presents distributed by my grandmother in the household and the village, but as regards my small self, beyond a dim feeling of holly, I have no recollection of Christmas at all. A birthday was truly memorable, a dream of drums and trumpets, of paint-boxes and tin soldiers, but what was Christmas ? If it produced as much as a single robin or a frosted churchyard it was as much as it did.

By the time I was ten I had a half-sister, and with her coming came Christmas. Presumably, by the time she was three she was old enough for a stocking, but then I was thirteen. That is by no means too old to continue the rite of the stocking if you have been well broken in to it, but it is too old to begin it. It is an age of knowingness and of some contempt for childish things. I cannot say that I had been brought up

as an infidel as to Father Christmas, for you can hardly
be an infidel as to a belief of which you have never heard,
but an agnostic I assuredly was. So, though I took an interest,
perhaps rather a patronising interest, in my sister's stocking,
there was never any suggestion that I should have one of
my own and I should probably have poo-poo'd it as a
piece of mumbo-jumbo if there had. Presents were highly
agreeable things, but they appeared in proper grown-up form
on my plate at breakfast. I am glad to think I was not base
enough to explode my sister's infantile beliefs ; I played a
perfectly honourable part in the stocking conspiracy, but
it is obvious that you cannot be suddenly converted to a
belief in people coming down chimneys at the mature age
of thirteen.

At what age that beautiful faith is shattered it is hard to
say, and in any case " shattered " is not the right word. It
fades away painlessly, the believer, by a merciful dispensation
of providence, scarcely realising that he has lost it. These
words are written at Christmas time and there is in the house
a young gentleman of four who is, as far as can be judged, an
implicit believer, a true fundamentalist. He goes through a
number of small tin motor cars on the floor one by one,
attributing some of them to Father Christmas and others to
mere earthly givers, and the fact that they are, save in colour,
exactly like one another appears to arouse no suspicion. He
had intended to hang up one of his own small striped socks,
and only after prolonged argument was he persuaded to
substitute a long grown-up stocking. The sordid advantages
of the plan were obvious enough, but it was thought that
Father Christmas might not like it. There is another little boy
in the house comparatively stricken in years ; he is six. It
appeared at one time likely that he would be elsewhere and
he expressed great anxiety lest Father Christmas should not
have learnt his new address. That seems convincing evidence
of an unhesitating faith, but six is perhaps approaching the
dangerous age. Even in the very young that matter of the

chimney provokes uncomfortable questions but they can, as a rule, be fended off by general references to magic.

To-day there must be peril in the fact that children go to some form of kindergarten so very young. If there be one child that has lost its innocence, it will desire to exhibit its superior knowledge by corrupting others, so that unbelief spreads rapidly like a contagion through the school. I have lately listened to a discussion between grown-ups as to the precise age at which they became aware of the horrid truth, and there were two who stoutly maintained that up to ten they had had no doubts. It is at least certain that they hung up their stockings with no perceptible diminution of the thrill till some time later than that. No doubt in the end there is a mutual conspiracy of silence, in which neither side makes any crude admission. And that is the best way. Even when faith is wholly gone there remains a sensitive love of the shrine where once we worshipped. " Of course I knew," said a small girl between her sobs, " that Father Christmas didn't really exist, but I did not want any one to tell me so."

There is another devil of doubt perpetually lying in wait for the modern child, or at least the urban child. To-day there is no big shop that has not a private Father Christmas of its own. It was recorded lately of one such shop that it had a large placard bearing the lamentable words, " Queue here for Father Christmas." I have even known a gentleman who enacted this sacrilegious part, and very hot he found it to be wrapped up every afternoon in layers of cotton-wool. What is to be said about these benevolent impostors ? How can their existence be reconciled with the tenets of the true religion ? There seems to be only one way out of it, to say simply and directly that they are only pretending and have no connection with the genuine article. To the grown-up this explanation may sound altogether too thin, but it is accepted readily enough. When it is considered how much of early life consists in pretending, there is nothing inherently impossible or even improbable in pretending Father Christmasses.

The Yule-Tide Spirit

If you have once believed there remains something holy even about the tangerine which so usefully fills up the extreme toe ; but never to have believed at all, never to have woken up in the dark and felt for the stocking weighted with unseen treasures and exercised an heroic self-restraint till the right time came—that is a permanent loss for which nothing can compensate. There was once a small girl who was seen creeping up the stairs at eleven o'clock at night to whisper urgently at a smaller brother's door under the impression that it was morning and that the hour for comparing stockings had come. It was a sad little figure that was escorted back to her bed again, with all those weary hours to wait. Yet how much better to have yourself endured such a supreme tragedy than only to have felt for it a condescending grown-up pity. So much is it better to have loved and lost a stocking than never to have loved it at all.

Yet for all their glory stockings are only in the nature of hors d'œuvre that whet the appetite for the feast. They keep a person in bed and wile away the time very pleasantly till breakfast, but once the real *pièces de résistance* appear in all the delaying fascination of brown paper and string they vanish from the mind. Not wholly indeed, for later in the day, when the time comes for taking stock and marshalling all the presents, they and their source will be duly acknowledged, but for the moment they are rather ungratefully forgotten. What with wondering, undoing, exhibiting, kissing and thanking, the human intellect can only take in a limited number of presents at once.

It cannot be denied that stockings make for a certain lack of tranquillity upon Christmas Eve, or so at least it seems to the more comatose and less conscientious givers of presents. These grave matters, as far as he is concerned, have been long since composed. That is to say, he has bought one or two essential presents and after that has determined to take it out or make it up in tips, a contemptible subterfuge. For those on whom the real burden of the festival falls, Christmas Eve is a time of dreadful restlessness, of endless tying up and labelling, of checking lists, of suddenly determined exchanges and last minute rememberings of having forgotten. The lazy present-giver has not the face to wonder aloud why they have not settled it all before, but that is probably what he thinks in the recesses of his black heart.

His own conduct has been deplorable, one long-drawn-out course of futility and procrastination. As long as possible he has shut his eyes to the approach of Christmas. When a flow of cards has forced it upon his attention, he has taken yet another week to think about it. Then at last, when the sands have almost run out, he has made a hectic rush of it. At that moment there occurs to him the luminous and original notion of books. It is always pleasant to browse in a book-shop and, unlike other shops, it is not necessary to go there with any pre-conceived ideas. As Kipps, who kept a book-shop, remarked, " One book's very like another—after all, what is it ? Something to read and done with. It's not a thing that matters like print dresses or serviettes." And then it possibly occurs to him that there are things still more like one another than books, namely, book tokens. Clearly it is much better and kinder to let people choose their own books than to thrust on them those they do not want. Thus he salves his own con-science and gives himself the least possible amount of trouble, which is likewise very soothing.

Coming to the day itself, which of the four meals constitutes its supreme glory ? There is much to be said for all of them. Breakfast as regards its actual components is only breakfast, but it is the time of the explosion of secrets. There is a cheerful and continual popping of presents in the room. Lunch is incomparable for solid eating, and supper, with cold turkey, for conviviality. But for a Christmas with children—and they are needed to give it its full poignancy—there is much to be said for tea, tea with a Christmas cake crowned with candles, tea with crackers and squeaky whistles in them. There is a mistaken belief that only alcohol can intoxicate. It is sugar and almond paste that go to the youthful head and induce frantic assaults upon uncles. Turkey and plum pudding demand too strict attention to business to permit of such a sudden ebullition of spirits. Only seen through a haze of cake and jam does an aunt in a pink and green hat attain the quintessence of absurdity. It is tea that rings all the changes on the emotions, for it begins with an awe-stricken silence at the glitter of the Christmas tree and ends with tipsy jollity.

Between lunch and tea there are two obvious alternatives, slumber or exercise. Of all the errors for which history is responsible there is none more palpably outrageous than that on the wedding day at Dingley Dell, the 23rd of December, the males of the party undertook a twenty-five mile walk to get rid of the effect of the wine at breakfast. Of course they did nothing of the kind, and indeed in point of time it is demonstrably impossible. As for Mr. Pickwick himself, I am sure he put his handkerchief over his head and his toes on the fender and snored happily. If the others got as far as Muggleton by the field path it is all that they did, and for my part I am extremely sceptical even as to that. But this monstrous fiction does at any rate inculcate a sound principle that a walk after lunch is a good thing. To come tramping home through the dusk, with the feet ringing in cheerful unison on the road, to see the light shining in the window and think of the tea well earned, that is to taste one of the intensest joys of living. How shameful then to recollect that I have not always shared those delights but have sometimes, feeling a sudden need for solitude, retired to my own room and gloomily practised putting on the floor. That was not the Yule-tide Spirit, but then, much may be forgiven me, I never had a stocking.

Frank Fairlegh

IT is as nearly true as makes no matter that *Frank Fairlegh* has just attained its centenary. " Scenes from the life of a private pupil," the modest beginning from which it sprang, were published periodically in *Sharpe's London Magazine* from 1846 to 1848, without Smedley's name, and the full-blown novel, into which he expanded them, appeared in 1850. At any rate, these dates give me an excuse to write about it, as indeed I am determined to do, for I have known it from early youth and owe it a deep debt of gratitude. To say that I have just reread it would not be accurate, for I have never ceased from reading it, but I have now been browsing over it more attentively, in a spirit not less affectionate but, I hope, a little more critical than usual. It may be that someone will try to read this tribute who has not read the book. If so I can see no manly course open to him save firmly to skip, unless indeed he repairs his previous error and reads *Frank Fairlegh*. In that case I shall feel that I have done my Boy Scout's one good deed for the day.

It is no doubt possible to pour on it contemptuous epithets. It is in places excessively melodramatic and indeed it is founded on the grand principle of melodrama of mingling in regular proportions scenes of blood and thunder with those of, as some will say, an equally crude humour. In the one the writing is often turgid and in the other it sometimes borders on the facetious. In many ways it is, I suppose, a ridiculous book, and yet it has some qualities that appeal successfully to simple tastes and emotions. To compare small things with great it possesses attributes that might almost be called Dickensian. Some of the things that can justly be said against it are often said, whether justly or not, against Dickens, and, like Dickens, *Frank Fairlegh*, in its humbler way, " gets there all the same."

Let me begin by setting down another's tribute to the book, which gives me both pleasure and encouragement. It is from the *Dictionary of National Biography*. " To give a satisfactory picture of youth in a state of pupilage, which should entertain at the same time boys and their elders, is a difficult if not impossible task ; but, after *Tom Brown's Schooldays* (and excluding *Vice Versa*), it is probable that no book has arrived nearer a solution of the problem than *Frank Fairlegh*." That is high praise. Some may think too high. Certainly there are many other stories of school and university life which have not the more obvious defects from which Frank Smedley's book suffers. They are more realistic, less melodramatic. It is possible to think of some that err too much on the side of realism, giving an excellent photograph rather than a picture. Life at school or college is generally one of trivial routine rather than exciting incident, and so the conscientious realist is in danger of being dull. Smedley certainly avoided that danger, for he piled up incident and excitement in reckless profusion. An artistic weakness no doubt but, as his lovers are convinced, an amiable one.

Frank Fairlegh, the book's eponymous hero who tells the story, does not go to school. He goes first, as Smedley himself had done, to a private tutor, or, as we should now call him, a coach, at Brighton, thinly disguised in the book as Helmstone. Thence, after a short interval, he goes to Trinity at Cambridge, as do two of his companions at Helmstone, the beautiful, magnanimous and slightly tiresome Oaklands and the horsy young blood and elementary humorist, the Hon. George Lawless. Smedley himself did not go to Cambridge, but he lived and read for some while with his uncle, the Vicar of Chesterton, nearby, and so saw at least something of University life. That undergraduates of those days regularly shook hands when meeting in the street and called each other " Sir " on such slight provocation it is a little hard to believe, but we may give him the benefit of the doubt. He did not go into his hero's doings at Cambridge in much detail and this, according to his own account, was not owing to any lack of familiarity with them, but because so many others had exhausted the subject. The story is in fact taken up more with events in vacation than in term time. In any case, I respectfully agree with the *Dictionary of National Biography* that the original germ of the book, the scenes at the private tutor's, " represent the summit of Smedley's literary achievement." They are the real fun ; by them the book stands or falls, and if any new reader, on his voyage of exploration, does not enjoy them he had better go no further. I grieve for his misfortune but *Frank Fairlegh* is not for him.

Despite its absurdities the book is in some ways a touching one, not because the author was a master of the pathetic, for he certainly was not, but because the pathos of his own life so clearly influenced his writing. He was from his early days a cripple and so could not go to Westminster where his grandfather had been a master. He had a natural love of life in the open air, but could not himself take part in the normal sports and exercises of youth. To this may be attributed the tremendous powers with which he endowed his young men, six feet or more in their shoes, and pictures of manly beauty, and the ease with which they achieved all manner of heroic feats. Harry Oaklands, though by nature indolent, could excel all rivals, no matter what the accomplishment demanded of him. Nor was Frank far behind him. He had learned to ride as a boy, and so may be allowed his conquest of the vicious mare, " Mad Bess," and his leap over a vast chalk pit on her back. But there is no evidence that as a boy he had ever played cricket, and on his own testimony he could only row " a little " at Helmstone. Yet at Cambridge he could, if he had a mind to it, " cross a country, pull an oar, or handle a bat with the best of them." The author would so dearly have liked to do such deeds and the next best thing was to see himself in the guise of his hero, doing them in imagination.

Smedley has a raciness and vigour in describing these achievements ; he so passionately believes in them himself that he makes his readers almost believe in them too ; but he is at his best in his humorous rather than his dramatic scenes. His humour is of a simple, almost a rudimentary character, but as far as it goes it is genuine and, as a rule, unforced. It must be admitted that it does not often go beyond practical jokes of a more or less elaborate character. Set down in cold print by another hand they will perhaps sound inexpressibly dreary but in their proper context they make us laugh. A fair sample is the trick played on poor Frank on his first morning at the house of his tutor, the Rev. Samuel Mildman. It is simplicity itself. A conspirator creeps into his bedroom in the early morning and secretes all his trousers up the chimney in Mr. Mildman's study. He is then told by his tormentors that for various reasons, such as old-clothes men being seen on the premises and a pawn ticket falling out of their tutor's pocket, it is regrettably clear that Mr. Mildman has himself stolen the trousers. The joke is prolonged by such ingenious means and the whole story told with such palpable enjoyment through a whole chapter that for my own part I am resolutely and unashamedly amused, and indeed this chapter is my favourite reading in the book. Entertaining too, in its way is the scene in which Frank and his friends, after rather too much champagne, ring the church bells and awaken the inhabitants to the belief that the town is on fire. Nothing could be more reprehensible, nothing could sound stupider, but—well, the reader must judge for himself. If he is fair-minded he will at least admit that the joke is carried through with unflagging spirit. By setting out these escapades in my own bald and prosaic language I may have implanted in his breast a lasting resolution never to read the book, but it is only fair to let him know the kind of thing he is in for, if he does.

There are plenty more of the same kind, which I will spare him. The two chief actors in them are Freddy Coleman and George Lawless. Freddy, though I endure him for old sake's sake, is rather a vulgar little creature who makes the most excruciatingly bad puns, but Lawless is, I will maintain, good value in his way. It would be excessive to say that he carries the book along on his back, but it would be dry work without him. It is not perhaps too fanciful to see a resemblance between him and the delightful Harry Foker in *Pendennis*. It is a likeness that is naturally flattering to Lawless but it exists. Probably it is quite a fortuitous one, for Lawless came into existence before Foker by a year or two, and nobody would accuse Thackeray of borrowing from Smedley. On the other hand, *Pendennis* was written before *Frank Fairlegh* appeared in its expanded form, and the success of Foker may have encouraged Smedley to make more of Lawless than he had once intended. In their double capacities as patrons of sport and agreeable rattles, in their love of driving tandems and of screwing up doors, in their terror of ladies and their ultimate subjugation, they are unquestionably like one another. There I leave it.

There is another more or less humorous character whom I do suspect of being borrowed, and that is Mrs. Coleman, Freddy's mother. She bears unmistakable signs of Mrs. Nickleby. To be sure there are in the world many kind-hearted and muddle-headed old ladies ; the type is far from unknown ; so the debt may have been an unconscious one. Moreover, Mrs. Coleman has none of the greatness of Mrs. Nickleby with her gorgeous irrelevancies and her mazes of memory, in which one partially developed idea is constantly being driven out by a supervening one. She is simply a lady who becomes pleasantly and inextricably entangled between the children and pigs belonging to another lady. " Four pigs, did I say ?—but it doesn't much signify, for the youngest is a boy and will soon be fat enough to kill." That is a fair instance of the humble foothills she scales. We grow in the end a little tired of her machine-made muddles, as we do of old Mr. Frampton's grunts. He suffers from a Dickensian weakness in that since he has begun by grunting it becomes what we should call to-day his signature tune.

No account of the book would be complete without its two villains, Richard Cumberland and Stephen Wilford. Between them they provide nearly all the melodrama, Cumberland the plucking of a pigeon at the sinister game of billiards and the abduction of an heiress, Wilford the attempted seduction of a virtuous pastry cook's daughter, the horse-whipping and the duel that ensue. Cumberland is merely squalid and disreputable but Wilford—ah ! here is one in the best Adelphi tradition. His dark, piercing eye (he had high-bred Italian blood in him), his withering glances, his contemptuously curled lip indicative of the bitterest sarcasm, his faultlessly-cut black clothes, showing never a speck of white as a mark for the opposing pistol, the coal black mare which he rides with such perfect address—these are one and all the real thing. As he stands gazing sternly on his prostrate enemy with the words, " Thus perish all who dare to cross my path," he reaches the very pinnacle of sublime absurdity. He is marked out for death of course, and does die murmuring Italian words, but I wish he could have survived in some villainous little kingdom of his own, ever young and beautiful and wicked.

I have said little of Frank himself, since for all his heroism he is, to tell the truth, something of a stick and a prig, neither better nor worse, let us say, than Nicholas Nickleby. I ought to add in bare justice that he was Fourth Wrangler. That is not necessarily an attractive trait, and I only introduce the fact for the chance of a small boast by the way. I believe that I am probably the only living man who can recite the names of the first three Wranglers in his year. At any rate, while smarting under some Dickensian defeat at his hands, I asked the late Dr. M. R. James, who knew everything, whether he knew that, and he did not. There is likewise very little to be said of the young ladies. Clara Saville, with her sad dog-like eyes, is as worthy of Frank as Madeline Bray was of Nicholas, and as supremely uninteresting, but there is something comparatively human and pretty about Fanny Fairlegh, and she ought to have married Lawless instead of Oaklands. Did he not write her a poem containing these engaging lines :

> *Dear Fanny, there are moments*
> *When love gets you in a fix,*
> *Takes the bit in his jaws, and without any pause*
> *Bolts away with you like bricks.*

Unfortunately she never saw them or she must have yielded.

I am sadly conscious that I have not done *Frank Fairlegh* justice. I am afraid I have laughed at it too much, and, though the laughter is inevitable, it should be gentle to the point of tenderness. Moreover, there is a quality about the book which defies expression, or at least my limited powers of expression. I feel about it as did poor little William Dent Pitman as he gazed at the beautiful waxen lady in the hairdresser's window and saw in her " a haughty, indefinable something." Smedley has a gift of narrative ; he gets along at a round, cheerful pace ; there is movement and " go " in him, and there is the spirit of youth that calls to youth all the world over.

Perhaps I never fully realised how excellent was *Frank Fairlegh* until I read a nearly contemporary work constructed on somewhat similar lines. True, this comparative method of criticism is not conclusive, for I think the other book is the worst I ever read in the whole course of my life. I chanced to tell a kind friend that I was going to try to write about

Frank Fairlegh

Frank Fairlegh, whereupon he lent me this rare treasure from his library. He admitted that it was fearfully and wonderfully bad, but said that reading it gave him the sort of self-torturing pleasure that a man derives from passing his tongue over a jagged tooth. It is entitled *The College Chums—A Novel in two volumes by Charles Lister, Esq.,* and was published in 1845, the year before Smedley began to write his original scenes. The young gentlemen are at Oxford instead of Cambridge ; otherwise the ingredients of the cup are in each case much the same. There is a good deal of hard riding, a genteel card sharper like Cumberland, a duel, a seduction, an infanticide and a murder trial. There are ladies of incredible beauty, one of them possessing " the most patrician nose ever seen," and they nearly all die in a lingering and painful way. I lost all count of the death-bed scenes. But Lister Esquire, for I would not insult him by calling him Mr., has not the saving gift of humour, even of the most primitive kind. He remains tragical and portentous throughout, and I cannot even derive my friend's perverse gratification from reading him. I believe him to have been the solemnest ass that ever lived, but I am nevertheless grateful to him ; he sent me back to *Frank Fairlegh* with a fresh ardour, a more burning admiration than ever.

The Boyhood of a Hero

ON the 18th of July, 1848, William Gilbert Grace was
born. To those who saw him play it is hard to believe
that, had he lived, he would have been a hundred years
old to-day. Those to whom he is only a name, however great
a name, may be startled to find him no older. Once they are
no more seen, past heroes and their times and generations,
grow strangely confused in the mind, and to many people it
would probably come as no greater surprise to be celebrating
the centenary of Alfred Mynn or William Beldham.

There is a form of speculation common enough no doubt,
and yet never indulged in without some pleasing effect. It
consists in wondering what those unwittingly present at the
making of history would have said and thought if they had
only known. And so, with a certain agreeable futility, I find
myself wondering about the neighbours in one small Gloucestershire village. They heard the hoofs of Dr. Henry Mills Grace's
horse as he came home from his round, and, soon after,
breaking out among the Downend apple trees, the crack of the
bat and ball and the barks of Don, Ponto and Noble, that
immortal trinity, as they raced to and fro, opposing to the ball

their dauntless breasts. How little they knew that those every-day sounds would go to swell the eternal murmur of the undercurrents of history !

Comparisons between game players kept asunder by the years are useless and irritating, even if made by those qualified by knowledge, and I am very, very far from possessing the knowledge necessary to appraise the greatness of W. G. It is easy indeed to point to the figures, to the immense proportion of runs in the whole side's innings that he constantly made, to the almost fantastic gap between his average in his best years and that of his nearest pursuers. Anybody can do that, and to those who are sceptical about the illustrious past a study of the records may often be salutary. It seldom wholly persuades, but it ought at least to inculcate in too confident youth a decent reticence. Yet statistics, even though they be convincing, are dry work. For my own ignorant part, I am content to leave the surpassing greatness of W. G. to the testimony of those who played with him. Enough for me is the vast legend of which he is the central figure, in which those three dogs who fielded his first childish strokes, and his uncle who supervised them, and his mother who watched them with a clear appraising eye, have for ever attained their niches.

The time may come when nearly all the cricketers of his long day will only be remembered, save by assiduous students of Wisden, not on account of their own achievements but because they appear in one of the many W. G. stories. Tom Emmett was a great bowler and a great character, and yet some day perhaps he will be known for one thing, that he said of the youthful hero, " I call him a non-such ; he ought to be made to play with a littler bat." Shrewsbury may have lasting fame only because W. G. when asked to rank his con-temporaries among batsmen replied, " Give me Arthur." And then there are those figures who from the very beginning were nameless. There is the boy, introduced to the great man because his father had played with him, to whom W. G. remarked (it is one of the stories of him I love best), " I hope you're a better fielder than your father was, for he was the worst I ever did see." Doubtless the boy had a name once, but it has long faded. Yet he himself will be as unfading as that other nameless boy who described his head master at Rugby as " a beast but a just beast," and so immortalised not only himself but an Archbishop into the bargain.

In this legend, no one is more secure of his place than is Uncle Pocock, who gave his young nephew his first and only lessons. He is remembered, to take an example from another game, as is Stewart Maiden, because the infant Bobby Jones followed him round like an adoring little dog and took him as his model. He is a mysterious and fascinating figure, and I only wish I knew more about him. His very name has an antique thrill. To-day he would have been simply Uncle Alfred, since we have given up calling uncles and aunts by their surnames, though I think the custom still survives in America. How much he would have lost by the exchange ! As Uncle Pocock he is with Uncle Glegg or Uncle Pullet in *The Mill on the Floss* ; he belongs to remotest ages. He seems to have played little cricket in his youth but to have caught fire from his brother-in-law and made up for lost time by assiduous study of the game's theory. By 1854, when the small Gilbert was six years old and ready to take his place in the family practice, Uncle Pocock came out regularly from Bristol to preach patience and the straight bat and the left shoulder well up.

We really do not know a great deal more than that, but surely it is permissible to imagine a little more. I believe that Uncle Pocock with his sister Martha, Mrs. Grace, as a staunch ally, had early determined that Gilbert should be *the* one. I fancy that he was a little jealous of E. M., and so of his brother-in-law, the Doctor, who thought the world of him. Very well, then, he, Uncle Pocock, would produce a pupil who should put E. M. in the shade. I am encouraged in this invention— for it is really no more than that—by an experience of my own. At my private school, the top form, in which were all, or nearly all, the Scholarship boys, was taken by the Head Master. I, who was to try for a scholarship only as a trial run, was in the second form, taken by a much younger brother-in-law. He took a fancy to me, resolved to show what he and I could do, and gave me a great deal of private coaching. When, to the general surprise—I fear it was a fluke—I beat two of the Head Master's best boys, that young brother-in-law enjoyed an unholy triumph. I am conscious that in this belief my later understanding comes to my aid, but I am sure it is well founded.

So in my story Uncle Pocock resolved to show Dr. Grace what he and the small Gilbert could do. It is to be remembered that E. M. was by seven years the elder, and seven years make an enormous gap. When W. G. was ten and could already, in his own words, " play a ball from his wicket with a fair amount of confidence," E. M. was almost a young man, seventeen years old, already dealing out death and destruction among the local bowlers and of a determined character, not likely to take too kindly to any uncle's advice. Already he had developed the gorgeous heterodoxy of the cross bat which was to stay with him through life. When very young he had been given too heavy a bat. Mrs. Grace had doubted, Uncle Pocock had hinted his disapproval ; so had Ponto, who growled whenever E.M. hit a vast pull into a quarry where the ball took a great deal of finding. Despite all their protests, Dr. Grace had refused to take a firm line, and here was the deplorable though superficially successful result. So Uncle Pocock was determined to devote himself to Gilbert, who was still young enough to be malleable and do what he was told. He was to play with a small bat until he was old enough and strong enough for a bigger one ; he was to concentrate on defence and the hitting would come ; he should walk before he could run in the way he should go, and in due time there should emerge such a batsman as the world had never seen.

It is curious that, considering his debt to Uncle Pocock, which he handsomely acknowledged, W. G. as a grown-up cricketer had not much belief in coaching and thought it often did more harm than good. The late Admiral Edgar Grace told me that his father seldom if ever gave his sons any teaching beyond taking a bat, and saying, " This is the way to do it." Perhaps it was because, according to Canon Edward Lyttelton, " No one ever had a more unanalytic brain." Perhaps his knowledge of cricket though profound was instinctive. As Hazlitt wrote of Cavanagh at fives, " he could do what he pleased, and he always knew exactly what to do." Such a man might find it hard to appreciate the problems of the less gifted or to find their solution.

Whatever he came to think in later life, W. G. in his youth clearly suffered the drilling of Uncle Pocock gladly, with a keenness and in particular a patience that never failed. No doubt it was a hard school and if there was a little favouritism on Uncle Pocock's part we may be sure there was none from the rest of the family. Those practices were stern and strenuous. The grown-up members had a quarter of an hour's batting a-piece, the juniors five minutes ; there was not a moment to waste and, we may feel very sure, no slackness permitted in the field. If sometimes in later life W. G. seemed a little too fiercely right as to the letter of the law, perhaps that Spartan upbringing at Downend had something to do with it. In other and lesser departments of life there might be such things as minor points to be carelessly or gracefully conceded, but there were no minor points in cricket. Rules were rules. The rule for boys was five minutes and not five minutes twenty seconds, and if Ponto could not find the ball you must go and find it yourself and pretty quick too.

Everybody must have played, strictly by himself, that game of the imagination in which, by means of some enchantment, he can turn back the clock and call up scenes long past. I have a whole theatre full of them in the domain of sport alone, the centuries sadly mixed up. There is George Osbaldeston after his great ride on Newmarket Heath and John Gully to force a way for him through the cheering crowd ; Allan

Robertson playing at St. Andrews ; M. J. Brooks jumping six feet for the first time, when it was deemed impossible, and, for cricket, of course Hambledon against All England, and my own Kent with Alfred Mynn and Fuller Pilch in their pride. But perhaps best of all I should like to see that family game in the orchard, with a cousin or two, a Rees or a Gilbert, thrown in, and to hear what they all said with their pleasant touch of Gloucestershire accent. " These Graces chatter so," was said years afterwards by a fiery and much tried batsman. I don't imagine W. G. saying much then, but no doubt there is plenty of cheerful noise from the elders. The small W. G. shall be batting, with Mrs. Grace holding the still smaller Fred by the hand, and Uncle Pocock looking on with mingled pride and anxiety, and the daughters, the poor unconsidered daughters whose names are almost lost, throwing up the ball if it comes their way. And then the boy's five minutes are up and my picture melts away and dissolves.

I have been told by one who played against Gloucestershire in Mr. Jessop's first match how some of the other side, seeing only the rough-hewn and almost rustic hitting and not discerning the greatness that lay beneath, dared gently to chaff W. G. and to ask him, " What have you got here, Old Man ? " Thereupon W. G. turned on them truculently and told them, " Ah, you'll soon see what I've got here." Uncle Pocock might have used those very words, and he had not long to wait for his prophecies to come true. Let any one look at this briefest record—I must have a few figures here—and then talk of any other youthful prodigy if he dare. In 1858 when he was ten young Gilbert played his first match for the West Gloucestershire Club. Two years later, at twelve, he made fifty-one for the club against Clifton. In 1863, just before his fifteenth birthday, he faced the All England eleven, with the two famous fast bowlers of the day, Tarrant and Jackson, and the bowling had to be changed and Tinley put on, with his cunning lobs, before the boy was out, for thirty-two. He was still only fifteen when in 1864, he played for the All England eleven himself, and then, a month or two after his sixteenth birthday, he made 170 and fifty-six not out against Sussex. By 1865 he had played twice for the Gentlemen against the Players, and for England against Surrey. As far as such representative honours were concerned he had no more worlds left to conquer, and he was but a little over seventeen. And yet to-day the world is greatly impressed if a boy after his last summer at a public school is given a trial for his county. Was there ever such a " riband in the cap of youth ? " If Uncle Pocock nobly refrained from saying, " I told you so," he must at least have sung in his heart a " nunc dimittis."

When I try to summon up for myself that scene in the Downend orchard I frankly admit myself defeated. The Gilbert of twelve years old is beyond my powers of imagination, and remains a dim and shadowy figure. I simply cannot conceive of a little W. G. I had the delight of a slight acquaintance with him when he was already over sixty, a vast monument of a man, with that mighty beard, " a sable silver'd." That is the portrait of him that I have in my head, and without any help in the form of a childish photograph I cannot reduce it. On the other hand, when the small boy has become the conquering hero of 1865 there are some data from which to picture him. By that time we know that he was a big, strong boy, over six feet high. He was tall and lanky, with no promise as yet of the massive and almost ponderous figure of later years, but he already weighed eleven stone. We may fancy him rather sprawling and colt-like, and one observer, Lord Cobham, detected as he thought " some appearance of delicacy." It was probably a deceptive one, and those long legs of his had plenty of strength, for he was in his day a winner of many races in the sports in his neighbourhood. Moreover, at an early age he showed unmistakable signs of manhood ; those who then played with him remembered afterwards a black scrub on his chin, the herald of the *promissa barba* of later years. The researches of historians seem to show that not till he was twenty-one or so did he begin to shave, that he kept it up for a year or two and then cast aside the razor for ever and let the jungle tide of nature have its way. As to his demeanour, we have again the authority of Lord Cobham (C. G. Lyttelton) for saying that he was " quiet and shy in manner." In this respect he was, Lord Cobham noticed, in marked contrast to E. M., but by that time E. M. had headed the averages and toured Australia, while Gilbert was only emerging from the schoolboy. It was small wonder if he was a little shy, thrown suddenly from a quiet, countrified home into the company of those who had seen a larger world and been brought up to a more spacious way of life. " Quiet " is hardly the epithet to be applied to him in later years, but he was always modest ; if he talked, and he liked talking, it was never about himself, and he had a delightful lack of self-consciousness and a great natural dignity.

So here, by the time he was sixteen or seventeen, we can make some sort of picture of him ; a simple, unaffected boy but looking like a man, so that those who watched him could hardly believe he was so young ; very anxious to do well (he described himself as " anxious " when he met Tarrant and Jackson) but never nervous ; a wonderfully good enjoyer, so that all the new glories that had come upon him never ceased to be fun ; finally, with a great love of home and a clannish feeling for his family.

There is a temptation to extend this modest paper and to follow W. G. through his long career, but I mean to resist it. The spring time is best, and in many ways, I think, W. G. remained all his life the same big boy of those early years. I once wrote a little book on W. G., and the late Admiral Edgar Grace, a truly adoring son, was very kind in helping me over it. When I sent him the book he was once more kind, but said that I had " made too many excuses " for his father. I will not fall into the same error again. No doubt he had his faults, but they came from his intense keenness on the game, and those who knew him best not merely condoned them but loved him, I think, almost better for them. He had a wonderful power of inspiring affection, and to know him ever so slightly was to understand and to fall under the spell. When my eldest daughter was two years old W. G. kissed his hand to her in the prettiest way, as she gazed at him through the window. I have always impressed on her that if she lives to a hundred she can never have paid her a pleasanter honour.

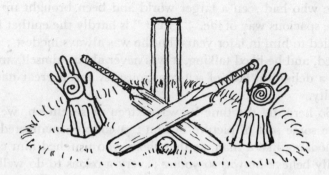

Heat and Cold

"FINE time for them as is well wropped up, as the Polar Bear said to himself, ven he was practising his skating." At first sight it would seem that the Polar Bear was an eminently sensible animal, giving vent to a sufficiently obvious truth. And yet this question of wrapping up, and indeed the wider one of being hot or cold, produces the bitterest feelings of hostility. The cold-blooded despise the warm-blooded as fools for not putting on enough clothes, and this contempt is returned with interest on the ground of cowardice, stuffiness and senility. It might be thought that it was a purely personal matter, which each one of us might decide for himself, but this is not so ; it is a matter of principle, in defence of which many are prepared to die. When, as now and again the question is mentioned in the House of Commons, the strength of feeling on one side or the other becomes apparent. An innocent question is asked as to long-sleeved vests and long pants, and the answer, awaking derisive merriment, is that youth declines to wear such things. Another question suggests that woollen underclothing is " in short supply," and a lady member leaps to her feet to ask whether it is not a fact that people only mollycoddle themselves by wearing these garments, and would not be much better without them.

Even those who are not in a general way averse from keeping warm are often martyrs to their own rules and shiver on principle. They very likely obey the wise saw bidding them not cast a clout till May is out, but once having cast it they are adamant. The clouts have been carefully put away in a drawer exuding a pleasant scent of moth balls, and there they must stay till autumn comes again. No matter how icy may be one of Mr. Buchan's cold spells, these rule-ridden persons decline to interfere with matters long since tranquilly folded and disposed of. They will not follow that which I suggest is in this country the only reasonable rule, namely, to treat each day as a new one, and, having taken a purely impartial and objective view of the weather, with no regard to the time of year, to dress themselves accordingly.

Sometimes they advance an argument, which on a first hearing has something to recommend it. If, they say in effect, we wrap ourselves up now, what shall we do when it is really cold and we have nothing more left to put on ? The answer is first of all that it may never happen and to suffer certainly now for fear of suffering possibly more in the future is the height of folly ; second, that there is no limit to the number of garments that a man may wear, unless he has a craven fear of appearances. I write as one who is not ashamed either of feeling the cold or of taking all conceivable precautions against it. In Macedonia in the first war I lived in a tent and when the Vardar wind blew nobody could possibly deny that it was cold. I borrowed six army blankets from a kindly brother officer who kept the blanket store, and devised for myself a suit of woolly night armour, including long stockings. And as a result other people came to breakfast declaring that they had not been able to sleep for the cold while I, like Mr. Mantalini, " laughed demnably." I am prepared to be as sorry as need be for poor wretches who are cold and cannot help it, but with those who, having the money and the coupons, know that lovely long pants are to be had in the haberdasher's shop and pass by on the other side, I resolutely decline to sympathise. And, apropos, the most beautifully snug night I ever spent was on a lonely Macedonian road, in a lorry-load of blankets. What a nest I made for myself amid those grey bales ! How pleasantly rough and warm were those blankets' kisses, and with what a soothing dreariness the wind whistled round my lorry of refuge !

The thought of that wind opens up the question of how far it is licit to heighten our own sensations of comfort by contrasting them with those of others. To me the sound of the wind adds, I freely admit, to my happiness when I snuggle in bed or crouch close to the fire. I do not find the thought of the unfortunate X or the deserving Y out in the storm by any means unpleasant. On the other hand, there are those, to be admired but hardly to be envied, who are made miserable by the thought of that solitary and hypothetical wanderer fighting his way head on against the gale. If I feel at all uneasy on this score I always take refuge in Dickens. Two things about him are axiomatic ; first that he was a very kind-hearted man who felt intensely for other people, and second that no one could ever compete with him in contrasting the cosiness of indoors with the rain and the snow and the fog without. If anybody tells me that Dickens did not revel yet a little more cheerfully in the glow from the knowledge, perhaps largely unconscious, that somebody was plashing along a miry road, wet through and in the dark, I am afraid I do not believe him. Think of just one among his many gorgeous descriptions. The landlord of the Jolly Sandboys is leaning against the door-post, looking lazily at the rain, while within a fire is roaring up the chimney and a mighty cauldron is bubbling and simmering. Now, since Codlin has arrived, the landlord knows that Short is outside getting unpleasantly moist, but Dickens does not reprobate his enjoyment of the rain on that account. Far from it, his own palpable enjoyment of the fact heightens the enchantment. It is quite true that it does not really matter how wet Short may get or little Nell who is with him, because a Dickens fire possesses a magical property of instantly drying people and preventing their catching cold ; but as to liking it, why of course he liked their getting wet. He himself was safe indoors and defied the rain to make him wet, let it batter at the window never so loudly. That was the point, and Tom Smart's glasses of hot punch would not have tasted nearly so good if it had been a fine, calm, starlight night on Marlborough Downs.

Dickens (having once dragged him in, I must have yet a little more of him) is invaluable in showing how maddening are the people who will not put enough clothes on. There is that insufferable Mark Tapley, with no waistcoat and the bosom of his shirt exposed to the winter blast. " Lord love you, sir," he exclaims. " *My* chest don't want no warming," and goes on to explain that inflammation of the lungs would tend to jolliness. I have in my mind's eye one friend who never by any chance wears a waistcoat and in all weathers has a cold white shirt, and, worse than that, openly boasts that there is nothing underneath it. He is in all other respects an estimable Christian gentleman, and yet it is hard to forgive him. He is like a draught of icy air blowing into the room. That great and delightful man, the late Mr. Wilson Steer, was much frightened of draughts (which he pronounced with a characteristic short " a "), and was popularly believed by his pupils at the Slade School to wear " two of everything." How far more endearing a quality is this ! I remember once to have played on the windy heights above Huddersfield with a golfer whose preparation for the game consisted in putting another pair of trousers over those which he already wore. That was the right spirit.

Those abominably hardy creatures who wear the same thin under-garments all the year round, or even none at all, are doubly offensive. Like those who have cold baths, they produce an involuntary shudder of pity, and at the same time they put us to shame. To say so much is to be inconsistent, since one ought to pity nothing but their folly, but I freely confess to some little inconsistency. There remains in every one of us something of the small boy that once bitterly resented being sent out wrapped up to the eyes and then saw another boy, of the same age and size, flaunting the glorious circumstance of having no great-coat. In my own case, I incline to attribute this feeling, after the manner of the psycho-analysts, to the hatred I conceived very early in life for the good boy in Miss Edgeworth's, *Waste Not, Want Not*. The two nephews, it will be remembered, were each given a handsome tip by their uncle. The good one first showed his detestable qualities by spending part of the money on a suit of clothes for a poor boy, and with the rest bought himself a nice, thick great-coat. The bad one expressed a natural preference for a green and white archery costume. And what happened? Why, the bad but essentially deserving nephew fell into some red mud, his lovely costume was bedaubed with clay and he was laughed at by that heartless aristocrat, Lady Diana Sweepstakes. The good but loathsome one kept warm and actually won the archery competition by means of the string which he had saved off the parcel containing his great-coat.

In the first place, to be given a purely useful present, one of necessity rather than charity, which ought not to be a present at all, is a gross fraud, and therefore repellent to every properly constituted mind. In the second—here is a little more psycho-analysis—I much desired white flannels in which to play cricket, and this repressed longing found an outlet in admiration for the green and white archery costume. So no doubt when I had to wear a great-coat I saw in myself a reflection of the good nephew and hated myself accordingly. And so much of that small boy that once was me, still remains that I like to go out without a great-coat if I possibly can, and make up for it by layers of invisible and more intimate garments.

But then, and here is a branch of the subject which I approach with a truly missionary fervour, I am sure in such circumstances to be wearing my mittens. If there is one crusade that could induce me to carry a fiery cross about the country it is on behalf of mittens. I have preached them all my life, but with sadly little success. People will not believe that a little circlet of wool encasing the wriṣt can not merely warm the hands but impart a delicious glow to the whole frame. A man may accurately regulate his temperature by mittens. If he ever grows too warm, let him take them off and he instantly cools down again. I believe that golfers stand almost alone in appreciating the mitten's worth. They have learned it the hard way by being unable to hold their clubs in an icy wind. They do not wear mittens, which cover the palm of the hand, but rather muffetees, which shelter the back of the hand, but leave the palm bare. Among them I am proud to think that I have made at least a few converts, but I go far beyond them, for in cold weather I wear my mittens both indoors and out of doors, whatever I may be doing. I am writing this very sentence with a mittened hand. If any kind female relative ever suggests knitting me a Christmas present, I have my answer ready. No man can have too many pairs of mittens.

Mr. Squeers remarked of Nature that she was a rum one, and it is curious that those who have cold hands do not necessarily suffer tortures from cold feet. But this is not to say that there is not great joy in warming the toes at the fire. It is not only a pleasant action in itself ; it is a symbolic one. It signifies the day's work done and the world shut out ; it has a vague but agreeable suggestion of crumpets for tea. To be enjoyed to the full it demands privacy, in which a stockinged foot can be extended towards the blaze, so near that it smarts and tingles when replaced in the shoe. And yet, here is another inconsistency, he who likes to warm his toes does not necessarily enjoy a hot-water bottle. Perhaps in this matter too, I suffer from an infantile inhibition or repression. I had an uncle and aunt who were given to strange accidents. He poked himself in the eye with a folded copy of *The Times* and she burnt her feet on a hot-water bottle. I was never in the least afraid of the first mischance, but I may have been of the second. At any rate I have no affection for a hot-water bottle ; it distracts my attention when reading in bed, and my last action before putting out the light is to drop it with a sonorous thump on the floor.

It is not, I fancy, a merely personal prejudice. This piece of domestic furniture marks one of the greatest gulfs dividing the sexes. Women, so much hardier and braver and more patient than men in a hundred ways, are lamentably dependent on hot-water bottles. They never travel a yard without one and if they surrender it to a still chillier sister it is as a supreme act of self-abnegation and with all the air of a Sir Philip Sidney. Moreover, they are not content with " warming their pretty little toes " like little Polly Flinders ; but, if accounts may be trusted, clasp the hot-water bottle passionately to their breasts.

This again opens up the question of another mysterious difference, not between the sexes but between human beings in general. There are some who never cast clouts because they never put them on, who in the daytime are so Spartan that the very thought of them gives a pain in the head, even as does an ice too precipitately eaten. Yet, when they go to bed their whole nature seems to change, and they retire under a mountainous pile of blankets and eiderdowns. Conversely, those who have all day been lapped in wool grow suddenly hot-blooded and only venture on the very minimum of blankets lest they awake raving after frightful dreams. There may be some reason for this phenomenon, but nobody has ever succeeded in explaining it to me.

It is then admittedly possible in certain circumstances to put on too many clothes. If I were to choose one race that appears to do so I should name the professional cricketers of a past generation. Unless my memory plays strange tricks there was the glimpse of a jersey to be seen underneath the flannel shirt even on the balmiest day, and an inch or so of grey drawers above the tops of the trousers. I have a vision of one in particular thus attired, bowling away for ever with his economical little run of two or three steps, and freely larding the lean earth. And yet perhaps these disciples of the polar bear really knew best and did not catch so many chills as the lightly-clad amateur. Those who live in treacherous climates are apt to wear more than mere visitors, and the Macedonian peasant wraps a scarlet sash round his waist in numberless folds. It looks oppressively hot, but he probably knows his own business.

One thing is surely incontestable, that for feeling a little more brave, or rather perhaps a little less horribly frightened, too many clothes are preferable to too few. There is nothing so destructive to the manhood as feeling cold. Give me the golfer who wears mackintosh trousers, two concealed woolly waistcoats under a mackintosh coat and the longest mittens that money can buy, stretching far out of sight up his arms, and if he has not wholly paralysed his power of swinging the club I will back him against any more scantily-clad champion. Yes, even if, like some of the cricketers of Dingley Dell and All Muggleton, he resembles " half a gigantic roll of flannel elevated on a couple of inflated pillow-cases."

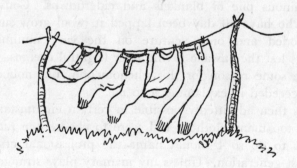

Games on the Air

WE are often accused of becoming a race of watchers instead of players. It is a grave accusation and perhaps a true one. Yet there is a lower depth to which we may sink; we may become a race of listeners. The B.B.C. and its body of breathless but unflagging commentators have much to answer for. When we consider the difficulty of getting tickets, and the difficulty of getting there and back with sixteen people in the carriage and the weary waiting beforehand and the feeling of utter helplessness in a heaving, swirling crowd, there is at least something to be said for a more tranquil manner of enjoyment. In the first world war a battalion after a thoroughly unpleasant spell in the trenches were luxuriating in their first day's rest behind the line, when they were suddenly ordered to march several miles, in a mutinous frame of mind, in order to be addressed by a Bishop. The Bishop began brightly, "As you can't come to Church, the Church has to come to you." At that moment there was nothing so revengeful and malignant that those listeners would not have done it to him if they could. Fortunately we who listen to games can have no such grievance; the match really is brought to us in our own homes.

For my part I ask nothing better than a Saturday afternoon, an arm-chair, a blazing fire and a Rugby International or the University Match. As a rule, I am, I trust, a tolerably complaisant and even unselfish listener. Give me a bound volume of *Punch* on which to browse, and even Bach may be said to slip off me like water off a duck's back. Those various and improving items which a small daughter once comprehensively described as " Man talking " have little effect on me, save sometimes an agreeably soporific one. Let others listen to what they will, but there is one point on which I am resolutely selfish ; if there is a Rugby match I am going to turn it on, and those who do not like it can lump it. If in consequence, as is sometimes the case, I get the room to myself, I can bear the implied reproach and can writhe in anguish or break into silent but vehement cheering in happy solitude.

It is to the eternal credit of the commentators—and I make them one and all my grateful and respectful compliments—that the anguish is so great. " Fool," exclaims the listener passionately, as he hears that a penalty kick has been given against his side. " Has he got it ? " says the commentator. " No, it's gone wide." And he sobs with relief. When one of his own men has actually got over the line, and then, *then* he hears in calm and abominably dispassionate tones, " No, the whistle had gone first," I should be extremely sorry to set down his remarks in print. Several times I have vowed that I could and would bear it no more. The famous Bob Grimston was known to walk out of Lord's, unable to endure the agony of Eton and Harrow. Hoylake supporters were unequal to following John Ball to a nineteenth hole, but went back to the clubhouse and, like Mr. Winkle on a famous occasion, buried their heads in the sofa cushions and groaned dismally. Therefore, I suppose that patriotic listeners have before now rushed to the infernal machine and switched it off, their feelings being too much for them. Personally, I have always so far been able to stick it out, but it has sometimes been a hard struggle. Only the other day I was listening to a match at Cardiff. Wales were leading by six points ; the referee was, so I was told, looking at his watch ; there were only two or three minutes to go ; the enemy were attacking with the courage of despair. " It must be all right now, they can't do it, it must be all right," I murmured over and over again to myself, touching wood with feverish fingers ; and when at last that blessed whistle did go I collapsed in a heaven-praising heap upon the sofa.

I take Cardiff as an example because, with the humility of one who never played this great game, but with the pride of half a Welshman, I regard it, as far as Rugby is concerned, as my spiritual home. I can picture the whole scene there more clearly than elsewhere. There is first the drive from the country with people pouring in from the mining valleys, a dozen or so all packed into Dai Jones's taxi. There is the intensely patriotic atmosphere, prayerful rather than truculent. There is the band marching round the field, and finally drawing up in the middle for the great moment of " Land of our fathers " that goes on and on, rising and falling round the ground, so inspiring and so unbearably near to tears. And at last come the two teams filing out one by one down the narrow alley between the stands, and the flash of red jerseys as they scatter to their places across the green field. I can deliberately heighten my emotions by imagining these things so as to attain to a delicious misery before ever the commentator has started.

And what a stirring pace he maintains when he does start ! It may be that he who describes ice hockey gets more words into the minute, but then I do not happen to care who wins at ice hockey and now I care desperately. Fast as he travels, he does now and then get left behind. There comes a try out of the blue for which the listener is unprepared, but this happens very seldom. Sometimes, I suppose, he names the wrong man, but what of that ? What the eye does not see the heart cannot grieve. There was once a too conscientious commentator, an Irishman, who being imperfectly acquainted with some of the opposing players used to say, " Wait now, till I look at my programme." He would have done better to chance it, for by the time he had identified his man, the tide of battle had swept to the other end of the field leaving him high and dry. His was an amiable and also a rare weakness, and as a rule, the commentator is so splendidly, pantingly up to date that the listener feels himself in the forefront of every rush. It cannot be denied that there are moments when we want most ungratefully to murder the commentator. That is when the poor man, performing his bounden duty to the late and lazy listener, insists on repeating the score, which the virtuous and punctual listener knows perfectly well. " Here at Cardiff in the match between England and Wales the score is still——" he repeats at intervals. " Idiot ! " we shout and how we wish he could hear, " we know that. You've said it before." This is thoroughly unjust conduct, but it is sometimes beyond our control.

One great advantage that the football commentator possesses is that his description is so powerfully reinforced by the crowd. Here I write with some little envy, as one who has sometimes tried to broadcast on the most silent and decorous of all games, golf. He who describes a golf match must generate all his own excitement, for he will get no outside help. His football brother, on the other hand, has only to keep quiet for an instant and say, " Listen to the cheers," and he may be sure of " getting it across." And if cheers are good, boos are almost better. A penalty kick given against the home side produces a low angry murmur, so formidable as to send a shiver down the spine. I suppose, for I am a child in these technical matters, that the use of such effects must depend on the position of the microphone, whether it is, relatively speaking, in a secluded eyrie or in the heart of the crowd. At any rate, that crowd, if it can be prayed in aid, is as effective an ally as it is to Mark Antony making his funeral oration on Cæsar.

It may be judged from these remarks that I am a listening partisan and being so I like my commentator to be a partisan too. Away with the hollow pretence of impartiality which imposes on the occupants of the Press stand the etiquette of a gloomy silence ! I was once smuggled into that stand at the University Match and was the victim of hushing and pained glances when I shouted for a Cambridge try, but I remained unrepentant and unashamed. I am all for a commentator who now and again lets his natural feelings get into his voice, who is a man first and a commentator second. It is one of the reasons for preferring Cardiff, that human nature is more likely to break out there than anywhere else. " Tanner to Cleaver, Cleaver to Bleddyn Williams, Bleddyn to Les Williams, and —oh ! a lovely try for Wales." When a year or two since I heard those words, or something like them, in a voice which flaunted beyond all doubt the glorious circumstance of a Welsh origin, I clasped its owner in imagination round the neck. And let me be fair to myself ; if it had been the other side that scored and he had been their partisan, I should still have felt towards him as a man and a brother, and should have preferred his enthusiasm, misguided though it was, to any more objective description.

These views of mine, to which I am entirely wedded, doubtless will not do from a practical standpoint. A too partial commentator would rouse violent emotions in those who did not agree with him. But at least let us have a little outburst now and then ! I remember once to have listened to the Derby (I think it was), which, like all other horse races, finds me in a state of odious and contemptible calm. Yet when my friend, the late R. C. Lyle, permitted himself to say, " It's the hell of a race," he communicated his emotion to me and fairly swept me off my legs. For all I know, half the old women in England rang up the B.B.C. to protest indignantly against such language, but those six simple words, coming so clearly from the heart, were worth all the dispassionate narration in the world. So it was with Harold Abrahams describing Wooderson's final and triumphant spurt, when all the Finns and the Swedes "lay withered and strown." His words tumbled over one another in his excitement and he stammered out as magnificent a description as any one could wish to hear.

Admittedly, he who describes a race has a great pull, and the longer the race the better. A sprint is over in a flash, and even a quarter does not give him a real opportunity, but the excitement mounts with the mounting laps, until those blessed words, " He's got him now, he's coming right away," can bring balm to the tortured spirit. Doubtless these remarks would apply to the University Boat Race were it ever close enough, but it so seldom is, and the listeners' hearts go out to the poor commentator trying vainly to excite them with, " In, out, in, out." Man cannot live by " In, out " alone. Even such well-meaning " stunts " as a gentleman perched in an aeroplane above the river somehow fail to thrill. There is a mild, but only a mild, interest in wondering whether he is feeling sick. Some day something tremendous will really happen ; Cambridge will win, perhaps after being behind at Barnes Bridge, and then I shall not be listening.

I feel much the same about broadcast cricket, as to which I am a hopeless infidel. Exciting things do happen at cricket but never when I am listening. Given a match likely to end in a draw, a fast bowler who takes a twenty yard run and a batsman who either lets the ball pass on the off side or prods it gently to point or short leg, and between them they " shed a gentle melancholy upon the soul." The commentators try most nobly. They tell us how the batsman takes a look round the field and pulls down his cap, how the bowler hitches up his trousers and then " over comes his arm." All that can be done in the way of verisimilitude they do, but the narrative remains—for me—bald and unconvincing. I know that people in Australia sit up in their thousands into uncharted hours of the night to listen to a test match here ; so I must be wrong and permanently unlucky into the bargain.

Yet if listening to cricket seems dry work, how incomparably drier and duller to listen to golf. It may be that some day a means of describing golf stroke by stroke will be discovered,

and some great artist arise to put it into practice. I believe
that in America the commentator has been known to follow
the game on some kind of moving tower. Perhaps he makes
it exciting, but my own experience of attempting a running
commentary has been a bitter one. I was once teed up on a
sandhill to describe a hole played by two or three successive
couples. Every time each player hit the ball a long way down
the course and then walked slowly after it while I padded in
a vigorous and futile manner. Then both played iron shots
to the green and both, after an interminable time, took two
putts a-piece. It was all I could do not to yawn in the middle
of my own description, and the listeners doubtless did not
refrain. As far as my own experience goes, golf and a running
commentary are wholly inimical. A description of the match
after it is over can be made tolerably interesting, and if the
describer can break off suddenly to picture something crucial
happening under his eyes on the last green, so much the better
for him and the listening earth ; but the golfing Fates are very
spiteful ladies, and always arrange for the really exciting things
to happen somewhere else.

My one wireless distinction, and that an equivocal one, is
of having said " Damn." That was in the course of a running
commentary, in so far as I was trying desperately to see through
a window what was happening on the last green at Carnoustie.
The regrettable exclamation did not arise from any of the
partisanship I have advocated. It was wrung from me by an
enormous back which suddenly obscured my view at the
moment of a final and critical putt. It was not a very loud one,
but there was no possible doubt about it. Once, years before,
I had been reproached in a letter from an old lady for referring
" to a devil of a long putt." She would not defile her pen with
the word but indicated it by asterisks. If one devil produces
one letter, how many does a damn produce ? It is a fair rule
of three sum. I expected to be inundated but was in fact left
severely alone. An expert in these matters accounted for this
by saying that " devil " is profane and " damn " is not. I

prefer the kindlier explanation that the listeners understood—
for I explained about that intrusive back—that the provocation
had been great.

Perhaps the dullness is only in myself and I have claimed
too much sympathy for the golfing broadcaster. At any rate,
I can think of another game, which I annually report in
writing, which would make a far sterner test. Let any one go
to Eton on St. Andrew's Day and try to describe a good long
bully in the wall game in a vivid, picturesque and enthralling
manner, and I will hand him the palm. He will be a truly
great artist, and even so I think I shall switch him off.

The Magic of a Name

IN a letter to my grandmother when I was a very small boy
my father recorded that I had been discovered wandering
in the garden, murmuring to myself in tones of dreamy
ecstasy, "The Duke of Hamilton and Brandon." Thus I
showed early in life a taste for names, and I venture to think
that in this instance at least it was good taste. It has stayed
with me ever since, growing if possible stronger with the years.
I scarcely dare open Burke or Debrett, however legitimate the
purpose, lest I lose myself in a fairyland of names, taking no
count of time, browsing for happy hours on the great-aunts
Dulcibella and Annabella, for ever grateful to one imaginative
and unresting clergyman of Saxon lineage, who had innumerable children and gave them all some fifteen christian
names apiece. It is almost equally dangerous to look up a
train in the outwardly prosaic A B C railway guide, for that too,
is a repository of fascinating names, and it is an amusing game,
though difficult to play without peeping, to guess from the
sound of them to which counties they belong.

Even the persons in my dreams often have elaborate names,
but let not the reader fear lest I commit the bore's supreme

crime of narrating his dreams, for these names, though they
seem to me enchanting when I wake up, are of that " baseless
fabric " that no clutching effort of the mind can retain. To
those who love them names are beautiful for their own sake,
full of an inextinguishable romance, almost wholly divorced
from reality, far more enduring than any vision of the places
or the persons which they represent. To forget a face may be
momentarily embarrassing but is accepted as inevitable ; to
forget a name is an agony and a sad wound to the vanity as
well ; it causes an unceasing itch and the making of frantic
casts through the memory, trying the alphabet letter by letter.
Only those who have suffered know the feeling of intense and
triumphant relief when sometimes in a sudden flash of en-
lightenment, sometimes through sheer hard work, the prodigal
name returns.

I have mentioned the A B C game and there is another
equally seductive, which can be indulged in every morning
over the toast hot and newspaper. It is simplicity itself. The
player takes the first column on the first page and goes through
the marriages one by one, deciding after due deliberation in
each case whether the lady has made a better or a worse
exchange in the matter of names. He keeps the score in golfing
fashion, wives two up, down to one, all square, husbands one
up, and so on. The issue is nearly always close and sometimes
positively thrilling, as when one side comes with a great rush
at the end and snatches victory out of the very jaws of the
other. The player tries to be honest but naturally likes the
husbands to win so that if he cheats at all it is in favour of his
own sex. The births are also interesting since so many parents
nowadays, anticipating the ceremony of baptism, announce
the christian names of their children as soon as they are born.
It is interesting to see how the wheel of fashion is forever turning
and how the well tried Marys and Annes are holding their own
against the invading hordes of Jennifers and Gillians, while the
Ethels and Gladyses after a brief heyday are now one with
the Adelaides and Almas. Again, the appropriateness of the

christian name to the surname must be given due thought in appraising the parents' choice. That delightful essayist, " The Londoner," took a high line in such matters. He complained bitterly of half the babies in England being called Derek, which he held to be suitable only to those families who had come over with William of Orange. He poured contempt on one who was named Frederick Lionel, a combination, as he said, of eighteenth-century German and " Gothick romance." Frederick, he held, should have been accompanied by Augustus or Adolphus. It is true that in that instance the gentleman's surname was Wickramasinha, which was certainly exacting. Those lacking " The Londoner's " erudition cannot rise to such critical heights, but we can all appreciate the rhythm and flow of a name, observing how trippingly some run in double harness while others are heavy, awkward and spondaic. This form of the game is perhaps unworthy of the title since it has not the competitive element which renders the other so exciting. It should rather be termed a pastime and a very pleasant one. There is much cause for gratitude to those who are in such a hurry that they cannot wait for the blessing of the Church.

The name-lover follows these agreeable if childish pursuits in private. He wants no sharer in his pleasures, if only because two or more players must become involved in a series of palpably insoluble arguments. We all have our own likes among names and mine run in the direction of the sonorous, even the grandiose. It is perhaps because I have a far-away minim of gipsy blood in me that I love the fantastic beauty of Romany names. Jasper reeled off a list of them to George Borrow—Pakomova, Sanspirella, and the rest. Very fortunate was Jasper's sister-in-law, born Ursula Herne, then Ursula Lovell and finally Ursula Silvester. How exciting was the name of a gipsy queen, buried a few years ago not far from my own Kentish village with much sable pomp of plumes and velvet and prancing horses amid a great concourse of her own people. Urania Boswell was her name. Has it not a truly regal sound? It seems to me to touch the very highest point. Holding these views, it may be imagined that I was thrilled to the marrow of my bones not long ago in Berkshire. In a cottage near my host's house there lived a pretty little girl who used to pass the time of day to us very confidently, yet had something whining in her voice and fawning in her way. She had, we were told, gipsy blood in her, and what was her name in a thousand guesses? It was Cleopatra.

Urania and Cleopatra are sublime in themselves, or it may be, according to individual taste, ridiculous. We can at least look at them more or less objectively, with eyes unblurred by use and wont. It is in the realm of the more familiar, and commonplace that we find it hard to judge. We come to connect names with people, and can scarcely disentangle them from their originals. We like or dislike them accordingly, and, more than that, we think of those particular names as signifying particular types. Neither can we ever exorcise such notions however absurd. An aunt of mine had, early in life, taken it into her head that a certain cousin was like Elizabeth Bennet in *Pride and Prejudice*. The cousin, when I knew her, was a little brown puckered old lady who showed no signs of having possessed Elizabeth's beauty and, I can take my oath to it, had none of her wit. My aunt was as fully aware of this as was anybody else, but the idea had taken too firm a hold, and she could not drive it out. So it is often with the names of our friends and relations. John must be long and thin, or Henry short and fat, and there is an end of it. All others seem to us impostors, misnamed for their aspects or their characters. Venus herself might appear plain if we had ever chanced to know a young lady with whom her parents had taken so desperate a risk. If indeed she had been Victoria Venus—and I once found one in Somerset House of my own surname and born in the year of my own birth—there would at least have been alternative suggestions.

The earlier we adopt our mental pictures the more ineradicable they are, possibly because we had then but a limited experience and so believed that any particular name belonged to that one person alone in the whole world. The servants whom we adored in extreme youth affixed their qualities to their names as firmly and adhesively as anybody. I have since travelled much in the realms of Freds but the name instantly conjures up a little thin-faced, clean-shaven man (he was a groom) with a horse-shoe pin, and all subsequent Freds must conform to that pattern or be just the least bit inappropriate. Harriet must be plump and comely and kindly, with a laugh that rings through the house (it penetrated regularly from the kitchen to the dining-room), while Tommy holds himself for ever with a military carriage, being a mysterious person who had dropped from nobody knew where and was suspected of being a deserter. I have known other Tommies since, cast in a different mould, but they cannot oust that early original, now grown dim and yet so very clear.

We are in much the same quandary over the names in books, which in themselves form an extensive and difficult study. We know some of them so well that it is impossible to say whether they are good or bad names. Some, such as many of Scott's, are obviously bad, being formed on the analogy of Mr. Bung the Brewer in the game of " Happy Families." Scott was very far from being deaf to the sound of a splendid name. Chesterton said of him that he valued a plume because it was a plume and a dagger because it was a dagger. So he doubtless valued Brian de Bois-Guilbert because it was a fine name, with a fine swagger in it, and loved the stately music of Ellangowan for its own sake. Very often, however, he was too hurried or too lazy to think of a good name for some relatively unimportant person and gave him the first, suggestive of his occupation, that came into his head. Mr. Saddletree, the harness-maker in *Heart of Midlothian* may stand as an illustration. That is a thoroughly bad name, nor is Jonathan Oldbrick much better. Plenty of other authors have fallen into the same trap. Trollope's Dr. Filgrave is an example, taken at random.

There is about such names a crudeness of invention which instantly condemns them.

It is when we come to familiar names, having no deliberate significance, that we are utterly at a loss. Is Micawber a good name? It seems to us now quite admirable, and, granted so much, there can be no doubt that Wilkins is perfectly adapted to it, but of its intrinsic merit we are really as incapable of judging as of that of Gamp. Both have become proverbial, each has given its name to a type, and our critical faculties are disarmed. Is Uriah Heep ideal for a monster of meanness? I think it is and I feel almost sure that Heep is perceptibly better for the purpose than would have been Heap. The double " e " seems to double that insinuating villainy. I likewise feel that Traddles is a good name because it implies just that touch of the ridiculous in a delightful and eminently sensible person; but this may be the purest delusion.

However we are getting on too fast. Let us consider if there are any rules that can be tentatively laid down as to what constitutes a good or a bad name. I venture to assert that if a name is to suggest the nature or the occupation of a character it must do so with a certain delicacy, and further that the name must sound as if it might conceivably be met with in real life. Take for example Sheridan who so conspicuously gave his characters such names. I should say that Languish and Surface were permissible, because they are within the realms of possibility, but that Absolute goes too far. It has not, in my ears at least, a sufficiently genuine ring. Acres is as thoroughly sound as O'Trigger is unsound. Crabtree skilfully suggests a sour, rancorous old gentleman, but Backbite is too obvious. As for Mrs. Malaprop, I admit I am in difficulty. Here is a borderline case. In principle I am against it, but might there not be such a name? What else could you call her? She must be given the benefit of the doubt.

It would be easy to go on and on illustrating these principles of mine, but I will magnanimously refrain. The mere exceptions to the rule could be multiplied almost for ever. What, for instance, of Trollope's Duke of Omnium ? It is hard not to have a liking for him, and still harder to reject Sir Omicron Pie, the eminent physician from London who attended the aged Bishop of Barchester. It is a preposterous name and yet it does pleasantly remind us of those resounding ones which seem to help physicians and surgeons on their way to baronetcies and glory. The world would be a little poorer without Sir Omicron, and after all Pie is genuine and even familiar. Two more instances I will give, both of them arguable, and, since I have dared to criticise Scott, both shall be culled from *Guy Mannering*. Glossin is to me an eminently good name subtly conveying a smooth and silky villain. Dandie Dinmont too, seems to have the right robust quality. As far as its implication is concerned, I at least only found through an accidental glance at a dictionary that a dinmont was a wether between the first and second shearing. I rather wish I had not made the discovery. I like the name better purely as a name.

Those that are names and nothing more, having no ostensible reason, present altogether too large and too discursive a subject. It is perhaps worth noticing—I hope I am right in this generalisation—that the three great women novelists, Jane Austen, George Eliot and Charlotte Brontë, attempted no flights of suggestive fancy. They gave their characters plain straightforward names suited to their station in life or the parts of the country from which they came, but having no hidden meanings. Lady Catherine de Bourgh and Mr. Fitzwilliam Darcy have more aristocratic names than the Bennets and the Bingleys, as is right and proper, but we can read nothing into them. Sir Christopher Cheverel has the right sound for a baronet but no more, and so we might go on ; the rule seems to hold good. These three great ladies played no tricks with their names and might have taken them, with a good ear and good taste, out of a directory.

Dickens's names are interesting in that he would appear to have adopted a variety of principles in their choice. Some of them are wholly of his own invention. We know, for instance, that he debated between Chuzzlewit or Chuzzlewig and a number of others equally fanciful which I have forgotten. Is Chuzzlewit a good name? As far as it is possible to view it with clear eyes I should cast my vote against it. So I should against Pumblechook, which is too laboriously fantastic. Now and again his " judgment goes out a wisitin " utterly and hopelessly, as in the Slummintowkens. To be sure they are only mentioned once but even so they are wholly indefensible. For that matter, Copperfield is, I believe, a non-existent name ; I have hunted for it in vain in telephone books ; but in any case it is colourless, neither good nor bad. Swiveller is presumably invented, but who shall appraise it? It is one with Micawber. How hard it is to judge of Dickens's names I realised the other day when a friend exclaimed ecstatically, " Oliver Twist ! What a perfect name." He was in fact praising Mr. Bumble's powers of invention, for it was he who named the foundlings as they arose. But there is surely no particular merit in the name. It is purely a matter of old affection. At any rate, I know where Dickens got it and it is my one literary discovery of which I am immensely proud. Wandering through the churchyard at Chalk, where Dickens spent his honeymoon, I came across three neighbouring tombstones bearing the names of Flight (not Flite), Guppy and Twist. The first two he kept in cold storage for years, till the time of *Bleak House*, but Twist he used almost immediately.

Dickens was likewise fond of what may be called trade names, and some of them are capital. Nothing could be better than Veneering for the newly rich with their brand-new house and plate and friends, their gold and silver camels and their brand-new crusading ancestor. Scrooge is a little more dangerous perhaps, but it is most effective, and so are Dedlock and Jarndyce, in their respective ways. Sir Mulberry Hawk is excellent, a far better name than that crude and melodramatic person deserved, and Dickens clearly appreciated, as witness also Sir Leicester Dedlock, that the best baronets have surnames as christian names. Yet in the same book Lord Frederick Verisoph represents a distinct lapse. We know Bob Sawyer so well that we almost forget that his name has any meaning and only fully realise it when read over the shop his succession to Mr. Nockemorf. Whether Podsnap and Pecksniff come under this heading it is hard to say. Both seem to convey something of their owners' characters, but they cannot be precisely analysed and perhaps in this lies their unquestionable merit. Dickens did not have too many of such names, and on the whole his successes in that direction are more numerous than his failures. In a more general way he undoubtedly leant towards the fantastic in names, but then so he did in his characters.

The greater the author, the more credit, sometimes not wholly deserved, he is given for his names. If Dickens had thought of Bultitude we might now regard it as an example of his inimitableness. So let me here put in a word for a lesser but still delightful writer, Mr. Anstey. He did not indeed invent the name, for it is a real one ; I have had the inexpressible happiness of seeing it over a shop ; but it has all the virtues of a superb piece of fancy, and its adaptation to our old friend of *Vice Versa* was a stroke of genius. It sounds for all the world as if it signified a quality, and moreover the precise quality, of its owner. If we say it to ourselves two or three times it becomes impossible to believe that we should not find it in the dictionary. There is about it the pomposity, with a touch of what we should to-day call " blimpishness," which distinguished that unfortunate merchant of Mincing Lane. In its own particular line I incline to think that it stands alone.

Finally, there is Thackeray, who for me is the greatest name-maker of them all. He has a taste for the ducal and the much-sounding which appeals to me. Not only did he revel in noble names but he had an unexampled skill in devising them. He was as adroit as need be in what I have called trade names. Newcome, in a quieter way, is as descriptive as

Veneering ; Mr. Wenham and Mr. Wagg, Lord Steyne's two aides-de-camp, are exactly worthy of their names ; Lord Bareacres and Lord Levant make the ideal impoverished noblemen. But I like him best when he is guided only by his fancy, at once so opulent and so ingenious, which yet functions always in the realms of the possible. Dickens had two excellent baronets, but Thackeray has more and better ones. Sir Pitt Crawley is in the very best tradition and so is his grandson, Sir Rawdon. Sir Huddleston Fuddleston and Sir Giles Wapshot are equally admirable in a more light-hearted vein. And then how delightful he is when he exercises his imagination on family trees ! I am sure that it gave him the keenest pleasure to make Lord Walham the eldest son of the Earl of Kew, and that he was thoroughly amused with the bear motif running through the family of Fitzurse, with Lord de la Pole as its head and Lord Cubley his eldest son. He indulged in such recondite antics in this direction that there are probably many little innuendos that the reader never discovers. They lurk un-revealed even as does a priest's hiding-place in some ancient house that is known to have existed and yet defies all search. I believe there is some reason of infinite subtlety why the family name of the Rockminsters should be Pynsent, but if there is a secret it for ever mocks and eludes me.

I have but scratched the surface of this great Thackeray mine. Let me end by copying out, purely for my own sensual satisfaction, the titles and honours of Lord Steyne when that nobleman expired, regretted by a numerous circle. It combines the beauties of Debrett with those of his own *Rose and the Ring*. " The Most Honourable George Gustavus, Marquis of Steyne, Earl of Gaunt and of Gaunt Castle, in the Peerage of Ireland, Viscount Hellborough, Baron Pitchley and Grillsby, a Knight of the Most Noble Order of the Garter, of the Golden Fleece of Spain, of the Russian Order of Saint Nicholas of the First Class, of the Turkish Order of the Crescent, First Lord of the Powder Closet and Groom of the Back Stairs, Colonel of the Gaunt or Regent's Own Regiment of Militia, a Trustee of the British

Museum, an Elder Brother of the Trinity House, a Governor of the White Friars and D.C.L." Here is richness indeed ! That roll of splendour must have given him the intensest æsthetic pleasure, and I like to think that he murmured it to himself as he walked in Kensington Gardens.

The Spirit of Picnic

THE essential quality of a picnic is the doing of perfectly
normal things in an abnormal place or manner. Those
who prefer the beaten track of meals, the seedy, commonplace
round of every day, will never be happy at a picnic. A famous
Cambridge character of bygone days, on being bidden by an
eager hostess to some such enterprise, replied in the single,
devastating sentence, " But the bread and butter will be so
smeary." Persons having souls so dead will never enjoy lunch
out of a paper bag in a third, or even a first-class railway
carriage. But to those of a more youthful spirit there is something positively holy about a hard-boiled egg eaten in such
circumstances. Nobody wishes to devour hard-boiled eggs forever, nor to have the salt wrapped up in a screw of newspaper.
Neither in ordinary life do we live for choice on sandwiches,
which if eaten rapidly one after the other, as they invariably
are, produce a curious sensation of breathlessness. Yet on a
journey they are infinitely exciting, and it was one of the few
good things about war-time travel, when restaurant cars either
ceased to be or were unattainable through the solid mob in
the corridor, that sandwiches came into their own again. They

could no longer be made of ham, and it is, to me at any rate, one of the unsolved mysteries of life that whereas cold beef is among the most divine of foods, cold beef sandwiches are among the least appetising. Still the old childish joy was there.

There were other circumstances in war-time far less attractive in which something of that ancient sensation could be recaptured. During the Battle of Britain a good many of us spent broken, " noisy " nights in the cellar, trying to sleep uneasily in easy chairs and periodically declaring that the latest crash came from several miles further off than it palpably did. Nothing could be more odious and yet when at some uncharted hour of the night cocoa was made and biscuits handed round there was more in them than mere comfort. There was romance, the ineffable romance of a picnic underground. Not far from my home are the famous Chislehurst caves, where during the war so many people spent their nights that for several months a special train ran every night from Cannon Street to take them there. That they were originally driven to this city of refuge by romantic motives I would not go so far as to say, but that the children at least must have derived an unfading delight from their surroundings I cannot doubt, especially if they were told the pleasing legend that the caves had been made with the antlers of deer by the Druids. At any rate, I like to think that some day they will say to one another with a great thrill of speech, " Do you remember what fun it was having our supper in Chislehurst Caves ? "

It cannot, I suppose, be denied that a love of picnics is not an irrefutable evidence of character, that sometimes the very best of people do not like picnics and the very worst do. There is a passage in *Emma* which always makes me rather uncomfortable. There is to be a party to pick strawberries at Donwell, and Mrs. Elton, after descanting on the bonnet she will wear and the basket she will carry, the one with the pink ribbons, declares that it is to be " a sort of gipsy party—a table spread in the shade, you know. Everything as simple and natural as possible." Mr. Knightley coolly replied, " My idea of the simple and the natural will be to have the table spread in the dining-room." Now it was delightful to have Mrs. Elton snubbed, so far as such a thing was possible, and we know besides that Mr. Knightley had other motives ; he knew that poor Mr. Woodhouse would be made ill with unhappiness at the idea of a meal out of doors. And yet purely on a matter of principle I cannot get out of my head the unworthy notion that for once Mr. Knightley was wrong and that insufferable Mrs. Elton was right. To be sure she would have spoiled the party wherever it was, as she did at Box Hill, but—well, I am never wholly easy in my mind about it.

Leaving that particular example on one side, it will be generally admitted that the best picnics are out of doors. I have always felt both envy and admiration for the old golfers of St. Andrews, who did not, as men do nowadays, play out their morning round to the home hole and retire for an excellent lunch to the club-house. No, they stopped and had their snack at the hole that is called the ginger-beer hole to this day, and then off again for their second round. That they drank only ginger beer I do not suggest. They would have said, as Dandie Dinmont did of the claret, " It's ower cauld for my stomach ; " but I am sure they enjoyed their lunch with its *al fresco* jolliness and, in theory at least, I should like to emulate them. I still have ecstatic memories from more than forty years ago of a day's golf on a little course at Macamish, on the shores of Lough Swilly. Some sailed across the Lough from Buncrana, others drove innumerable miles from Portsalon : every one brought his own lunch and we ate it on the edge of a putting green under the lee of a sandhill in blissful peace and solitude.

Solitude is essential to the full enjoyment of a picnic. This is a point on which even the most unselfish sometimes belie their beautiful natures. As for those whose natures are less beautiful, is there any hatred deeper and more venomous than that which we feel for a rival party that has had the effrontery to choose the very same place ? It was only lately that I was taken on a picnic to a most enchanting spot, on the shores of a little

160

lake, secluded, bowered in woods. And there, on the other side of the lake to be sure, was another party already encamped. They were wholly quiet and innocuous, they did us not the faintest harm : it was their audacity in being there at all that was so hard to bear. If scowls could have killed across the water, they would not long have survived, and doubtless they directed the same malignant glances at us. I said I was taken on a picnic, and I carefully chose my words, for a picnic requires considerable energy and organising ability, neither of which I possess. That picnic basket which disgorges an endless wealth of good things must be a fairy basket. And yet, in point of prosaic fact, somebody has had to cut the sandwiches and fill the thermos and pack the bottles of beer and not forget the opener and do all the other benevolent things which we are too apt to take for granted. And sometimes the most dreadful mistakes are innocently made, which threaten to wreck the picnic.

I have vivid memories of a picnic party up the river at Cambridge when someone had blundered and made the tea, in a thermos, with the sugar irrevocably in it. If there was one thing my father hated more than another it was sugar in his tea, and, though he was normally sweet-tempered, this was almost more than he could endure. I can still hear him protesting in a tone of deepest gloom that he did not mind the tea in itself ; " What I mind is the folly of it."

The size of a picnic is a matter of individual taste. I cannot wholly agree with the too hospitable Mr. Weston (also in *Emma*) that " such schemes as these are nothing without numbers." I am disgracefully inclined to hold that this policy of the more the merrier is a one that can be overdone. Picnics on a large scale can be very good fun, but they demand strong nerves. I remember to have heard that the illustrious family of the Graces used once every summer to have a mighty nutting party, in which the whole clan, and they were essentially clannish, used to sweep across Gloucestershire, forty or fifty strong, sisters, cousins, and aunts, in an irresistible flood.

It has, and no doubt it made, a jolly sound. The Doctor himself would have been in his kindest, friendliest and most cheerful mood. And yet my mind misgives me that at any rate, for a stranger it might have been just a little prostrating.

I confess that there is one great man with whom I should like to go on a great picnic, and that is Dickens. He was filled, I am sure, with the very spirit of picnic. We have only to think of two or three that he describes, that in Mr. Wardle's carriage at the Chatham review, the shooting lunch near Bury when Mr. Pickwick took too much cold punch, and Dora's birthday party. There are no doubt others that I have not thought of, but those three will serve. With what inimitable gusto he would have made the party go ! He would have organised everything to perfection and made wine cellars in hollow trees. For all I know he would have sung comic songs after lunch. Yes, and made us sing them too. He would have made us do all manner of things that we should have believed ourselves to detest, and for that once we should have loved them. He would have swept us clean off our feet into rapturous enjoyment, and when we woke next day we should have felt that the picnic had been a dream and we had been bewitched.

That picnic being unattainable save in Elysian fields I cast my unadventurous vote for the small, select and peaceful variety. If I dare to describe briefly two of my own favourites, let not the reader be angry but rather let him translate my words into terms of his own doubtless far superior picnics, and do his private gloating as it were by proxy. My first is an exceedingly select one as it consists, as a rule, only of two roysterers, myself and another, though there has once or twice been a third. It used to take place regularly once and often twice a year and was part of a solemn rite, which I am conscious of having described elsewhere, the drive to Wales. Everything was done according to a strict tradition, and the lunch on Bromyard Common was as unvarying as the " elevenses "—a glass of beer, and that the " genuine stunning "—at Broadway. It was not merely on Bromyard Common, which is a large and noble expanse ; it was on a particular piece of turf by the side of a particular piece of the road, soon after it passes through a particular piece of woodland ; I could find my way blindfold to it at this moment. Sometimes on a fine day we could sit upon the grass ; sometimes we must stay in the car. That was the only difference. The sandwiches were always of the same scrumptious quality, and, for no precise reason save that we had done so once, we always washed them down with perry—a drink in my mind solely associated with this festival. Whatever were our other topics of conversation, we tried to recall the name of the inn in Bromyard (yes, now, after an effort, I have remembered it) at which we must take a sharp turn. I am ashamed to think how regularly I expressed the wish to let loose a golfing architect on that gorsy, undulating stretch, clearly designed by Providence for one end. If we concealed any remnants of our meal (though I hope we packed them all up tidily in the car) then I am very sure that it was in the heart of the very same bush. We may never be able to go that journey again, but if ever we do, then, touching wood, I know where we shall lunch. It would be far better to starve than break so sacred a tradition.

My other very particular picnic is of quite recent memory and happened but once ; yet it was so enchanting that I cannot for the life of me refrain. This too, was within sight of a golf course, not imaginary this time, but a very real one, for it was on the Pebble Ridge at Westward Ho ! I suppose it broke one of the regular rules, whether Mrs. Elton's or any one else's, that a picnic should be in the shade, for a blazing sun beat full upon us. Neither did we sit on soft, caressing turf, but on the hard stones of that famous ridge. I remember that on that very day the great J. H. Taylor told us how when he was a boy the ridge had been so tall and steep that it must be scaled on hands and knees. Time has mysteriously mitigated these rigours, for the five of us clambered up comfortably enough, and once we were there the stones made kindly resting places for baskets and glasses and bottles. To find an entirely

lonely piece of coast in high midsummer is something to be
grateful for, and that was our happy lot. We were as Byron
on Sunium's " marbled steep."

> *Where nothing, save the waves and I,*
> *May hear our mutual murmurs sweep.*

Our own murmurs were louder than those of the waves, which
made but the gentlest lapping ; yet the air was filled with the
great, vague sound of the sea, and such a blue and shining sea.
And when we had eaten all the sandwiches we threw stones
at some mark on the beach below, in a heaven of laziness and
digestion.

It may be that a truly scientific and analytical student
would put in different categories picnics which are the sole
object of a " party of pleasure " and those which are, however
pleasant, merely incidental to a journey. I have, having no
claims to such depressing epithets and having let my pen run
on at random in the realms of memory, will draw no such
distinctions. Some may be better than others, but all picnics
possess an essential beauty and romance, and any true lover,
as he falls on his first sandwich, will never fail to say his grace, in
Mr. Wardle's words at Chatham, " Now an't this capital ? "

Reading Aloud

No questionnaire, Gallup poll or other form of domestic "quiz" has ever revealed to the world to what extent reading aloud still flourishes in English homes. Has the wireless killed it? Does the family circle of to-day "deem the pastime slow?" If not, what is read and who does the reading? These are secrets which every household keeps to itself, so that the subject is one that must inevitably be treated in an egotistical manner and from a limited experience.

Despite Dick Barton and the Children's Hour, children, we may hope, will always enjoy being read to. The reading to them is an occupation at once lazy and prostrating. It is lazy because children agree wholeheartedly with Hazlitt's fine sentiment, " I hate to read new books ; " they are wonderfully faithful to established favourites. It is prostrating because the grown-up tires of the very best of books long before they do. Only the other day I heard an enslaved grandmother, with a proper admiration for perhaps the greatest of all children's authors, the late M. Brunhoff, admit that it was just a little fatiguing to read one or other of the immortal series of Babar books every single day. And yet the reading can never become, by way of compensation, mechanical and unconscious, for one wrong word will bring a bitter cry of protest. And the protest is always justified. A grown-up with the best of visual memories might read one book in bed every night for the rest of his life with the most passionate attention and yet could never hope to rival the diabolical accuracy in quotation of any small critic, picked at random.

Leaving on one side this reading of picture books to the very young, we come to the next stage. A friend of mine assured me the other day that, apart from purely infantile works read to him, he began life by reading *Great Expectations* to himself. This is desperate work and I can make no such precocious boast. *Masterman Ready* seems to emerge from the fog of memory as one of the very earliest books read aloud to me, with the harrowing death of Ready invariably left out. Then follow *The Little Duke*, *The Lances of Lynwood*, *The Children of the New Forest*, extracts from *Pickwick* (the review and the cricket match), some Scott, and then—doubtless there came a now obliterated interval—*The Moonstone*. I have the clearest vision of myself curled up in a particular corner, falling asleep over that truly noble book and waking with a start as the voice of the reader reproachfully ceased. At least I have been making penitent amends ever since by reading it times beyond number. G. A. Henty, I think, one read to oneself. There were heights of devoted boredom which the grown-up could not scale.

I am clear too, about Scott ; the order in which he was read to me was *The Talisman*, *Quentin Durward*, *Ivanhoe*. In my family—one feels like Mrs. Micawber in using those words—there was an inexorable tradition. *The Talisman* was the book on which the young must be broken in. My knowledge of it is now so vague that I cannot say if the tradition was well founded, but my personal and maturer judgment would favour *Ivanhoe*, subject to one condition. The tedious explanation as to Normans and Saxons must be left out and the reader begin with Gurth's words (no, I have not looked them up though unworthy suspicion may think I have), " The curse of St. Withold upon these infernal porkers."

That opens up the question of skipping, a most important one in reading aloud, on which I hold the strongest and, as I hope, the soundest views. There are those who are too much " hadden doun " by the sacredness of the text ; they lack either the imagination or the courage to skip, and plod their weary way through the most lamentable morasses of dullness. From a reading aloud point of view there is no book so good that it cannot be a little better for judicious skipping. Judicious it must be, for I have seen a child's *Ivanhoe* in which the whole of Locksley's archery at the tournament, one of the most romantic passages in the world, was left out. Whoever did that ought to be barred from his occupation for ever more like a drunken motor car driver. He had given his proofs once and for all. Fortunately his must have been a character that only occurs once or twice in a century.

Some skipping more or less is, I maintain, essential. In reading to ourselves we may skimp (a less thorough-going measure), but in reading aloud it must be one thing or the other, and there are passages which, whether they are maudlin or merely stodgy, are too agonising to read aloud. Once the reader is conscious of a lack of sympathy in his listeners, his voice trails away into nothingness and both he and they are plunged in melancholy. Therefore it is better for all parties that the reader should have at least a tolerable working know-ledge of the book. Even so his task is not easy. I have read much aloud in the family circle and am still painfully conscious that I cannot skip in the grand manner. The heaven-born skipper has that quality which has been attributed to so many great men, that no one would know from his angelic smile that someone was kicking him behind. He can see at a glance the bad patch that is coming, make up his mind on the instant where to take off and make so swift a jump, perhaps over several pages, that no one is a penny the wiser. The con-scientious but ungifted skipper cannot rise to this. He either finds himself bogged before he realises what has happened or, if he resolves to jump, does so in a painfully obvious and hesitating manner. " There seems rather too much love-making here," he observes, " I think we'll miss it," or perhaps he tries to paraphrase that which cannot be read, in a few too palpably fictitious sentences. His own doubts beget doubts in the listeners ; they cannot trust him and believe themselves to have been defrauded of some vital excitement.

Even in books I know very well indeed I have never been able to avoid such errors. Knowledge alone is not enough nor, though it is extremely valuable, is that eye for country by which the best skippers can tell instinctively when to beware. They are useless without a high courage and a power of instant decision. I have known readers, especially well practised aunts, who had these gifts in such a supreme degree that they defied detection even by those well acquainted with the book. The listeners were perhaps a little surprised that a particular passage had never come, but believed the mistake to be in their own memories, so smooth and unbroken had been the reader's flow. This is greatness. I have never come near to attaining it, if only because I am a bad pretender, but there are just one or two books in which I can make shift. Every year on Christmas Eve and Christmas Day, almost from time immemorial, I have read aloud the most appropriate of all literature, the festivities at Dingley Dell. I have at last learnt to cut out some superfluous sentences at the beginning in favour of Christmas in general, and one in the middle about a gush of silent tears which annually caused my auditors to writhe, not wholly in silence. If this be deemed an arrogant tampering with sacred things, I cannot help it. In a private circle I conscientiously believe it justifiable. Were someone to allow himself such freedom in a public reading, as on the wireless, we should want to lynch him, but circumstances alter cases.

Just because such occasional liberties are desirable it is as well that the reader should know his book, and there is the further advantage that he will stutter and correct himself the less ; if he does make a slip he can cover it up. It is not easy to attack an unfamiliar country without a fall or two. In the classical reading aloud, that of Gibbon by Mr. Silas Wegg, we know that he was " getting rather shaken by Hadrian, Trajan and the Antonines ; stumbling at Polybius ; heavily unseated by Titus Antoninus Pius ; up again and galloping smoothly with Augustus." That was to be sure a hard test, but even less exigent works can be trying. " How wise of you not to attempt the French accent," said a once famous Eton lady to someone who had been striving with every nerve and sinew to read her part with propriety and distinction in a French play. To read some of Scott aloud, whether the Scottish accent be attempted or not, is for an Englishman a stammering and self-conscious business.

Again the reader who knows his book can get along at a good round pace, and here is another difference between private and public reading : I heard lately of an eminent person who said, " I am getting to the time of life when a man thinks his wife talks indistinctly." Many people, eminent or otherwise, have arrived at the time when they think that speakers on the wireless talk too fast, so that they cannot hear a word. It is an entirely unjust accusation, but that which is a pleasant, leisurely pace on the wireless would probably seem slow in domestic reading. Even a good solid spell of reading aloud gets through such a comparatively small amount that the book appears to the more impatient to stretch away for ever in an unending vista. So it is a good plan, short of absolute breathlessness, for the reader to put on a reasonable amount of steam and get along.

There are some listeners who like deliberately to pause now and again, as it were to pull up in the middle of a drive to look at the view. These are chiefly people who pay the authors the sincere compliment of taking his story as if it were literally true. They are like those who cannot enjoy a melodrama without hissing the villain. They want to know and argue the question at some length why the characters behaved as their creator made them, why, for instance, the hero shilly-shallied through several chapters when it was obvious that the heroine would have accepted him with open arms. Why on earth did not David Copperfield propose to Agnes and be done with it? How could Emma be such an idiot as not to divine Mr. Elton's intentions? On what conceivable grounds did that greatest of detectives, Sergeant Cuff, suspect Rachel Verinder of having large unknown debts, and make no effort to verify his suspicions? Why, oh, why did not beloved Mr. Harding accept the Deanery of Barchester when we and the Archdeacon so dearly wanted him to and it would have been such a delicious sell for Mr. Slope and Mrs. Proudie? These are undeniably, and sometimes maddeningly, interesting questions, but even if the author deserves no consideration, the reader does ; their discussion should be reserved till the reading is over for the night.

Then there is the question of what Mr. Wegg called " the needful implement—a book." It is dangerous to embark on too long a book unless there is a prospect of reasonably un-interrupted reading. The very best of books must suffer if there are too many intervals. The broken thread needs too constant mending ; the most placid listener comes to long almost venomously for the end. To me *Wives and Daughters* appears by far the longest book in the world, merely because it was read thus, piece-meal, in a particular aunt's house. It had admirable things in it and I have no reason to believe that it is really any longer than any other novel, but I have never had the courage to put my belief to the test. It remains a discouraging foretaste of eternity. War-time, when the only probable interruption was a bomb, made an excellent time for reading aloud and gave it a peculiarly soothing quality. In my own household we read the whole of Miss Austen through at a heat without taking breath, and when we had come to the end we should have been quite happy to begin again with,

" It is a truth generally acknowledged that a single man in possession of a good fortune must be in want of a wife." There was no profane skipping there.

It is not easy to predict what books will read aloud well. Both parties, reader and listener, may know a book reasonably well ; both may come to a simultaneous conclusion that it would be just the thing ; and yet disappointment awaits them. There turns out to be more flat country between the peaks than either had expected, and once this is apparent it is wiser not to persevere, but to acknowledge defeat. I cannot reasonably be accused of not liking Dickens, and yet I would hesitate to read any of him aloud, except Pickwick, and then with all the interpolated stories, save only Tom Smart, relentlessly left out. I would venture on *David Copperfield* and *Great Expectations*, but not too confidently. There is too much in him that produces, if not a mutual boredom, a sort of mutual shyness ; each party is conscious of the other growing hot all over. It is possible to have readings from him—the Crummles part from *Nicholas Nickleby*, Boffin and Wegg and the Veneerings from *Our Mutual Friend*, Mrs. Gamp from *Martin Chuzzlewit*, but this is not only to treat him without a proper respect ; it often involves too much explanation of what has been left unread. Scott is, I suggest, better for the purpose. There are appalling *longueurs* in him, but they can be clean cut out as if with a knife, because they have so little to do with the story that they will never be missed.

Short stories make good reading and so do essays. A night or two with Charles Lamb or Hazlitt cannot be bettered, but there is the disadvantage that we have constantly to be beginning again and deciding which one to read next. Moreover, we can hardly stop in the middle of a short story or an essay and must either stop too soon or go on too long. It is otherwise with a good long book, on which we embark deliberately in the reassuring knowledge that it will keep us going and that we shall not soon be called on to rack our brains and make a fresh choice. When bedtime comes, the mark goes into the book, to await us on the morrow. We are as those who have settled comfortably down for a whole day's railway journey with no changes and no agonising decisions. It is true that the listener is sometimes apt to say, " Oh, you simply can't stop there. I must know what happens." It is better and more calming to stop at the end of a chapter, and this affords yet another reason for the reader knowing his book well and so being able to lay his plans accordingly.

There is another advantage of reading aloud to be mentioned with all proper delicacy ; it does away with the need for conversation. This does not apply to family gatherings ; they can shift for themselves and are not bound by too strict rules of politeness. But in the case of a visitor, when talking for talking's sake has reached its limits, the resource of reading aloud, more particularly in bridge-less households, is not to be despised. It may be said that it would be far less painful for everybody to sink into his or her own book, but there is about a roomful of silent readers something a little too despairing, a too palpable throwing up of the conversational sponge. It will be remembered that this simple artifice was employed by Mr. Bennet on the occasion of Mr. Collins's first visit to Loughbourn. Having sufficiently enjoyed his conversation he was happy to lead him into the drawing-room and invite him to read aloud to the young ladies. The manœuvre was not so successful as it might have been, because Mr. Collins chose to read Fordyce's Sermons, but the intention at least had been excellent. If the visitor falls asleep, and there is something suspicious about the way in which people settle down to listen to reading, the main object has nevertheless been attained.

I said in the beginning that since there were so few data to be obtained, this discourse must be largely of an egotistical character. It has fully lived up to my expectations in that direction, nor can I deny that if there is reading I like to do it. For one thing, nobody can decently be asked to read a book which he does not like himself. For another, the comparatively slow progress is not so apparent to the reader as it is to the listener. But, above everything else, the reader exercises almost totalitarian powers. He can do his own skipping.

Hard Hitting

WHETHER it is some inheritance of primeval savagery from remotest ancestors or whether it is no more than a natural healthy instinct, let the psychologists determine; I do not know. All I say is that for the normal human being the moment of keenest, sensuous pleasure any game has to offer is that of hitting as hard as heaven and his bodily powers will allow him. As he grows older and feebler he must taste it vicariously in watching the hitting of others, yet that thrill of quivering joy is still essentially the same.

> *But whatever fame and glory these and other bats may win*
> *Still the monarch of hard hitters, to my mind, was Alfred Mynn.*

There spoke natural, primitive man by the voice of C. H. Prowse, the author of the most rousing of all cricketing verses, at any rate in Kentish ears. Let others praise whom they would for qualities to which he paid his tribute, but that which stirred him to the profoundest depths of feeling was the sheer elemental force of the Lion of Kent.

He chose the right epithet when he wrote " hard " hitters.

It is the vehemence of the blow rather than the consequences that produces the ecstasy. I never received a more vivid impression of hard hitting at its exciting best than in watching the champions of badminton attack so murderously the poor little shuttlecock that is only capable of fluttering a few yards. In the making up to strike, as it were the drawing back for a spring, in the throwing of every ounce of muscle into the stroke at exactly the right instant, in the sense of zest and power, here was as much to enjoy and admire as in the longest drive at golf or a hit into the highest point of the pavilion at Lord's. Within a few days of that almost terrifying experience I watched by happy chance the great men of table tennis, and came away equally stunned and overpowered. Nobody who has not seen the modern game—and I have seen it but once—can realise how different it is from that which he played himself in ancient days, perhaps on no more formal or statutory battlefield than the dining-room table. Gone are those interminable bouts of neat little back-handed half-volleys in which he used complacently to indulge, deeming himself something of a triton among the domestic minnows. The rallies can still be long, since there are spells of comparatively defensive play, and the power of retrieving the apparently impossible is beyond belief ; but that which primarily strikes an awe and terror upon the sight is the tremendous driving. On the sight, I say, but it is but a form of words, for the ball travels at times invisibly fast. To hit so hard and yet keep the ball within those tiny bounds is such a marvel as the stranger thinks he has never seen before. " This," he exclaims with Hazlitt at the prize-fight, " is the most astonishing thing of all : this is the high and heroic state of man."

As far as I needed any convincing, those two brief experiences convinced me that it is the hardness that counts and not the distance that results from the hit. I must not allow myself to become too technical on my own particular subject, nor to drag in King Charles's head. Yet, consider for an instant the question of the golf ball. Whenever it is proposed to keep its flight, and so incidentally the dimensions of the course, within reasonable limits, golfers are up in arms, each man fearing that his own drives will be clipped of a few yards of distance. Now and again they can reach a particular land-mark at a particular hole. If they could do so no more they fancy their little world would come toppling in ruins about them. Fools that they are ! they do not realise that length is relative ; the positive pleasure is in the hitting. The distance that the ball travels may vary but that physical satisfaction is constant and unvarying. It would be idle to deny that it is good fun to see the ball go swooping away over hill or valley for enormous distances. We cannot refrain from the same child-like " Oh " of delight with which we greet a rocket at the fire-works. But if the ball were ever reduced in power we should quickly readjust our standards and be equally swept off our feet by an achievement in point of mere yards more modest. The greatest drive I ever witnessed—certainly it gave me the greatest thrill—still seems to me one made by a pro-fessional on Coldham Common at Cambridge over sixty years ago. I can still see in imagination the ball soaring into the mist which hung about that place of mud and gloom. Yet to-day the same length would doubtless be attained with a light iron. Einstein's theory of relativity is of course beyond my comprehension, but I have my own theory of relativity in regard to hitting to which I am indissolubly wedded.

Some of us cannot hit as hard as others, but the joy is in hitting as hard as we can. Whatever the game, that is not to be attained unless we do it in the right way, for hard hitting is not, as the envious sometimes allege, only a question of brute strength, though strength is important ; it is also and most emphatically one of skill. Much of the pleasure of seeing it is in the poise and rhythm of the hitter. There is a moment of bracing, of tension, and then everything the player possesses pours in a smooth, yet irresistible flow into the ball. " One of the most beautiful sights that can be imagined," wrote Nyren of William Beldham, " and which would have delighted an artist, was to see him make himself up to hit a ball. It was the beau ideal of grace, animation and concentrated energy." That description might serve for any great player and any kind of ball. The instant of " making up " is but as a flash ; if it be more there is a suggestion of heaviness and effort, but just that instant there must be for the perfection of the mysterious and heaven-sent gift that we call timing. The more clearly inspired the hitter, the more conspicuous is the appearance of leisure, that he has all the time in the world in which to hit. " Even in his hard hitting," wrote Alfred Lyttelton of William Gray, " there was an ease and grace delightful to watch. . . . In games he would frequently use old rackets apparently as unfitted for active service as the seats of old cane-bottomed chairs. But in his hand those veterans seemed to renew their youth and drove in a manner that was both astonishing and mortifying to an opponent who, with an incomparably superior tool, produced most inferior results." There is a fine relish in the words, a picture of genius given only to the very few.

Granted that perfection of method there is a fierce satisfaction in seeing someone who palpably intends to kill the ball. If he be graceful he can scarcely be too murderous for our bloodthirsty taste. I doubt if any game has ever provided a more truly awful spectacle than that of Mr. Edward Blackwell driving a golf ball ; a big man with a big, heavy club which he wielded as if it were a toy. His swing though extremely rapid was smooth and lovely and, while there was no undue appearance of effort, he was yet so palpably out for blood. He put everything he had into the stroke ; as one admirer wrote, he even put his eyebrows into it, and they were essentially formidable eyebrows. There was about him the same " divine fury " which Horace Hutchinson attributed to James Braid, and Braid, tearing a ball away from a hanging lie, going down to fetch it, as it were, with his knees buckling beneath him, provided a sight comparable in magnificence.

" Elegance, all elegance, fit to play before the King in his parlour." That was said of Joseph Guy, one of the batsmen, by the way, to whom Prowse awarded a rather grudging meed of praise in his poem on Alfred Mynn. It is a charming picture. But we, the great mass of hearty, ignorant spectators, want something more than that ; we want venom. It is noteworthy when we watch cricket how swiftly and greedily the appetite for hits comes in the eating. One boundary may receive little more than a formal acknowledgment, but if the next ball goes the same way our spirits and our tributes rise immeasurably. In the summer of 1947 I watched a day's play in the test match against the South Africans at Lord's, in which Compton and Edrich were making a big stand, running neck and neck in the matter of runs, with Compton a little ahead. The scoring was of a good pace but always discreet. We were all happy and all liberal with our applause, but in a comparatively restrained manner. Then there came on an unfortunate slow bowler and Edrich suddenly cut loose and hit his first four balls for four of the most exhilarating boundaries. The first was clapped, the second cheered, and the third and fourth produced a crescendo of shouts and crows and delighted laughter. That cheerful hitting had gone to our heads like wine.

In all four of the strokes the ball had clung virtuously to the ground. We should, I fancy, have crowed still more loudly if in one of them it had soared into the air. It is perhaps a confession of weakness but the most inebriating of all hits is undeniably one that climbs the sky, and the higher the better. A series of perfect shots along the floor leave on the memory, when the day is over, only a blurred and general vision of magnificence, but one outrageous six may remain for ever. It is doubtless very wrong, but then, contrary to all propriety, we do remember the wrong things. " Almost twenty years since," wrote Mr. Thomas Fuller, " I heard a profane jest and still remember it. How many pious passages of a far later date have I forgotten ! " So it is sometimes with these profane strokes. I still recall a square leg hit over the ropes at Lord's in the first Eton and Harrow match I ever saw. And it was

made by an Harrovian, confound him ! If in later years I had
seen an Etonian friend knock out an old lady—not severely—
in the back row of a stand, I should doubtless remember it still
better ; but that happiness was denied me.

Something ought clearly to be said about lawn tennis, for
its champions hit the ball blindingly hard. And there can be
no stroke in any game so suggestive of pure savagery as the
whole-hearted smash executed by a master hand. It seems
almost too brutal.

> *It's like hitting of a gal,*
> *It's a lubberly thing for to do.*

But it must be productive of the most exquisite sensations,
over which to lick the chops of memory. How sad that, save
on the rarest occasions, they are out of the reach of the common
man. When I used sometimes to play lawn tennis, to give my
form of it that courtesy title, I found that by a niggling, sneaking
game of ineffable meanness I could sometimes beat those of
more soaring ambitions, because their strokes soared far out
of court. I had a profound contempt for my own methods, but
I had also a shameful and irrepressible desire to win, and in
the humble circles in which I moved those methods were not
wholly unprofitable. Without descending to that " Gamesman-
ship " which my friend Mr. Stephen Potter has made famous,
they had a power of irritating and distracting the opponent.
Those who could play the game even in the most modest sense
of the words, could drive me out of court in less than no time,
but then I seldom encountered them. There were moments
when I almost resolved to try for nobler things and, come
what might, to play the man. If I could have done it successfully but a single time I might have persevered. But it was not
a case of taking a gallant risk and failing ; it was not danger,
it was certain destruction. The ball inevitably buried itself
in the laurel bushes far beyond the confines of the court.

This bitter personal experience has probably coloured my

views. It seems to me that for those who have not learned and probably never will learn to hit the ball properly, that is for the great mass of mankind, there is much to be said for a game played in a court wholly surrounded by walls. To say so much is not to insult one of the noblest of all games, rackets. Rackets has a splendour that explains itself to the least educated eye. The glory of hitting reaches the highest possible point, and the ball travels almost at the speed of thought. In thinking over the gratification derived from all kinds of great hitters, I incline to put first that of the only occasion on which I watched Mr. J. C. F. Simpson in a racket court. Neither for the world would I affront Squash, truly exciting when played by the best, while for the worst it is, to quote Peter Latham's scornful aphorism, " banging about in a box ; " and that in a most cheering form, for at least they do bang. That is why I am upholding for the humble and meek those surrounding walls. They will not help the weakling to win, for his most violent blows will only present his enemy with an easy chance off the back wall, but they will help him to enjoy himself. He will now and again give the ball one blow with all his might and main ; most likely to no purpose, but it will afford him a sensation of virility. In that ecstatic moment at least he will have lived. For this reason I have always thought it a pity that there are so few courts in existence for the game of " sticky," or should it perhaps be spelt " stike ? " since its name is presumably derived from " sphairistike," as Major Wingfield's embryo game of lawn tennis was classically called. It may be that some have never heard of it, and few have seen it. Almost the only courts are, I believe, those made by the British Army in foreign stations, though I have seen one built by the R.E. in Lancashire, and I know one private court in England. Briefly and inaccurately the game may be described as lawn tennis in an indoor court with a pent house, side walls and back walls. Well played it clearly demands a high degree of skill : and for the unskilful player there are at least none of those humiliating laurel bushes. He ought, as I judge, to play a heavily cut stroke into the corners ; he will, in fact, if he hit the ball at all, drive it full pitch against the back wall. No matter ; he has given it what the Rev. Robert Spalding called " a good, hard knock." Mr. Spalding was but an innocent curate, but he had his feelings as a man and so have we all, even the mildest of us.

I have said nothing of the great game of tennis, of which I know too little to dare it ; nor of pelota, which must give almost unexampled opportunities, since I have seen nothing but a casual knock up. Let me not be thought to depreciate the subtler points of skill and finesse in which all great games are rich. In my own game I hope I am not without appreciation, and in others I can at least see something of them, if through a glass darkly. On this occasion I have deliberately essayed the part of the simple, barbarous, uninstructed creature that lurks within every one of us and rejoices in his strength. Hard hitting has some of the great qualities of obloquy. It is like telling a man for once in a while what we really think of him. It may be that from Christian or even prudential motives we had better have refrained. Our vocabulary may have been miserably inadequate but we have done our best. We have screwed ourselves up to the effort which imparts a glow to the still trembling frame. In that supreme instant we reck little of the consequences. So it is with our more passive enemy the ball. We have let it have it for all we are worth, we have got under the tail of that one. Let it vanish into the thickest whins or the depths of the sea ! *Ruat coelum !* We have hit it hard.

At the Club

IN the spring of 1892 I became a member of my first club and was much uplifted accordingly. It was neither a distinguished nor a venerable one, nor did it demand any social qualifications whatever, but still to be a member of a club at fifteen appeared a step in life. It was the Aberdovey Golf Club, then springing into being and holding its first Easter Meeting, and, as far as I know, there was no formality of election of any kind ; we simply elected one another. Having begun to play golf at eight I was tolerably familiar with clubhouses, but only as a small boy allowed to come in with his father, like a privileged little dog. To be on a sudden a member of such an institution—not a boy member nor the son of a member, but full blown—was unquestionably soothing to the vanity. I remember very clearly our first general meeting in which the entire membership was crowded into one room, its windows looking out on the pier. There is still in my ears the sound of footsteps and of Welsh singing, as the young men and boys of the village pass and repass the window and look in curiously at our gathering. This they are not allowed to do for long, for there is to be seen the immoral spectacle of a bottle of whisky on the table, and one of our Vice-Presidents, a local timber merchant, hastily draws the blinds before helping himself. Since those days I have travelled much in the realms of clubs and attended a good many committees, but in my memory there is a halo round that first meeting, which belongs to no other.

Not only was I a brand-new member but the club was a brand-new club. In that respect it differed from most clubs, since it is of their essence that they appear to have existed from time immemorial. The date of their foundation is known, and it may in fact be an extremely recent one, but that is really an illusion. More notably perhaps than any other human institution, a club is a type of eternity. It is difficult to imagine a time when it was not ; it is impossible to conceive that it will ever cease to be. The mere thought of it is calculated to reduce the self-importance in a highly salutary manner. There are some places in the existence of which a man scarcely believes ; if he is not there to see them they simply cease to be. There are others, in particular his own house, which he fancies must be perceptibly different when he is away. But the most arrogant cannot pretend to think that his presence or absence can in the slightest degree affect the placid, perennial routine of his club. At any hour of the day he can picture to himself exactly what is happening there, and he will almost certainly be right.

Should he go there in person, perhaps after months or even years of absence, he will find the very same people asleep in the very same chairs, just as he has imagined them, and if by any chance they should wake up, they will show no more surprise than if he were his own ghost. My grandfather had a story of his dog, which I have always liked. When he came home to Shrewsbury, after several years of absence on the voyage of the *Beagle*, he went into the stableyard and gave his own peculiar call. Instantly the dog appeared and started out for the familiar walk without the slightest display of emotion of any kind. It was as if those years had been obliterated and their last walk had been only on the day before. That story seems to me perfectly typical of all clubs and of the welcome that the visitant may expect there.

Everybody must have experienced this sensation, but each one of us is most acutely conscious of it in one particular club. Never does it come over me with such overwhelming force as when I visit a club, to which I have belonged for something over forty years and for which I have a great affection, the Dormy House at Rye. Twice I have been away from it for several years owing to a war. In each case I retained a definite picture of my last moment spent there, in which somebody was extended over the corner of the billiard table, watching with apprehensive eyes the black ball heading for the wrong pocket. Each time when I came back and looked through the little hole in the door before entering, there was the very same player in the same agonised attitude, or if he was not positively the same, at least his back view encouraged the illusion. In the course of time the players must have changed but they do not seem to have done so, and there is certainly no other change in the room save that once we could watch the sparks disappearing up the maw of the giant chimney. We can still sit in the chimney corner, and somebody always is sitting there, but the fire has been reduced in splendour and some economical device now intercepts the sparks as they fly upward. That is a fine changelessness after forty years ; the most resolute lover of everything that is old could hardly ask for more, and the same beautifully immutable atmosphere pervades the rest of the house. Only the other day I arrived at the slack time of day and wandered upstairs into the smoking-room. There were three figures ensconced in large arm-chairs before the fire, and of those three I could have laid considerable odds on two of them being there. Not one of them looked up and I must needs break into their combined reverie with unseemly heartiness. Some might deem this a mortifying reception. Not at all ; it was entirely soothing and as it ought to be, full of the essential and lovely tranquillity of the place. Properly considered there can be nothing more flattering than to be taken as a matter of course. It is only when people look up at him as if to say, " What the devil is this fellow doing here ? " that the newcomer can feel any discomfort.

During the last war some evacuees who had been taken into a country house insisted on returning home, and on being asked their reason said they did not like the way the butler looked. They were probably quite unjust, and yet it is not to be denied that butlers have a way of looking. It may be only a bad conscience as to the contents of our luggage, in particular the raggedness of our linen, that gives us sometimes a wrong impression, but nearly all of us, especially when young, have quailed before the hooded, impersonal eye of a Littimer or a Jeeves. Whether or not butlers can look, there is no doubt at all that the members of clubs can. Can we lay our hands on our hearts, and declare that in our own clubs we have never too emphatically looked at some unoffending stranger ? If we have ever done so, it is due, I fancy, to one of the virtues of clubs that can be exaggerated into a vice. We are all possessive and patriotic about our own clubs. By a merciful dispensation of Providence, we believe that they are the best clubs, not on account of any particular qualities, but on much the same grounds that everybody, who has the least spirit in him, thinks that his county is the best county. This intense patriotism can spring up almost in a single night. Once we were tremulous candidates ; now that we are elected the pictures and the traditions and the hall porter—we are nearly always proud of the hall porter—belong as fully to us as they do to the oldest member. Perhaps so many great possessions all at once go a little to our heads, and unfortunately in some not very large or wise heads they persistently remain.

If we incline to be too possessive it is a very natural sentiment, for one of the great charms of a club is that it is our very own ; it is our home in which we can, within reasonable limits, do as we please. How intense is this feeling of home we can perhaps only appreciate when we give up a club and return to it as mere guests. To have to go through the formality of asking whether our host is in the club, to have our name put down in a visitor's book, to take our meal perhaps in the Jews' Quarter of the Strangers' dining-room—these are things hard to endure in the house where we were once fractional monarchs of all we surveyed. We may have had the most virtuous and economical motives for resigning but now we have a sensation of disloyalty, almost of treachery. What were a few guineas more or less compared with this wound to the heart, this consciousness of a sceptre departed? It is generally thought that many members keep their names on the books of a club, which they visit scarcely once a year, from a constitutional laziness which forbids them to cancel the banker's order for their subscription. Some such there are, no doubt, but it is pleasanter to think that there are more who simply cannot bear to take the irrevocable and ungrateful step. They will die at last still hoping and intending to come back, and their names will be formally " noted with regret " by a Committee that wonders dimly who they were.

If this is a weakness, it is at least thoroughly amiable. A much less admirable one is that which makes us hate the members of another club, who are temporarily billeted on our own. These migrations during a spring cleaning are sometimes necessary but always painful. It is to be hoped that we do our best to be civil, but we do look at them and they in their turn are conscious of being looked at, of not knowing the ropes, of exercising rights and privileges to which they are not fully entitled. It is a brave man who does not feel just a little frightened of someone else's club. The going up the steps and asking whether Mr. So-and-So is in the club is a test of courage never to be faced without a little flutter of the heart. It may even have happened to us to go into the wrong club by mistake—a thing that might easily befall in Pall Mall —and to depart covered with shame and blushes, under the hall porter's pitying eye. Take it at its best and friendliest, we must sit up in somebody else's club ; we can sprawl in the arm-chairs at our own.

At the Club

A remarkable, and on the whole a good, feature of our possessive patriotism is that once we have been elected we are disposed to think the other members the best fellows in the world. Some of them, if we met them elsewhere, we might deem a little tiresome but inside the portals a certain glamour is over them, and their jokes have a quality not perhaps intrinsically their due. There are exceptions to every rule, and there are club bores, among whom, mercifully unknowing, we may ourselves be numbered. There are those who from excess of caution ask at the door whether a certain member is in the club before entering, but this is a dangerous habit. If indulged in to excess it tends to sap the manhood and produce an almost hysterical state of mind. One friend of mine, now dead, who did not suffer bores gladly, used to tell of the dreary hours he had spent tramping between his two clubs, driven to and fro by an ever mounting terror. Finding that A was at the first club, he set off impulsively for the second, only to discover that B had just arrived there. There was nothing for it but an about turn back to the first, and there was C, a devil worse than either. So back again, and, if the story improved with telling, there is no reasonable doubt that he ultimately lunched extremely late and very hungry.

Of course such tragical comedies can only happen in an essentially clubbable club, where, broadly speaking, everybody talks to everybody else, and it is almost a duty not to seek seclusion but, subject now and then to a little reasonable manœuvre, to fall with a good grace into a vacant chair and make the best of it. Whether the more friendly or the more formal is preferable must clearly be a matter of individual taste, but I have personally no doubt and am all for friendliness. The occasional risk is a hundred times worth the taking, and if we are not all quite so amusing or such good company as we think we are, our friends' loyalty will conceal our deficiencies from us.

If perhaps the members of a club are not quite so interesting as they deem themselves and each other, neither perhaps are they quite so important. But that is unjust ; let me rather say that the club is not quite so important, that they sometimes take it and its affairs a little too seriously. There are times when members, chiefly those with not a great deal else to do, are to be seen in small knots, their lips pursed and their brows furrowed, murmuring low, with an air confidential and solemn in the extreme. Experience tends to show that it is often about nothing in particular. These periods more often than not synchronise with elections. Then, rumour is apt to rush through the club. There is a malicious excitement in the thought of someone being black-balled which makes a lively appeal to those immune from such a disaster. It is one of the features of a club that the greatest man in the world cannot enter its gates if the members do not want him, and sometimes perhaps they enjoy this thrilling sense of superiority a little too grossly and palpably. It is probable, however, that the thrill has diminished with the power to exclude, since, I fancy, election at nearly all clubs is now by the Committee and not by the whole body of members. To allow any and every member to vent some imaginary or momentary spite was to put too high a price on virtue's head. It is almost bound to produce lobbyings and conspiracies. A Committee has often difficult and unpleasant duties to perform in this matter, but it does them conscientiously and after open discussion. To read the old histories of clubs is to gain an impression of attacks and counter-attacks by opposite parties, which threatened sometimes altogether to check the flow of new members. Things are better and more civilised than they used to be.

This extreme solemnity has, I fancy, decreased in other respects besides that of elections. There are fewer club rows than, judging by the historians, there once were. The most famous of all such rows, that at the Garrick over Edmund Yates, which led to the estrangement of Dickens and Thackeray, strikes us to-day as deplorably gratuitous. A modern Com-

mittee would, one may surmise, have declined to rush in, have
prudently declared it was no business of theirs and let the
protagonists settle it amongst themselves. There may be one
reason for the rarity of rows in that the great battle of smoking
which raged intermittently for years, has now ended triumphantly for the big battalions of the smokers. Once in private
houses the smoker must practise his vices in the harness-room
or the kitchen, and now there is no room sacred from him.
So it is in clubs ; the weight of perhaps inconsiderate numbers
has prevailed. In a London club, to which I once belonged,
the last desperate stand of the non-smokers was made. There
was a large room on the ground floor where smoking, save for
pipes, was allowed, and there was another upstairs where even
pipes were licit ; but between the two stretched the no-man's-
land of the staircase, and over that the battle raged. It was
more than a battle as to tobacco, which became little more
than a formal *casus belli* ; it was a fight to the death between
insurgent youth and long enthroned age. Some three hundred
new and youthful members, of whom I was one, had lately
and reluctantly been admitted and we wanted to smoke.
Our elders, thinking us impudent young dogs—perhaps we
were—mustered their reactionary ranks against us and we
were heavily defeated. Yet, as so often happens, the victory
was short-lived. In a few months the motion that had caused
all the pother was carried without any row at all, and he who
now puffs his cigarette on the stairs—it is to-day in a different
house—probably does not realise that the smoke rises metaphorically from heaps of the slain.

I began by saying that one could with tolerable confidence
prophesy as to any particular members who would be there at
any time of day and what they would be doing. To that
proposition may be added a corollary, that for us they have
often no existence save in that club, nor we for them. In all
other walks of life we mutually cease to be, and if by chance
we meet elsewhere it is with a shock of unreality. This is, I
think, especially true of golf clubs, of which my knowledge,

if by no means peculiar, is certainly extensive. Within it we are all golfers and this is the link that binds us together ; its gates close on us and we take our separate ways, nor perhaps does either of us know whether in that unseen private life of his, which we dimly presume to exist, the other is a tinker or a tailor, an apothecary or a thief. When we meet again in the club it seems both natural and agreeable to do so, and it is only afterwards that we reflect with shame that we have scarcely given each other a thought since we parted. Do we then, as the profane may think, talk about nothing but golf? It is not nearly so bad as that. On the contrary we may owe to meetings in a golf club much pleasant talk on subjects of which otherwise we should have known nothing whatever. Yet I cannot overcome the feeling that particular people belong to particular golf clubs and that away from them they become shadowy and unsubstantial. Is it that " my head has not many mansions, nor spacious ? " I am afraid that must be it, and yet when those shadows become for the moment solid again I am truly glad to see them.

To those whose way of life has taken them into many clubs it is strange to think that there are those, " beings erect on two legs and having all the outward semblance of men and not of monsters," who have never belonged to a club and never wanted to. They have missed, I think, a great deal of harmless pleasure and friendliness, that can give a glow to the heart. There remains one thing about clubs that puzzles me, though this may be a purely personal idiosyncracy. If the clubs are such agreeable places and " clubbable," so enviable an epithet, why is " clubman " so loathsome a word ? If Dr. Johnson, instead of saying that Boswell was " a very clubbable man," had described him as " a good clubman " should I have had the same feelings ? I do not know, but to me " clubman " is of all second-rate, vulgar, and generally detestable words in the English language, the worst and lowest. It suggests all the little childish vanities and squabbles and snobbishnesses and elaborate fussings about nothing which are occasionally to be found in members of clubs, as indeed they are in other mortals. If a man should know that he had been described in an obituary notice as a " clubman" he would be justified in haunting the writer of that notice and making night a misery and a terror for him. It seems probable that the knowledge will be mercifully concealed from him.

Hidden Treasure

"THERE!" exclaimed Mr. Boffin, who had been revelling in *The Treasures of a Dunghill* as read aloud to him by Silas Wegg. "There! see what men put away and forget, or mean to destroy, and don't!" His enthusiasm was, as we are bound to believe, only simulated, but at least it was very well simulated and evokes entirely genuine sympathy. Hidden treasure is to any properly constituted mind irresistible. Nor does it appeal only to what is miserly or acquisitive in us. We have no more seriously thought of finding any ourselves than we have of winning the Calcutta Sweep or a football pool. That is the kind of thing that only happens to shadowy people in the newspapers. Whether it be the treasure of the Incas or the jewels King John lost in the Wash or a mere pailful of old coins dug up in a field, we gain from it an altruistic and romantic emotion.

During the early years of the war a case was heard in the Chancery Division, which would have delighted Mr. Boffin and must have made a greater stir in the world at large had it not been occupied with matters it deemed more important. There was once a wood-turner called Nathan Perrott, a name fully worthy of *Caulfield's Characters* or *The Wonderful Museum*. He died at the age of ninety in 1912, and his wife died a year after him. Their daughter Elizabeth, who had lived with them, supported herself by charing and flower-selling until 1938, when she grew too old for work and must go into the workhouse. Probably in a moment of " clearing up " before her departure someone suggested breaking open an old locked box of her father's. She had kept it in her room since his death but had left it untouched since she had no key. In it were found securities worth some £20,000. For those six and twenty hard, barren years she might have sat back as a lady of means, watching someone else charing for her, buying flowers where she had once sold them. As it was she was like the last victorious survivor in a tontine whose good fortune is momentarily fluttered before him when he is too deaf to hear of it and too infirm to enjoy it. Within a year poor Elizabeth was dead.

It is a pathetic story without even, save presumably for Elizabeth's heirs, a happy ending. Therein it differs from that told in an old song, which is I believe still popular at penny readings. I have myself heard it given with great effect at a supper after a village cricket match in Hampshire. An old lady died and the grandson who had expected to be the chief beneficiary under her will was maliciously laughed at by his brothers and sisters,

> *When they heard the lawyer declare*
> *That Granny'd only left me her old arm-chair,*

Making the best of a bad job he sat consistently in it for years, until at last it had to be mended and was then found to be stuffed with banknotes. He who laughed last, at any rate, laughed loudest.

It is an excellent story, but for my part I prefer, and so I fancy too, do all who cultivate the mysterious and the sublime, that the treasure should be buried under the earth. So many things of value are constantly being found, turned up by the spade or the ploughshare, that it is hard not to believe that people bury them from a pure love of secrecy for its own sake. Perhaps they dig them up now and again to gloat over them, as poor Silas Marner did with his guineas under the floor, or as a dog disinters a bone from a flower bed for another succulent chaw. Of course there are often more practical motives. I have a friend who, when a German invasion seemed imminent, seriously considered burying his plate in his back garden. He even bought a receptacle for the purpose, but changed his melodramatic intention when Hitler changed his mind. Probably, if the truth were known, a good many people went one step further than he did, and have since had considerable difficulty in identifying carefully memorised landmarks. Some may have even forgotten their hordes, for judging by lost property offices men can forget anything : or they may have died without revealing the secret to their heirs. There will very likely be some rich discoveries to be made by future generations.

There is an eternal thrill in underground. It is arguable that the most romantic line in all English poetry is, " Over the hills and far away," and the words are full of ineffable things, of mystery and beauty and dim blue distances. Yet I venture to offer as an alternative two lines of Francis Thompson's :

> *East, ah, east of Himalay,*
> *Dwell the nations underground.*

There too are mystery and distance with the added subterranean enchantment. *Alice in Wonderland* was originally to have been called *Alice's Adventures Underground*, and though the name by which we now know the book is so familiar that we cannot judge it, it is by no means certain that the author's second thoughts were best. The first breathless pursuit of the White Rabbit down the hole under the hedge is never forgotten; it is one of the permanent charms of the story that all those lovely things happen deep, deep down under the earth, over which those less fortunate than Alice are walking, quite dull and unconscious with their umbrellas. In Hans Andersen's story of *Little Tiny* we were bidden to be dreadfully sorry for her because, if she married the mole in his rich black velvet coat, as the field mouse desired, she would have to live underground. It seemed to us on the contrary to be the most enviable and exciting lot. It is this same fascination which accounts for all the stories of secret passages. There is not, I believe, a village in England which has not the tradition of such a passage, dating vaguely back to " those old times." And what of the speleologists ? These are ostensibly grave, researchful persons, worthy of their scientific name, but it must surely be that they possess a perennially boyish imagination. As they crawl on hands and knees through an opening into some mighty cavern, as I suppose and hope they do, they must think of King Solomon's Mines or Dirk Hatteraick's hidden cave by the seashore, and forget all their solemnity in the playing of so entrancing a game. I have referred in another place to the pleasure of bolting underground in an air raid. It was a very moderate one to be sure, but having a measure of compensation for other unpleasantness. There was something more in it than a presumed security. The sensation was even to be enjoyed in that normally prosaic spot, Broadcasting House. I went there once or twice during the war and was escorted for what seemed a quite immeasurable distance below the ground floor. Down and down we went. It was so hot that we might have reached the fiery bowels of the earth. But it was unquestionably exciting, and when I saw in one room a tidy little white bed and knew that someone slept there in those fathomless depths, I was consumed with an envy which did not wholly come from a distaste for bombs. I like to think that there was in it something of romance.

Only once have I assisted in the digging up of buried treasure, to confer on it in this case an undeserved dignity, and that was for the most practical possible reasons. When I was a D.A.D.O.S. in Macedonia, my admirable Warrant Officer, with an air of some embarrassment, made one day a revelation to me. My predecessor in office had buried a director (an instrument having something to do with artillery) under my tent. He had indented for one too many, and having a well-grounded fear of Ordnance law had not confessed to the error, thinking no doubt that in time he could dispose of it to a unit in want of one. I had no mind to live over a mouldering director, like a murderer over his cemented victim, and decreed that it should be exhumed. There is a temptation to use the most poetical language my vocabulary affords, to describe how we dug it up, " the sods with our bayonets turning " by that wonderful moonlight which can make the grey-green stretches of Macedon as bright as day. In fact, we did it in a hole-and-corner fashion with a spade, feeling rather like resurrection men at their grisly task, and looking uneasily over our shoulders. The director was returned to the base (let no one ask me at this distance of time by what juggling it was " taken back on charge ") and its ghost never haunted me again. It was a great relief to my mind, but of romance, I must admit, there was none.

There was more in another and more genuine treasure trove in the same country. Near my encampment lay a deep dry river bed, which became after rain a rushing torrent. One day, when the torrent had abated, I saw a shimmering something in the shallow water which turned out to be a silver coin of Alexander the Great. Alas ! I had a companion who had seen it first by the fraction of a second, so that I had to yield to his superior claim. Perhaps one of the Macedonian phalanx had dropped it out of his pocket in crossing the stream and it had lain there ever since, or perhaps—but this is a shameful case of sour grapes—it was one of those forgeries of which the shops in Salonica were full.

I doubt if the most skilful of writers could have made much of either incident, but what a lot they have made of secret hordes better adapted to their purpose ! It is impossible that any one can ever tire of reading *Treasure Island*, and here by the way is an instance in which second thoughts as to a title were best. This immortal work was originally to have been called *The Sea-Cook*, doubtless a very proper compliment to John Silver, but in itself a dull name, not to be compared with one so perfectly suggestive of pieces of eight and the Spanish Main. I have just been looking at the pictures once again in my dear old edition of 1885 in its tattered red coat. They are all beautiful, but I am not sure that I do not love best of all that of Jim Hawkins in the cave delving deep into that heap of sequins and moidores and doubloons, and, as it were, washing his hands in soap-suds of gold. And what a grim and happy thought that was of Flint's to lay out the body of the last of the six men he had killed single-handed, as a compass pointing the way to the treasure. That was in the best manner, for a treasure should always have an ingenious clue to its discovery. " By thunder ! " as Silver remarked : " If it don't make me cold inside to think of Flint. This is one of his jokes, and no mistake."

And by thunder ! Stevenson knew his business. So did Sir Walter Scott, though in this regard not quite so brilliantly well, when he sent Sir Arthur Wardour and Edie Ochiltree and the egregious Dousterswivel treasure hunting in Misticot's grave. The lonely priory of St. Ruth makes the ideal setting for the search. Franklin Blake groping for the tin box under the Shivering Sand must not be forgotten, nor must Sherlock Holmes. The great Agra treasure is a very good treasure, and has the merit of a cryptic clue in the sign of four. It has also the virtue of extreme opulence. It is unquestionably irritating when Jonathan Small hurls that mass of splendour, that epitome of all the jewels of the world, into the Thames. Yet with some confidence I put forward the higher claims of the Musgrave Ritual. Here the clue is conceived in the very highest style of art. " Where was the sun ? Over the oak. Where was the shadow ? Under the elm," and ending with the words so pregnant with delicious meaning, " And so under."

The poor stupid Musgraves had forgotten what it meant, but their cleverer butler had discovered the solution and with it the precious thing they had hidden. Moreover I have made a modest little discovery of my own, bearing remotely upon it in *The Wonders of the Little World or A General History of Man* by Nathaniel Wanley, late M.A. and Vicar of Trinity Parish, Coventry. This engaging and comprehensive work, which I am happy to possess, has a chapter entitled " Of such Princes and Persons as have been fortunate in the finding of hidden treasures and others who were deluded in the like expectations." Among its pleasing stories is this one of a Prince of Apulia in the year 1060. It would be an impertinence to tell it save in Mr. Wanley's own words. " There was found in Apulia a statue of marble having about the head a circle of brass with this inscription : *Calendis Maii, oriente sole, aureum caput habebo* ; that is ' The first day of May at sun rising, I shall have a golden head.' There was not any that could solve this riddle that could anywhere be found. At last a Saracen, then prisoner, offered himself to expound the inscription, upon promise that when he had done it he should be set free and at full liberty. The Prince gave him assurance thereof, and at the first day of May having come, at the rising of the sun, the Saracen observed the shadow of the circle that was about the head of this image, and in the same place where the shadow was, caused them to dig. Which they did. And when they were come very deep, they found a mighty treasure, which came in good season for the Prince, for it served to defray the charge of the war he made at that time. The Saracen, besides the grant of his liberty (which he preferred before all things) was bountifully rewarded and sent away with many rich and princely gifts." I like to imagine that the first Musgrave borrowed the notion of the shadow from this source.

Wanley has other agreeable stories, such as that of Narses who having hidden an " incredible mass of gold and silver " imitated Captain Flint and killed all who knew the place, all unfortunately except one, a small boy. That was where he made a mistake, for the boy, when he grew up, broke his promise of silence and disclosed the spot to the Emperor Tiberius the Second of Greece. It seems that this sport of treasure hunting is one best confined to the imagination. In reality there is too much temptation to kill those who are in the secret and would claim their share of the profits. I have an adventurous friend who once went on a treasure-hunting expedition to an island in the South Seas. They came back empty-handed and I gathered that he was rather relieved than otherwise. " Look out for squalls when you find it," said Dr. Livesey to Silver, as he handed him the chart on which the hiding place was marked ; my friend was apparently of much the same opinion.

Perhaps, on reflection, I was wrong in saying that we never really believed that anything of the sort could happen to us. It may simply be that it has not happened yet, and that if we were once even on a fancied scent we should be consumed by a fierce lust for gold and dream of money to play ducks and drakes with ever afterwards. There was once a distinguished artist who, whenever he felt destitute, used to set out on a sovereign hunt through the pockets of all his clothes and was seldom disappointed. Those glittering days may never return, but there is an undeniable joy in lighting on even " the ridiculous amount of eighteen pence." A shilling saved may be a shilling gained, but a shilling found is worth at least half a crown. The chair in which I am now sitting has deep cracks between the arms and the seat, which are generally believed to be paved with small silver. A member of the family, knowing the male habit of lying on the shoulder blades and so tipping things backwards out of the trouser pockets, once undertook to make a thorough search on a commission basis. She retrieved, if memory serves, no less than fifteen shillings and sixpence. So modest a trove cannot compete with that in Granny's old arm-chair, but at any rate, this really did happen ; so there is always hope. The time for another hunt has almost come.

Crowd and Urgency

THE phrase, I need scarcely say, is not my own. It is
Mr. Churchill's, and until he used it many of us had
perhaps never fully appreciated the emotional value of being
packed like sardines, nor realised that we cannot have
a great occasion without a crowd. To see and hear in comfort
is a desire that grows upon us with age and laziness, but
comfort and excitement, though they may live together, can
never be true friends. The perfection of poignancy can only
be enjoyed by the uncomfortable, and the longing to wave the
hat in the air in an ecstasy of triumph is never so keenly felt
as when the arms are firmly pinned to the side by the pressure
of our next-door neighbours. We may and very likely do hate
those neighbours, but they contribute to our excitement for
all that, and we feel their thrills not only physically but
mentally. The blocked road, the railway carriage with ten
people standing in it, the fighting a way to our seats—these
are all exquisitely uncomfortable but they add an exquisite
flavour to our sensations. Once we grow frightened of them,
as I admit I have done, the game is up. I have said elsewhere

in this book that I have taken to listening instead of watching, and it is a pitiful confession.

Of the sights enjoyed in youth it is the excitement of the crowd that survives when the spectacle itself has almost wholly vanished from the memory. In 1887 I was taken to see Queen Victoria's Jubilee procession. Save for a general feeling of the unspeakable glory of the Life Guards all has gone. Even the tiny bowing figure in the carriage, the very heart and centre of all that magnificence, has grown very dim. But what remains distinctly is the staying the night before in Kensington, the thrill of early breakfast, the driving as far as the four-wheeler was allowed, and then the walking through yellow sanded streets already lined with people, till the appointed eyrie was reached. That was the crowded hour, there was the glorious life.

I am writing these words soon after watching, in the contemptible luxury of a garden on the river, the University Boat Race. If ever there was an example of the value of crowd and urgency it is this festival. It was a fine sunny day, but with a biting east wind. A million people were there to see, and of those all but the tiniest proportion were at least as ignorant as I am of the art of rowing and had no reason, but a purely artificial partisanship, to care who won. They stood in serried ranks for some hours, they saw the boats for little more than a moment, and for most of the race only the possibility that Cambridge might catch a second crab in that poppling water could avert the inevitable end. That does not sound a particularly enthralling entertainment and yet I have no doubt that those million onlookers found it good fun, and it was good fun. As far as the race itself was concerned it was all too soon over. There came the cry of " Here they are " from those perched on a roof nearby, and then the flash of the oars after Hammersmith Bridge, the light blue in front and sparkling cheerfully in the sunlight. For a minute or two we saw the boats and the crowd of following steamers ; then they were hidden from us by Chiswick Eyot. The great waves of the steamers surged and splashed against our guardian wall, and after that the river returned once more to comparative emptiness and placidity, the spectators began to disperse, and there was nothing for it but to return indoors to a fire and listen on the wireless to Cambridge—it was Cambridge and that was something—drawing comfortably away to victory.

Nevertheless, I repeat it was uncommonly good fun. There was the packing of the sandwich basket, the settling down to the drive, the wondering whether we should be blockaded as we drew near to Hammersmith, the sight of more and more people obviously making for the river, bent on a common enterprise. It was Hazlitt on the Bath coach going to see the fight at Newbury all over again ; on a rather mild scale admittedly, but much can be done by a little imagination. Just because it was a great occasion, the hours of waiting assumed an agreeable tenseness and things ordinarily dull took on a new and vivid interest. We called to each other to look at a procession of steamers, much as we should once have exclaimed at a traction engine thundering down the lane ; we felt sorry for the swans rocking in their wash. We watched the spectators accumulating ever more thickly on the Surrey shore and wondered maliciously whether the tide would rise high enough to wet their toes. In short we made the very most of a very little.

I confess that now and then I felt like the little boy in Hans Andersen's story of the *Emperor's New Clothes*. It will be remembered that two impostors professed to have discovered a fabric of great richness and beauty, invisible to any one that was either very stupid or unfit for his position. No one could see this miraculous fabric, but no one dared say so, and the Emperor, fearful lest he should expose himself, marched in a procession under a gorgeous canopy wearing nothing at all. At last a small child exclaimed, " But the Emperor has no clothes on," and then all the people, including the Emperor himself, saw that this was the truth ; but the procession went on to the end. So I said to myself that the great show of the

Boat Race was an imposition, that the onlookers were all pretending to be excited though they did not really care at all, that the procession still went on year after year because nobody had the courage to utter his real sentiments. But then I recalled the historic names of Harrods and the Doves and Duke's Meadow ; I looked again at the crowds and their rosettes and the swans and the steamers and the Stork gaily beflagged, and put such shameful thoughts behind me. It was not an imposition but an occasion, and it was the crowds that made it. We had all mesmerised each other.

Supposing—a singularly futile but pleasing speculation— that we were Hans Andersen's Emperor, who could decree anything he had a mind to, we might be tempted to order the Boat Race to be rowed for our private and imperial benefit. Even as William Rufus laid waste the New Forest for his hunting, the banks and the bridges should be cleared of onlookers ; all the houses along the river must keep their blinds down, and we should follow the race sitting under a canopy in a solitary launch blazing with gold. It is a thoroughly disgraceful project and would bring its own reward. We should be proved very stupid and unfit for our position, for the entertainment would fall as flat as a pancake and the oarsmen would scarcely trouble to row, except for the fear of having their heads cut off. And so it would be if any of our other selfish day-dreams could come to pass. A test match, played on the best wicket in the world within our own park palings would lapse into a mere exhibition of skill. Perhaps the most thrilling of all moments in any contest is that of the sudden hush that precedes it, but it would be as nothing if it were only the silence of absent thousands. We might as well hope to get the greatest of all orators to make a speech to us in an empty room as to enjoy a match without the barbarous yells of triumph that greet the fall of a wicket. Without the crowd there can be no urgency.

I, whose business it has been to watch golf, have superficially as good a reason to hate the crowd as have most people.

At other games it is kept within bounds but the golf crowd is fluid and pours over the field of play. By much shouting and stewarding and roping it is to some extent restrained, but ever and anon it breaks through and runs wildly and tumultuously. It prevents me from seeing what I want to see, and yet, on purely selfish grounds, I would not be without it, for it can be the most dramatic of all the crowds in the world. The great black ring six deep round the putting green, the silence unbroken save by the curlews calling overhead, is a sight infinitely and eternally exciting. In any golfing scene that I remember over the years the crowd plays its part. How often have I seen—how often, alas ! have I described !—John Ball starting down the first hole in a great match with a rose in his button hole, with the trampling and the hum of the prayerful Hoylake crowd behind him, held back by the blue-jerseyed fishermen manning the rope. To ancient hero-worshippers of my generation there never was and never can be again so moving a spectacle as that. But others, second only to it, come back. There is Bobby Jones winning the Open Championship at St. Andrews. His ball lies in the hollow before the home green, called the Valley of Sin. The crowd are halted solid behind him. The moment he has played his shot and scrambled up the bank, the crowd rush up irresistibly behind him and halt again, making a black fringe round the green. He taps in his winning putt and the next moment there is no inch of green to be seen, nothing but a swirling mob, with Bobby in the middle, perched on adoring shoulders and his putter, " Calamity Jane," held in precarious safety over his head.

Even more tremendous, in point of sheer numbers, is the scene of our lone victory in the Walker Cup, when all but one match is finished, and the individual crowds that have been watching the others come streaming over the burn, with divisions melting into corps, and corps into one great army, converging on the cockpit of the home green. Better a thousand times to have been crushed and buffeted, and to have seen little but " the 'oofs of the 'orses " than to have missed so splendidly terrifying a spectacle. To-day at St. Andrews we who watch are herded to the side lines among the whins. It has to be for the sake of the players and we ourselves see far more than we used to do, if at longer range, but something of the old drama has departed.

I have been " prophecyin' avay wery fine " about the crowds that go to see games, because it is chiefly these that I encounter. I welcome them, with modified rapture, because, however uncomfortably, they enhance the luxury of my own feelings. But there are clearly many people who love crowds purely for their own sake. They are enviable and admirable but to an opposite school of thought unintelligible. The other day I met a lady of whom, were it not unchivalrous, I should say that she was old enough to know better. She said that she was trying to induce her family to go for three days to the Channel Islands at a time of public holiday ; the proposal had not so far been received with enthusiasm, but she was not without hope. On my expressing strong sympathy with her family, she replied that " anyhow, travelling was such fun."

To the shrinking and misanthropic, and in this regard I name myself among them, it appears sheer, stark lunacy. Travelling is good fun—I could look out of the window for hours—but it must be done in reasonable comfort without too much rubbing of shoulders. Is it altogether too shameful an admission that one of the pleasantest things about the night journey to Scotland is to lie in your bunk and hear the clanking of milk cans and the scurrying feet along the platform and hug to yourself the knowledge that you are safe in your own little kingdom ?

The term " fellow-traveller " has to-day assumed a sinister political meaning, but, taken literally, fellow travellers are, except in the strictest moderation, to be deprecated. We admire that gallant lady of my acquaintance, but at the time of Easter holidays we cannot agree with her. Hers is the right and hearty spirit of travelling : she is what E. V. Lucas termed a " life-and-souler " ; she will not only be happy herself with other people squeezing the life out of her, but will make the whole railway carriage happy too. If only we could be like her !

" How nicely we are crammed in ! " exclaimed Lydia Bennet to her three sisters. " I am glad I brought my bonnet if it is only for the fun of having another band box ! Well, now let us be quite comfortable and snug and talk and laugh all the way home." I adore Lydia, though a little of her would doubtless go a long way, but I cannot share her views. The world is divided into two classes, those who like being nicely crammed in and those who hate it, and, incredible as it may appear, it is the former, the " intrepid hedonists," (again I quote E. V. L.) who must be in the majority. Witness the long-drawn-out horrors of the station queue. If, in the war-time phrase, their journey is really necessary, we may sympathise with them almost as wholeheartedly as we should with ourselves on being thus herded ; but those who must go are surely few compared with those who want to go, and regard the discomforts of the journey as part of the delights of getting there. For them the whole enterprise is one continuous joy in which there is no better and no worse. In fact, they carry to its logical conclusion that doctrine of crowd and urgency which I have been preaching in one solitary respect.

If they applied it only to a party of pleasure we should feel no sentiment but admiration, but many of them carry it one step further into work-a-day travel. They not only endure those human contacts from which we recoil ; they positively revel in sitting shoulder to shoulder. They have no taste for solitude and corner seats, but close up affectionately on their nearest neighbour. It someone gets out they never give as much as one painful inch to relieve the pressure, but remain firmly rooted. As soon as a door is open they pour in, reckless of empty seats in the next carriage, and leave the door open behind them as an invitation. In short, they carry Lydia's principle to the ultimate point, and we poor shuddering, unsocial creatures remain crushed and puzzled.

There is an omnibus by which I sometimes travel having

two attractive little separate seats, safely entrenched on which no man need fear his neighbours' elbows. It would seem certain that these would be the first occupied, but they are not ; rather are they left untenanted, so that I, coming almost last up the steps, can yet pounce on them in my misanthropic way. My only competitors have as a rule been small boys, and their motives are obviously quite different from my own, being purely romantic. It is hardly possible to play any game that is at all worthy if you are sitting next a plump grown-up who resents your jiggling, but a lone seat can from a pretending point of view be almost anything—a fortress, the box of a carriage, even a throne. I have felt so much sympathy with the small boys that on occasion I have deliberately abandoned those enviable seats and suffered next the plump grown-up.

Is that perhaps the secret of those happy voyagers whom I envy most when I am tempted to like them least ? Yes, they must be imagining lovely far-off things while I am only thinking of my own toes on which they are so good-naturedly standing. Theirs is that priceless gift of pretending that moved my spirited lady to say that travelling was such fun. She can go one better than Hazlitt. " It is hard," said he, " if I cannot start some game on these lone heaths." She can start some game in a crowded railway carriage. I only wish I had half her complaint, but at least I have braved the Boat Race.

Colour and Colours

THERE is a drive that a friend and I sometimes go in his car when we are nursing our respective aches in Worcestershire. After a few miles we both begin to look out eagerly on one side of the road for a particular spectacle and to betray the gravest anxiety lest we should have missed it. Such fears are quite unnecessary, for I defy the least observant to miss that sudden tremendous blaze of colour. There are two small houses, next door neighbours in an unimpressive row. Each house in the row has its little suburban garden sloping down to the road, and all the rest are drab and commonplace enough ; but these two hit the traveller straight between the eyes. Such flaming scarlets and blues and golds were surely never seen, and concentrated as they are into a small space they are overwhelming. It is as if some magician flying overhead had opened his box of the most blinding, brilliant jewels and tipped them out in a promiscuous heap.

We have never been able to make up our minds whether these two neighbours are devoted friends with similar tastes or the most deadly enemies, each consumed by a fury of jealous hatred and determined to out-do the other in flamboyancy of colouring. The second is the more dramatic supposition and seems to offer the material for a short story full of morbid emotions. That is one of the many talents that I lack, but I offer the plot freely to any one who can make use of it. Friends or enemies, the two must be devoted gardeners. More than that, I think there must be something agreeably childlike in their passion for gorgeous colour.

An affection for colours is something that remains with us from childhood. We lose many enthusiasms and curiosities, but of this one we may, if we are lucky, retain a little. Anybody who has ever tried to tell stories to children knows how important it is that the colours of all the clothes should be precisely given. That is not very difficult since the taste of the audience is not likely to be too exigent ; what is difficult is for the narrator to remember his first inspired description, for he will get into sad trouble if he varies it later. Of all the authors who grasped this truth, the greatest was Walter Scott ; but indeed he had no need to grasp it, for in this respect he had remained a child himself and nobody could have enjoyed colours more than he did. Let the reader take *Ivanhoe*, as good an example as any, and count the pages in the first chapter or two given to this entrancing topic. Wamba has a full page given to his bright purple jacket ornamented with flowers of various hues, his silver bells and best of all his parti-coloured legs, one red, one yellow. But it is when Brian de Bois-Guilbert comes riding down the forest glade that Scott really lets himself go. From his scarlet cap faced with fur (scrumptious !) to his large two-handed sword, he occupies two pages full measure. Second only to him, in point of detail, is Prince John caracoling round the lists at Ashby in crimson and gold and fur, with golden spurs and such a tippet and cloak—but I must not copy out all the lovely stuff as I should like to do.

At any rate, any one properly brought up on *Ivanhoe* ought to have imbibed a romantic taste for colour which will stand by him for the rest of his life. And there is another book which should likewise inculcate it, Edward Lear's *Book of Nonsense*.

Here the colours are not merely to be imagined ; they are to be seen. There are, I believe, many unfortunate persons who only possess the black and white version of this truly great work ; but the lucky ones have it in colour. And what colour ! So exquisitely pure, so beautifully bright ! Think, if you can remember it, of the balloon in broad stripes of red and yellow, built by the old man of The Hague in order to examine the moon. As to the flaming red waistcoats they are innumerable. The various old persons or old men of the West, of the Dee, of Troy, Peru, Calcutta and Dutton were all as so many robin red-breasts, but infinitely more fair, while the Old Person of Dover had purple trousers to bring tears to the eyes. And all the colours are so clean and flat, with no nonsense of light and shade about them, as if laid on by the paint brush of some inspired child.

Doubtless, those who only possessed the book in black and white did their best by painting the pictures for themselves. Even to-day it might be tempting, for there lives nobody with soul so dead that he does not love the thought of a paint box. How black and shiny it was outside when it was new, and how virginal the palette which folded back to reveal the two rows of untouched paints, each in its little white case, like flower beds in a formal garden. Their names have a strange, exotic charm. Superficially they may not be so rich as is the language of fireworks, with its clusters of jewelled serpents, but they touch profounder depths of emotion. They are full of the sound of rain falling, hard, friendly, persistent rain that forbids the interruption of a walk. Vermilion, emerald green, gamboge, burnt sienna, Prussian blue and indigo—why has nobody written a poem on a paint box, simply to bring in that roll of names ? Even as many people read the accounts of hunting merely to revel in the names of the copses and gorses and spinneys, so it is worth reading the list of starters for the Derby to enjoy the names of the colours and to think of painting them. Incidentally, it was, at any rate, to me as a Cambridge little boy, a sad defect in most paint boxes that they contained no light blue. Prussian blue, however well watered down, produced only a travesty of the right colour. The makers of paint boxes must all have been at Oxford.

I have kept for a separate paragraph of its own by far the noblest colour of all, alike in name and in intrinsic quality, Crimson Lake. God bless me, what opulence there is in the sound ! The case (casket is the worthier word) that contained it was always the first through which the white metal began to show when the vein was beginning to be worked out. For Crimson Lake would not keep. It was always laid on thick, with as little water in the brush as possible. Only the other day I came on an extremely early production of my own, a picture of the Forty Thieves, or as many of them as could be got into the paper. They all wear jackets of Crimson Lake, painted without the slightest regard to economy. They must almost have exhausted my store in one fit of profligate splendour, but there is an unctuousness of brush work about the picture that made it worth while.

Very splendid also were gold and silver paint. They were not to be found in the ordinary paint box and must be acquired separately at great cost, but they were essential to those who painted coats of arms. When the heraldry book prescribed *argent* it was a miserable business merely to leave the paper uncoloured or to resort, as a make-shift, to white paint ; nor was there in the box any yellow that made even a passable substitute for gold. A bend or a chevron *or* must not be so insulted. Far better give it up and fall back on the flags of all nations (which by the way make very pretty painting), than to desecrate the lovely, simple arms of Clare or the gorgeous complexities of Magdalene with common yellow paint.

To think of colleges is instinctively to turn to colours in the plural, which I have loved ever since I was first taken to the May Races and studied them, set out in language of magenta and old gold on the race card. To-day they must surely have reached their zenith and so may be near their decline, for there is scarcely an institution in the country that does not flaunt its colours. " Upon my life," said Miss Mowcher as she exhibited the trophies of her art, " the whole social system (as the men call it when they make speeches in Parliament) is a system of Prince's nails ! " And much the same may now be said of colours. They make a fascinating study and I am unashamedly an addict and a collector ; nor is this, I will maintain, in any way a disgraceful confession, so long as the collector is prepared to laugh at himself. Colours are not to be taken too seriously. I admit that there is hardly any sum of money which would tempt me to be seen in a colour to which I am not entitled, and there are many who share the feeling. But that is our own little absurdity which does no one any harm, as long as we remember that this is a free country in which the wearing of colours has not yet been controlled and a man may wear what tie he pleases. The nameless person stands gibbeted for ever who accused the wearer of a Guards' tie (or, in another version, that of I Zingari) of pirating the colours of the Upper Tooting Bicycle Club. And justly so if we execrate him for the right cause. His crime lay not in his ignorance of the Guards' colours : why should he know them ? It lay in his believing colours to be solemn and sacrosanct things.

That little homily disposed of, we can approach the subject frankly and freely. If ever I meet any one wearing a tie that appears to stand for something more than his private fancy, I make a practice of asking him what it means. Thus I hope agreeably to flatter the wearer and at the same time to increase my own stock of knowledge. The number of ties is so vast that the garner of memory cannot hold all its store. Yet some of the information sticks and may create a bond, or, if not that, a topic of conversation. The story is well known, at least to readers of *The Wrong Box*, of the two men who were sitting next to one another on the top of an omnibus. As they passed the Athenæum one of them murmured dreamily, " The Athenæum ! Golly, what a club ! " " My dear sir," exclaimed the other, " I perceive you are a Wrong Boxer." And they became fast friends ever afterwards. So with ties, to be able to say to a man, " Sir, I see you are a Boojum," or " A Goosler, unless I am much mistaken," makes an excellent opening.

At the same time it is rash to speak unless we are quite sure, for ties are very like one another and nobody enjoys being mistaken for somebody else. " Once when I was very young," said Sherlock Holmes, apropos of type, " I confused the *Leeds Mercury* with the *Western Morning News*." Similarly I confess to having had my doubts between Old Rugbeians and Old Cliftonians. Of course there are numerous points of difference, but I have doubted. The pink stripe on the black ground in the ties of the Old Westminsters differ in shade from that of the Old Cheltonians but may deceive the superficial observer. The Old Salopians and the Oxford Authentics, the Highland Brigade and the All England Lawn Tennis Club provide, as Holmes would say, parallel instances.

So it will be seen that there are many pitfalls for the unwary and these grow yearly more numerous. Only the other day I read of a new danger. The old boys of a certain school had suddenly woken up to the fact that owing to a hosier's error some of them were wearing their stripes in one order and others in exactly the opposite. Both parties presumably believed their version to be the correct one and neither wanted to buy a new tie. It was an impasse from which we can only hope some honourable way out was found. But the real difficulty about stripes is that, humanly speaking, all the possible permutations and combinations have now been exhausted, and the only resource left is the dotting of small objects in a specified pattern on a common background. I believe this happy thought first came to Vincent's Club at Oxford with their silver crowns on a ground of dark blue. By some incredible lapse of mind I once described them in print as silver lions, and it is never too late to apologise. That tie has opened up a new avenue. In my own tiny collection are lions, eagles, roses, bells, ships, saints, crosses, jugs and champagne bottles. I have seen, though I am not qualified to possess, elephants. Yet none of these pious imitations have ever quite come up to the original.

How happy then are the clubs of venerable standing who had the whole domain of colours open to them. The simplest coats of arms have always a severe beauty not to be equalled by the most intricate quarterings, and so it is with ties. The bold simple stripes are the best, such as the red, black and gold of I'Zingari. Incidentally, it is recorded that when the M.C.C. instituted their red and yellow stripes I Z. felt some indignation, since the new upstart colour worn on a black hat might be confused with their own. That mistake is not likely to be made again, for coloured ribbons on black hats are a thing of the past. Not such an incredibly distant past for all that, since at my private school we wore the black and yellow of Brasenose, our head master's college, round our bowlers. Even now I have some scruples of conscience at the recollection.

There are so many admirable colours of plain stripes that it would be impossible to name them all and invidious to name some. Yet I must put in a word for one to which I am myself entitled, though I never sat in a boat—the dark blue and silver of the illustrious Third Trinity Boat Club. It seems to me at once rich and austere. Now First and Third Trinity are fused and that colour will no more be freshly minted, but it is still mine to wear, at a safe distance from any river. One more, to my mind, " nice derangement " of stripes I can name with quite impartial admiration—the white, grey and black of, I believe, the Annandale at Balliol. There is about it a fine dignified sobriety. The more numerous and complicated the stripes, the less attractive as a rule are the colours, but there are exceptions to this rule and I will make so bold as to name as one example those of the Eton Ramblers. Stripes of purple, green and my old friend Crimson Lake, with a narrow line of yellow dividing them—they sound supremely hideous and in fact, they are generally admitted to be very pretty. And there are other colours to which the same remark applies ; mere description is utterly unjust to them. There are also some so repulsive that language fails in the other direction. I possess two radiant examples. One I have worn on a single occasion and on the other I have never ventured. Periodically they are thrown to the top of a jumble of ties in a drawer, as on the moraine of a glacier, and I turn shuddering away and bury them deep at the bottom again. Wild horses shall not drag from me their names, but I may say that one has now been superseded and its successor is both quiet and charming.

Colours have now become such an institution in this country that they seem to date back to a time beyond the memory of man. So, in a sense, I suppose they do, for the Knights Challengers in the tournament in *Ivanhoe* had their colours of russet and black. But as we know them to-day they are comparatively modern. Tom Hughes, writing of the football of his time at school, said with something very like scorn : " There is none of the colour and tastiness of get-up, you will perceive, which lends such a life to the present game at Rugby, making the dullest and worst-fought match a pretty sight." There were no plush caps and no uniform of any kind except the white trousers of the School-house, " But," he added, " we mean business, gentlemen." Well, business first and colours afterwards is a good sound motto, and business must be very good nowadays if we are ever to afford new ties. The one we first put on " That day we overcame the Nervii " is becoming terribly dingy, but at least it is still there in the drawer.

P.S. It will, I trust, be observed that I have not used that most detestable word in the English language—" colourful."

Instruction with Amusement

"'Peter, my boy,' said Compton festively, 'what do you say to this? If you will give me a guinea now, I will give you one thousand guineas on your wedding day.' 'Agreed,' cried Peter, and paid down the guinea, which Compton pocketed, thinking it good business." Was there ever a better beginning? How admirable an example of cutting the cackle and coming to the horses! With his very first sentence the author plunges into the very heart of the story. A whole picture leaps instantly to the reader's mind. He can see Mr. Peter and Mr. Compton—they lived in the seventeenth century—a little flushed and confused in their intellects after much friendly passing of the bottle, but each sufficiently master of himself to think that he has done the other in a highly satisfactory manner. And yet the sentence is culled from no work of fiction but from a dissertation on the Statute of Frauds and agreements not to be performed within the space of one year. The author is the late Mr. Walter Shirley and the book is his immortal *Leading Cases in the Common Law*.

My own copy, now in a somewhat disintegrated condition,

bears on its first page my name, followed by the words, " Trinity College, Cambridge," and it must have been acquired about the year 1896. For some twelve years after that date I studied the law with a temperate fervour, and yet such fragments of it as I still retain I owe almost entirely to Mr. Shirley. All else has vanished, but him I can still quote with reasonable accuracy and can pore over his book if not with profit at least with pleasure. He must have been a great man and as such I take leave to introduce him to any reader who knows even less law than I do.

No one ever succeeded so perfectly in blending instruction with amusement. He adopted a style which should in his own words " arrest the attention, aid the memory and make the study of the law less dry and repulsive," and nobly he succeeded. To him may be applied his own description of the gentleman in Scott *v.* Shepherd who threw a lighted squib into a crowded market house and so ultimately put out another gentleman's eye—" a man not destitute of humour." His humour tended towards the deliberately facetious. Admittedly also he sometimes wrote what is to-day called " journalese." But what if he did ? Did not an even greater humourist once refer to a hot-piemen as a " heated pastry-vendor," and do we not love him for it ? If Mr. Shirley likes to say of a ship that sank that it " had gone to the mermaids," why shouldn't he ? I protest that when a writer so gloriously attains the object he sets out to achieve, we must not be too priggish as to the means.

Let us try to see how he did it. He was essentially terse and he did not stick at a trifle. If he thought a case tiresome as in Bickerdike *v.* Bollman (the reader will forgive my particularity) he did not hesitate to say that " the narrative was too complicated to be worth giving," and simply gave its effect. Yet he could always find room for the three or four unnecessary but felicitous words which fixed the case for ever in the mind. He put himself in the student's place and made just the comment on the case that would have occurred to that young person. He sympathised with the lay mind and if he never

said the law was an ass he sometimes delicately implied it.
Take the famous case of Coggs *v.* Bernard. Coggs wanted some
hogsheads of brandy moved ; Bernard undertook to do it for
nothing and did it so badly that some of the brandy was lost.
Then, says Mr. Shirley, " Coggs was not pleased ; and as he
successfully maintained an action against Bernard for damages,
probably that gentleman never again volunteered rash acts of
friendship." That last sentence is strictly irrelevant and yet
how perfectly to the point ! The reader does not thereupon
know all about the law of bailment, a dreary subject to which
several more pages are devoted, but he has ever more before
his eyes a picture of Bernard telling all his friends in the city
what a dirty dog was Coggs. Something at least of the duties
of a bailee remain to him. The ordinary law reporter is a
miserable, unimaginative creature who is content with the
dry facts. Not so Mr. Shirley who never forgets the human
feelings of the parties. " Keech was very indignant ; "
" Thereupon the wrath of the College of Corpus Christi was
kindled "—these are happy little touches which make all the
difference. Even the lamentable subject of stoppage in transitu,
is cheered and lightened by the statement that the holders of
a bill of lading " rose to the occasion." Best of all in this
category is a little gem of eight words in Mountstephen *v.*
Lakeman. A certain Board gave notice to neighbouring house-
holders that they must connect the drains of their houses with
the main sewer or the Board would do it for them at their
expense. What could be duller and drier than that ? But see
how Mr. Shirley rises to the occasion. He says that the Board
did it " in the usual peremptory manner of local authorities."
Instantly the case comes alive. The reader's smouldering
hatred of bureaucracy leaps into flame ; he thinks of coupons,
of basic petrol, of tart young ladies on the telephone, of that
confounded Council that bothered him about cutting down
an overhanging branch. His sympathies are instantly and
warmly engaged on the part of Mr. Mountstephen, the builder,
and against Mr. Lakeman, the Chairman of the Board. He

rejoices that Lakeman had to pay, and so remembers how the base creature tried to get out of paying under the Statute of Frauds and why he was deservedly foiled.

Sometimes Mr. Shirley is amusing and sarcastic. At others he appeals rather to our love of the mysterious and the sublime, casting

O'er the dim page a gloom, a glamour.

By an apparently casual phrase he invites us to consider the darker, the more romantic possibilities of our society. The name of Mr. Gandasequi, " A Spanish Merchant," revives in my breast an ancient thrill—Hidalgos and toreadors and castanets—but perhaps this is a merely personal enthusiasm. At any rate, every one must fall under the spell of " a Leicester-shire baronet " in Cornfoot *v.* Fowke. A baronet by himself would be nothing ; it is the county that is so magical. Was not Sir Leicester Dedlock a Lincolnshire baronet and Sir Pitt Crawley a Hampshire baronet ? I like to think that this one may have hunted in Leicestershire when the famous Squire was Master of the Quorn. The dates make it at least con-ceivable. His christian name is not given but Fowke is in itself full of possibilities. Sir John Fowke would be good ; Sir Theodosius or Sir Emilius perhaps better still. Thackeray, an inspired artist in such matters, would have christened him by an uniquely apt surname, but I have no such gift. And yet what of Sir Harbottle Fowke ? I may be flattering myself, but that seems in the right tradition. At any rate, Mr. Shirley has given me a minute or two of unalloyed happiness in the exercise of my poor invention.

Moreover, that vision of a baronet galloping over midland meadows does not stand alone. There are other cases in which by a homelier title he can conjure up green lanes and woods, and a pleasant rustic England. Farmer Norton, Farmer Jordan, Farmer Wadsworth and Farmer Wigglesworth all play their parts, and above all there is Farmer Whitacre, whom

I love. "Farmer Whitacre," said the cunning Thornborow, "let us strike a bargain. If I pay you a five-pound note down now, will you give me two rye corns next Monday, four on Monday week, eight on Monday fortnight, and so on— doubling it every Monday for a year?" The poor innocent farmer found that he would have to deliver more rye than was grown in a year in all England, but fortunately for him the case was settled. I have introduced Farmer Whitacre for the particular reason that Mr. Tony Weller came near to being the victim of much the same manœuvre at the hands of Mr. Stiggins. "Borrows eighteenpence on Monday," Mr. Weller explained, "and comes on Tuesday for a shillin' to make it up to half-a-crown ; calls again on Vensday for another half-crown to make it five shillin's ; and goes on doubling till he gets it up to a five-pound note in no time, like them sums in the 'rithmetic book 'bout the nails in the horse's shoes, Sammy." I like to think that this celebrated arithmetical problem was originally founded on the machinations of Thornborow.

So much for Mr. Shirley's skilful use of men's names and occupations. Now let us turn to him in another mood, in which he gives to some of his characters symbolical names, somewhat in the manner of *The Pilgrim's Progress*. The best known example is to be found in Birkmyr *v.* Darnell, though in this case the joke may have originated before his time. "My friend, Mr. Lightfinger, wants a horse ; will you lend him yours?" said Darnell to Birkmyr, and the rest of the story need scarcely be told, for Mr. Lightfinger, true to his name, rode away and never came back. In another case—Bickerdike *v.* Bollman before mentioned—Mr. Shirley invents a series of imaginary persons to illustrate the perils of backing a friend's bill. First of all there is Mr. Spendfast, a young gentleman constantly in want of money. Then there is Mr. Lighthead, a weak, good-natured person always ready to do a friend a turn without counting the cost. He is assured by Spendfast that the whole affair is a mere formality and that he will never be called on, and so accepts the bill. Thirdly, there is Mr.

Thriftman, a more calculating and sinister character, into whose hands the bill ultimately falls. He sued Spendfast for the money, but it seems unlikely that he ever got it. I must not forget that too much married young lawyer Mr. Benedict, who was sued by jewellers and milliners for the debts of his extravagant wife. Here again, however, I think the joke was not Mr. Shirley's own, but that of Benedict's brethren in the law, who, in their reports and the kindness of their hearts, veiled him and his misfortunes under an alias.

I have but skimmed a little of the rich cream off Mr. Shirley. I could go on for ever, as, for instance, to the tempestuous gentleman, who rather than wait an hour at York ordered a special train to Scarborough ; but perhaps the reader may not share my passion. So I will give but two more instances of his skill. One is from Lampleigh *v.* Brathwait which has fully as good a beginning as Peter *v.* Compton— " Brathwait having committed a murder." That is stark and splendid, and now for my favourite among all his cases, Mitchel *v.* Reynolds. Here his method is different ; he allows himself a little embroidery or local colour in approaching his subject. " Leading eastwards from the Grays Inn Road," he begins, " is, or till recently was, a street called Liquorpond Street." There's a lovely name for you, to start with. He goes on to tell how there lived in that street a baker who " baked himself a fortune " and retired, selling his business to the plaintiff with a covenant not to bake again for five years in the parish of St. Andrews, Holborn. Then comes utter tragedy, the tragedy of those who retire too soon and feel time heavy on their hands. " His fingers were everlastingly itching to be in the pudding, and the end of it was that long before the five years were out he was baking away as hard as ever." He had to pay, which was doubtless right and proper, but it is impossible not to feel sorry for him. He was a martyr to the love of his art and if Liquorpond Street were still there I would pay a pilgrimage to his shrine.

I cannot for the life of me refrain from ending with a

Every Idle Dream

general and heartfelt tribute to Mr. Shirley. He was to my mind that very rare thing a great teacher. He knew how to allure his pupils. People with that gift are often ungratefully called crammers. I sat in my youth, at a private school, at the feet of one who was sometimes so termed by less successful rivals. He had an instinct for the sort of thing that would be asked by examiners for scholarships. Even at the very last moment, at breakfast of the appointed day, he would " pass round " to his young team some possible question with its answer, and behold there it was in the paper. But apart from that almost uncanny gift he had a far more permanently valuable one ; he could make boys think lessons the most thrilling of all amusements and the examination itself a splendid adventure. Half an hour's Latin grammar before breakfast has to-day a gloomy sound, and yet we went to it as to an exciting treat, revelling in the irregular behaviour of *jecur* and *supellex*. In short, he made us happy and interested.

Mr. Shirley seems to me to have the same gift. His picturesque phrases serve much more than the purpose of a mere *memoria technica*. His work is like that of the private schoolmaster in that he does not profess to do more than put his pupils on the right road. But he sends them off on that long, hard road of the law with gay hearts. For a little while at least they will think it is " all wery capital." Subsequent experience may temper that agreeable illusion, but well begun is half done and he has done his very best for them. As the most utterly " stickit " of barristers I pay him my devoted compliments and hope to browse happily on his pages again and again. If I still like listening to legal " shop," as I do, it is not due to my own wig and gown, sold forty years ago now, but to him. " Nobody but Pell——" said Mr. Weller senior, " nobody but Pell as a legal adwiser." For me there can be nobody but Shirley.

At the Junction

JUNCTION is an ugly word nor are junctions superficially beautiful places. The thought of them suggests the partial decay of that blessed institution, the through carriage, which used to carry us almost from door to door. It brings back memories of the agonies of Bradshaw and of cross-country journeys, of clambering up stairs and crossing bridges, of the frantic fussing after luggage and the cold-hearted calmness of porters with which it is received, of the solacing of the long wait with an arid bun and a sloppy cup of tea.

There are junctions of various kinds, from the great and busy to the tiny and deserted. Some appear to be junctions and nothing else, with no other object in life than to make us unpack ourselves and begin all over again. There are doubtless people who live at Bletchley, who when they get there know that their troubles are at an end and that they will soon be eating crumpets and toasting their toes before their own fire ; but to the great mass of travellers its name suggests nothing but changing, and even the fact that it is the half-way house between Oxford and Cambridge does not materially lighten its gloom. Then there are junctions—I have in my mind's eye two in Wales—where the traveller can only get out to get in again. If on some sudden impulse he decides to alight for any other purpose, such as exploring the country, he will be disappointed, for there is no road to or from that junction ; he is a prisoner, cut off on all sides ; he must either pace the platform till he sinks down and dies of old age at last, or he must own himself beaten and get into another train.

About such a junction as this there is, to be sure, a very soothing and peaceful atmosphere, which is to be experienced at its best perhaps on a Sunday afternoon. One train has gone, there will not be another for several hours ; the ticket office is shut ; the station-master in his gold hat has gone to cultivate his garden, and perfect tranquillity reigns. The idle metals go shining away in perspective, knowing that no distant puff of smoke above the trees will come to disturb them. There is not even a clanking of trucks on a siding ; they have all tucked themselves up to sleep under their mackintosh covers, and the lonely traveller, the only living thing in the landscape, feels a growing fear that he too must stay there for the night. It may be that it is a hot, drowsy afternoon, filled with " all the live murmur of a summer day," and in that case the traveller may yield himself up to its influence, or might if the seat were not so hard. But it must be admitted that this is not the sort of day on which we picture a junction. We think of it in a piercing wind or lashed by rain, not a straightforward rain that is intercepted by the roof, technically and humorously called the verandah, but slanting rain that attacks us on our own unprotected level. There are grateful exceptions to every rule, and I have once at least found a truly noble fire in a junction waiting-room, in which I read a considerable part of a Trollope novel during a little wait of two hours and a half. But too often a junction is a cavern of the winds, so that there are other memories of hiding from the blast behind an automatic machine, the last and slender refuge of the destitute. At such a moment, even the cold, clear voice, apparently from heaven, that articulates so beautifully, would be welcome, though it inevitably announced someone else's train, but that is never heard at the remote and solitary junction really worthy of the name. Only the sound of his own footsteps disturbs the traveller's despairing reverie.

It may appear from these remarks that I have no liking for junctions, but all that has gone before has been but an elaborate pretence, a mask for my true feelings. In fact, I have, not indeed for all, but for some junctions a sentimental affection beyond words. Their names sound in my ears as chimes, ringing me home to my own country. It is a singular fact that there is nearly always a junction on the way to the best beloved of golf courses, and it comes very nearly at the end of the journey. We have already worked ourselves up into a state of some excitement, looking out of the window for landmarks and up into the rack to be sure our clubs are still there, and then comes the change, which turns excitement into ecstasy. A change half-way through the journey is of no comfort at all ; it is merely a nuisance, but when the porter's cry is as the bell that announces to the weary runner the last lap, it is music indeed.

These entries to their respective paradises have no notably divine qualities in themselves, being for the most part drab and dingy enough ; they are gateways and no more. Yet to those who know them, each has some definite character of its own. There is first of all, for it cannot possibly occupy any lower place, Leuchars, change for St. Andrews. There is about it, at any rate, for the southern pilgrim, something of the freshness of the morning. He has had his night in the sleeping car (supposing those civil servants with their confounded " priorities " have allowed him to get one) ; he has eaten his breakfast while crossing the Forth Bridge and snuffed the fragrance of linoleum with distended nostrils in Kirkcaldy station. Now he steps out to find the air more " snell "—or is it " caller " ?—than at home, and to wonder whether the wind will be slicing him into the whins on the way out or on the way home. That sudden stepping out into the Scottish air is the peculiar charm of Leuchars, though it belongs also in a high degree to Drem. There, in happy days, the train used to halt on the way to Edinburgh, and the golfer, feeling exceedingly ducal, if not regal, at having the train stopped for him " on request " at such a tiny wayside station, found a kind car awaiting him and drove away through stone walls and pleasant dull East Lothian meadows, to his breakfast at North Berwick.

Now to turn from north to south, there are two great gateways, one busy and bustling, the other rustic and peaceful : Ashford, change for Rye, and Minster, change for Sandwich. Perhaps it is cheating a little to include Minster, for the trains, or at any rate my train, has not gone that way for a long while now, but goes without a change by Dover and Deal. Yet I know I have been in old days by Minster. Certainly I did the very first time I ever went to Sandwich, and ate ham sandwiches on the platform in a state of suppressed excitement, so that I should not waste a minute before I dashed out on to the links in a blue serge suit to get in a round before dusk fell. So Minster and its church are for ever mingled in a romantic dream with a first sight of the tall trees round the clubhouse and the Maiden towering in the distance.

The Ashford change is much more familiar. Even as I write I am hoping to make it again, and shall take my clubs with me for old sake's sake. On the surface there is nothing romantic about Ashford, but there is about the two ensuing stations which artfully enhance our sensations by a little delay, Ham Street, bowered in its orchards, and Appledore (change for New Romney) which provides yet another and subsidiary gateway for the golfers of Littlestone. There are those, I believe, who reach Rye by Hastings, and I have even condescended to return that way when romance is temporarily dead ; but there is only one way to go there. What would life be without Ham Street and the first sight of Romney Marsh and its lonely little farms and its sheep and its intersecting dykes, and the torpid, muddy waters of the Rother ?

There is a decency of tradition in these matters that must be observed.

Now we must flit for a moment to the noble golfing counties of Lancashire and Cheshire. In Lancashire there is Preston, change for St. Annes. It cannot be denied that what they actually say is " Change for Blackpool," but we, who have no desire to go to Blackpool, and should do so indeed with a perceptible shrinking, we know that St. Annes is on the way there. We know too that when we stop at Ansdell and begin to take our belongings down from the rack, we shall see the little short hole at the far end and shall continue our way along the course, so close to it that already, with a fearful joy, we see ourselves slicing into the line on the morrow.

And so to Cheshire and Hoylake, and here again I must be a little dishonest. To-day, unless my memory fails me, we get into a train at the Central Station in Liverpool which takes us in a relatively swift and quite unbroken journey to the shrine of John Ball. But it was not always so. Once we changed at Birkenhead Park, and we said to our porter at the Central, " Change at Park, I suppose ; " not that we were in any doubt but because we wanted to show that we knew the ropes, and that abbreviated " Park " was essentially knowing. In those days the Park station had a gateway feeling which a great big, bustling Central can never afford. Perhaps it is on that account, and because the old steam train rumbled and bumbled along so slowly, that Bidston and Moreton and Meols—I remember their names if not their order—had a sacred character that is no longer quite what it was.

Lastly, I come to the best of all junctions. I have seen it looming in the distance all the time, and so, I fear, must any one who has ever read any book of mine. I need scarcely say that it is Dovey Junction where there is, in a Stevensonian phrase, an infinite melancholy piping of porters : " Change for Aberdovey, Towyn and Barmouth way." There is, I think, something about the Welsh voice, or intonation, which has a natural melancholy. When the little boys at Moat Lane

Junction cry, or used to cry before the days of sweet rationing, " Papers, chocolates, cigarettes," it was with an unutterable sadness. So at Aberdovey, when the caddie, perched on the sleepered crest of the Cader bunker, announces, " On the green," it is not in a tone of triumphant delight but rather of resignation to inevitable fate. It is only when the cry is, " In the bunker," that a measure of cheerfulness seems to break in. I write in the present tense, but alas ! it should be in the past, for the more sophisticated caddies of to-day remain silent and only signal our fortune, good or bad, with the hand. At any rate, the porters at Dovey Junction make no invidious distinctions. They always sound heart-broken and our hearts almost burst with joy as we hear them.

There is much to be said for the journeys to these places of pilgrimage by road instead of rail, and there are villages on the way that have something of that heralding beauty. To Sandwich there are Littlebourne, Wingham and Ash ; to Rye, Peasmarsh and Rye Foreign—surely a name of unexampled charm. The whole road to Wales, once we have entered the Cotswolds, is one long eagerness of looking forward, enchantingly delayed. Yet, on the whole, for the absolute of poignancy, there is nothing like that last change at a good, old-fashioned, uncomfortable, draughty junction.

The Jubilee of a Society

IN the United States are many country clubs, but there is one at Brookline in Massachusetts that is called The Country Club. Nor is that name given it merely for the sake of brevity or honour : it is its official title. When it was founded it was the only one of its kind, and, though it has had innumerable imitators all over that vast continent, it is rightly proud of its name, so " simply and severely great," and scorns any more local designation. It is thus that we, who are its members, speak simply of " The Society." We have not so legitimate excuse, for our full name is " The Oxford and Cambridge Golfing Society," but that is too large a mouthful, and moreover ours is so far like The Country Club that it is the eldest of a great family. The word " society " was applied to golf clubs long before we were born or thought of. That charming and familiar picture of William Innes by Lemuel Abbot is dedicated " To the Society of Golfers at Blackheath." But our Society gave the word a new meaning. It has come to signify a body of golfers—nay, I will be honest and say predatory golfers—bound together by some link, educational (at least by courtesy), professional, regional or merely friendly, that is as a cuckoo among clubs, having no nest of its own and descending periodically on those of other people.

1948 is our jubilee year and the modest seed planted by John Low and Arthur Croome, at a dinner at Oxford fifty years ago, has produced not merely one fine beanstalk but numberless others that have grown up under its shadow. I am one of the now small and diminishing band who have O.M. written after their names in our roll. That does not imply, I hasten to add, any encroachment on the prerogative of our patron the King in respect to the Order of Merit. It signifies no more than fortunate survival, and stands for " Original Member." As, moreover, I have the great and pleasant honour of being its President in this anniversary year, the least I can do, from the great love I bear it, is to pay the Society my humble tribute.

Fifty years is a long time whether to look back or forward. To those who were at that Oxford dinner it would, if they had given the matter a thought, have seemed a wild dream that they would one day be acclaiming this jubilee. " The thoughts of youth are long, long thoughts," but not quite so long as that. To the survivors of to-day it is equally fantastic, though very pleasant, to reflect that the present undergraduate members, or some of them, will in 1998 be acclaiming the Society's Centenary. " Feeble of limb and rheumatic of shoulder " perhaps, but there, please heaven, they will be, on the edge of the year 2000, thinking much what we their predecessors are thinking now.

The conception of a nomadic band was not of course original. It had occurred to the players of other games. The cricketers have been wandering for years seeking whom and what they might devour. So have those distinguished football players, the Corinthians and the Barbarians, and all manner of " old boy " clubs. But in golf this notion of living on the land was as new as it was luminous. What, in Sam Weller's phrase, " a fat and happy living " it has been ! It is utterly impossible to be emphatic enough as to the kindness of our many hosts, and all the good fun and good golf we have had and the good friends we have made. Some people are born hosts and others guests ; we are indisputably and unashamedly guests, and the most we can hope is that we have been good ones. Grateful ones we assuredly are.

It may be that if our founders had not had this notion somebody else would ; but, however that may be, we have not lacked for imitators, and they, it is to be hoped, have had the same sort of fun as we have, though we shall never believe it to have been quite such transcendent fun. It was natural that all the old boys of all the schools should come in time to band themselves together for golf as for other games, and they have had an immense piece of fun in that great annual festival at Deal which owes its existence to Mr. Halford Hewitt, himself a member of the Society. For a combination of general friendliness and frantic school patriotism there is nothing like it. It has long since founded a tradition of its own, and the streets of Deal are yearly beflagged to welcome it. There is another respect in which our emulators have, as Sherlock Holmes would say, " broken fresh ground " in the annals of— well, no, not of crime, but of unblushing invasion. There is to-day hardly a profession, however recondite, that has not its golfing society, to swoop at intervals on the course of some amiable club. Only one profession, as far as I know, has not done so, and that is oddly enough the one whose members have long since obtained a reputation second to none for descending in hordes, whether on golf courses or on Hellenic cruises. Need I add that it is the Schoolmasters' ? So far they have, with an instinctive delicacy, abstained. And every one of these marauding bands has its colours. If the makers of ties rejoice, as they must, over a small but by no means negligible increase in profits, it is hardly too much to say that they have us indirectly to thank for it.

The original notion was then, obviously, a happy one, and in the Society's case, apart from many separate and agreeable matches, it has taken the form of tours to different golfing neighbourhoods, or, as they would to-day be called, zones. I know I have written of these tours before, and will therefore show a noble restraint or at least a tolerable brevity.

The greatest enterprise was that to the United States in 1903. It was on returning from it that our Captain, John Low, uttered his warning to beware of our coming conquerors from America. " Already," he exclaimed, in prophetic tones, " I hear the hooting of their steamers in the Mersey." Of that adventure I cannot write at first hand, but as to our more domestic ones I cannot wholly refrain, for the very word " tour " brings a whole series of pictures before my eyes, in particular from three hospitable regions. First come our oldest friends and opponents of all, in Lancashire and Cheshire. St. Annes, Formby, Hoylake, and later Birkdale—I put them in that order because that was the chronological sequence of our visits. They are all seen impartially now through a dim, beautiful haze of potted shrimps and blue Cheshire cheese, and of one thing more, hero-worship. Only those who went on our earliest tours there can fully realise what it meant to see for the first time, and even possibly to encounter, John Ball, Harold Hilton and Jack Graham. That was indeed " an awfully big adventure." To see Mr. Janion, in his invariable black and white check, walking with extreme deliberation to the notice board in the hall at Hoylake to affix to it the order of battle, and then to see one's own name opposite that of one of the great ones—that was at once to touch the stars with uplifted head and to taste an utter abasement of terror and humility.

Then there was the Scottish tour, also with its heroes to encounter—Maxwell, Laidlay, Leslie Balfour. That tour has become more and more strenuous as kind hosts have multiplied. First it was only to that circuit of famous courses in the Lothians, Muirfield, Luffness and North Berwick. Next there was added Gullane, and golf has no greater view to show than that from the top of Gullane Hill with the Forth Bridge, gaunt, angular and majestic in the distance. To think of it is to hear the curlews calling and calling in one's ears. Then to the east was

added the west with its equally great links that cluster so
thickly, cheek by jowl on the coast of Ayrshire : Prestwick,
Prestwick St. Nicholas, Troon and finally Western Gailes,
where we once met, and even defeated by a single shaky but
successful putt, the illustrious 32 Club, the picked men of
the west. As a separate enterprise too we have had the unique
honour of playing the Royal and Ancient at St. Andrews, an
almost too fraternal conflict, since so many were eligible for
both sides. Once too—alas, that I was not there—our team
made a pious pilgrimage to see the glory that was Musselburgh,
played there with gutty balls and had the ever famous Bob
Ferguson to carry our Captain's clubs.

Scotland is certainly rich in memories, and so is Ireland.
Portmarnock, Dollymount, and Newcastle—what a trinity of
fine courses ! I metaphorically drink their healths in the good
Benedictine to be for ever associated with them. In particular
I see myself in imagination sailing across to Portmarnock on
a windy, sleety March morning and profoundly thanking
heaven that the crossing was no longer. To-day we drive
prosaically round by motor car to that enchanted spot, but the
old island magic remains.

So much for our pleasures for which we owe so great a
debt to other people. Have we done anything at all to deserve
them ? I like to think that we have, though this may be a
vain delusion, and whatever it may be, it is very hard to
define. It is perhaps too portentous to say that our founders,
whom we others have tried to follow, faint but pursuing, stood
for a way of golfing life, and yet I scarcely know how else to
put it.

John Low, our first Captain, and Arthur Croome, his
faithful disciple and our Secretary, were steeped in the best
traditions of the older golf and resolutely preached and
maintained them. They had a great feeling for the dignity
of the game, though it never caused them for a moment to
lose their sense of humour. I have never known any man who
so perfectly combined, as did John Low, the serious and the

festive in golf. To serve under his banner was to learn, or at any rate to try to learn, valuable lessons. One, very salutary for the self-important, was absolute obedience in taking the place assigned to you and not merely never to whisper but never to think that it ought to have been a higher one. Another, which I fear I never wholly learnt, indeed I know I have not, I can best indicate by a reproof he once gently administered. I had written of some match as a great " fight," and he disapproved that word ; it never ought to be more than a game. He lived up to that precept himself. However hard he played, and he could be very solemn and take sometimes an exhausting infinity of pains, it remained a game with no touch of bitterness or hostility. He played it with a cheerful gravity and in a spirit that I can only describe as knightly. It was a demeanour as hard to attain as was his inimitable gaiety when the match (I had nearly written " fight " again) was over ; but at least his example was good for us all. If he was a staunch conservative, who did not like overmuch some modern development in the way of " popularising " golf, I am myself enough of a conservative to think that in that respect too he was good for us and for the game in general.

So far I have spoken of comparatively vague and intangible things, but there is one perfectly definite benefit that I dare to believe the Society has conferred on a wider world, again through the efforts of our founders. That is the spreading of the gospel of foursomes. At the end of last century foursomes had fallen from the high estate they had once held. Whether this was the fault of English golfers I am not prepared to say but it was certainly a fact. When we first went touring in the North of England, we were apt to play our matches by thirty-six hole singles ; it was good discipline, there could be no doubt, but it was comparatively cheerless. John, as a good Scotsman, loved the foursome for its own sake, and loved to play it with an elaborate taking council between partners. Further, a foursome was unquestionably the friendlier game after lunch and made for a better mingling of the opposing sides. Our leaders gently, tactfully but persistently insinuated these views and in course of time they prevailed, so that now, and for a long time past, foursomes have formed an integral part of all the Society's matches. And not only that, but the fire thus kindled spread over England and various foursome competitions were instituted. The Halford Hewitt Cup furnishes the most conspicuous example. I know that to-day there is once more a movement in favour of thirty-six hole singles, which are unquestionably good practice for the Walker Cup. They have a fine, hardening effect. But *neque semper arcum*, etc. ; I think these high principles can sometimes be carried too far. At any rate, on a tour which is just serious enough but not too unutterably so, a foursome enhances the vital element of friendliness and makes golf more of a team game. And heaven knows a foursome can be stern enough. The man who thinks of it merely as a post-prandial amusement has never tasted its ardours and delights ; indeed he has never played a real foursome in all his life.

So far I have been expounding what may be termed the external relations of the Society, and saying that perhaps we have done a little good in return for so much received. I may have imagined a vain thing, though I hope not. When it comes to our internal affairs, and in particular to our President's Putter, I am on sure ground. We have at least done each other a vast deal of good, and as for that festival of Rye, I believe that all who have ever been there are agreed that there are no other such days in the whole year. Here too we have abundant reason to be thankful, for the Rye Golf Club has allowed us to regard that noble links as in some sort our home course, and if each of us has one home of his own he has come to regard this as his second. At Rye we are " all together and nobody by," and the full tide of our communal life surges round the billiard room at the Dormy House. If that be too possessive a statement may it be forgiven !

We have often been deemed insane in choosing the stormy month of January for this our serious frolic, and we have assuredly taken risks. But though we have been battered by wind and rain and have twice played on ground stony hard with frost we have been spared the snow. Since 1920, only the war has broken the sequence. Darkness has once driven the finalists to retire, still locked in a deadly embrace, at the twenty-fourth hole and share the honours for the year, but no malignity of weather has ever caused the putting off of a single round or a single match. Providence has been wonderfully kind and has benignantly justified the risk we ran. And the fact that there are no other lunatics to hold a tournament in January has ensured that, humanly speaking, all our best men take the field.

To be sure the wind does blow cold and fierce, and Rye is at no time a course for weaklings. It makes considerable demands on the manhood to set out, if the draw so decrees, at soon after eight on a bitter winter's morning. Yet contrast can afford some of the intensest satisfactions of life, and these very hardships out of doors give to our indoor hours an almost unequalled glory of snugness. In a Pickwickian sense, not in the usually accepted meaning of the words, but in a strictly literal one, the Dormy House fire takes on a glow such as was never seen on land or sea. To stand before it after that battle with the elements, is to feel like Mr. Pickwick at Manor Farm when he exclaimed in the fullness of his heart, " This is indeed comfort." I have tried to say something of what we owe to our earliest leaders. There is much that could be said of those who in later years have slaved for us in many ways, and in particular over this Rye carnival ; but I am not sure that they would like me to say it. We all know who they are and they know that we are not unmindful of them. So I will not carry my catalogue of gratitude into the realm of the present.

There is one other thing ; perhaps it is superfluous and yet I want to say it. Since on two days of the year, the days of the University Match, I am, however unjustly, regarded as a gross and unbridled partisan, it becomes me to say it as well as another. The Society achieves the complete and perfect fusion of Oxford and Cambridge. Once a man belongs to it we forget to which University he belonged. There was a time when we had an afternoon to spare after the tournament was over and filled it by a foursome match between Oxford and Cambridge. Now there is no time to spare and that match is no more. It was played in the most fraternal spirit, but even so, to my mind at least, it jarred a little, and I think we are all glad that even that simulacrum of hostility is gone. One and indivisible may the Society flourish, and may those still sprightly old gentlemen of 1998 have a good dinner !

Father and Son

IT is an accepted fact that until the fifth number the fate of Pickwick hung in the balance. Neither the booksellers nor the general mass of readers had as yet appreciated its greatness. With that fifth number came Sam Weller and with him began to surge the vast wave of popularity. So it is an historic moment when Sam is discovered hard at work on the boots at the White Hart, and " Ask number twenty-two wether he'll have 'em now, or wait till he gets 'em," becomes one of the decisive speeches of the world. Yet to many people, all of them Sam's devoted admirers, it seems a still more transcendent moment when in the inn out of Cheapside a hoarse voice emerges from a cloud of shawls and smoke, slowly uttering the words, " Wy, Sammy ! "

Not until the book has run rather more than a third of its course are we introduced to the colossal figure of Mr. Tony Weller. Had Dickens thought of him earlier, he might have driven the Commodore Coach to Rochester, and we should not have had to wait for him for over three hundred pages. That is a saddening reflection, but we must be thankful for what we have. For all we know he may have been at first a suddenly improvised creation, a mere fill-up between the visit to Dodson and Fogg and that to the Magpie and Stump. At any rate, the inspiration was one of profoundest genius. *Filius pulcher, pater pulchrior.* Great as is Sam, he is not, to my mind at least, of the towering stature of his father. He may have grown to it in the end ; visdom may have come with vidth, as his parent prophesied ; but, judging them as we know them, there is an oracular quality about the father, an orotundity, an overpowering dignity which the son never attains. Sam has many delightful and admirable qualities but set beside that great creature he seems to shrink into the bright little Cockney. Even that particular form of expression generally known as a Wellerism, which has contributed to Sam's fame, was probably derived from his father. " I'm pretty tough," exclaimed Mr. Weller on one occasion, " that's vun consolation, as the wery old turkey remarked wen the farmer said he wos afeerd he should be obliged to kill him for the London market." That is the sole example handed down to us, but Sam may have heard others in his boyhood and founded his own style accordingly. Of this gulf between them nobody is more intuitively concious than Sam himself for in nearly all their scenes together he allows his father to take the centre of the stage. He may so far forget himself as to call that father a " perwerse old file " or even, however regrettably, an " addle-headed old creetur," but he realises that, as Mr. Turveydrop would say, there are things—things out of his reach. At all other times he may reign supreme, but now he knows and keeps his place.

Before going further into the characters of this immortal pair, let us deal briefly with one palpable fiction, namely that Sam was not the only son of his father. It is founded on a too literal interpretation of a single sentence on Sam's first appearance. " Ah," says Mr. Perker, " you're a wag, a'nt you ? " to which Sam replies, " My eldest brother was troubled with that complaint, it may be catching—I used to sleep with him." Here is indeed a slender foundation on

239

which to build a heresy. Of course it was only part of Sam's essential waggishness. The two or more elder brothers are never heard of again for the reason that they never existed. Yet in case any one clings to them let me laboriously demolish his belief from the words of Mr. Weller Senior who ought to know. When referring to the designing nature of ladies and the impossibility of escaping them he observes, " I wos married fust, that way myself, sir, and Sammy wos the consekens o' the manoover." That is plain enough, but if more be required there is first of all the warning to Sam, solemnly and impressively given, that " the family name depends wery much upon you," and secondly, his statement that, when he is " took off the road " all his property will come to Sam.

Incidentally, Mr. Weller's hostility to matrimony showed some little ingratitude. He certainly had a good deal to bear at times from his second wife, but he did uncommonly well out of both marriages. Sam's mother left him £400 and when he had realised the second Mrs. Weller's estate and sold the Marquis of Granby, he was altogether in possession of £1180. It was, also by the way, rather odd that, having already once been a legatee and attended Doctors' Commons, he had so completely forgotten all about the law of probate that he proposed to put his second wife's will into the fire.

That £1180 was a handsome sum of money, increased as it doubtless was by Mr. Pickwick's wise investment, for Mr. Weller, as far as we know, had begun life in quite humble circumstances. His education had been neglected since he always printed, having " learnt writin' from the large bills in the booking office." In mathematics his progress seems to have been more advanced, for he was acquainted with " them sums in the 'rithmetic book 'bout the nails in the horse's shoes." This was to be sure a problem that would naturally appeal to one of his tastes but how did he hear of it ? I find it hard to believe that he had studied to improve himself at evening classes. Some people may think that it was a lingering resentment at this lack of early opportunities that made his only political utterance of a distinctly radical nature. When Mr. Solomon Pell mentioned the Lord Chancellor's regrettable expression, " If I do, I'm damned," Mr. Weller appeared profoundly moved by the inequalities of human society and the licence allowed to the upper classes. " I say Parliament ought to have took it up," he exclaimed with heat, " and if he'd been a poor man they would ha' done it." There is no other evidence on the point, for, though we know that he accepted a twenty-pound note from one party at a previous Eatanswill election, to tip the opposing voters into a canal, we are not told which party it was. It may have been the Blues or it may have been the Buffs, and in either case he may not have allowed his political sentiments to interfere with his professional code of ethics. For my part, I shall always hold that too much weight must not be given to that one remark, that it was a sudden ebullition of feeling due to growing boredom with Mr. Pell's reminiscences, and that he was at bottom a good sound Tory.

One thing is certain, that Mr. Weller was perfectly well satisfied with his position in life. He laid no undue stress on it, but the fact that he once casually referred to himself as " the celebrated Mr. Weller of the Belle Savage " shows that he knew his own worth. He had no petty vanities and was one of the great men who take their own greatness for granted. And a stage coachman in his time was a great man. The dreadful day was coming when they would be deposed and driven off the road by the usurping railways, but it had not dawned yet. In his own words, a coachman was " a privileged indiwidual " and, if he drove long stages, possessed " insiniwations " that made him the object of universal respect and even adoration. Moreover, a coachman's wisdom was not confined to merely professional subjects. " A man," Mr. Weller laid down as a point of dogma, " as can form a ackerate judgment of a animal, can form a ackerate judgment of anything'," and Sam realised that this was one of the subjects, legal procedure being another, on which it was vain to argue.

This sureness of himself no doubt contributed to give Mr. Weller that unexampled dignity which was perhaps his strongest characteristic. He was a man with whom it was dangerous to take a liberty or attempt a correction. Mr. Pell twice tried it and retired abashed and beaten ; once when Mr. Weller demanded the " probe " of his wife's will, and once on the subject of the " prodigy son." On the one occasion Mr. ·Weller bluntly threatened to take his legal business elsewhere and on the other he remarked, " Never mind, sir, I know wot's o'clock, sir. When I don't, I'll ask you, sir." Who could stand against so crushing a rebuff? Certainly not Mr. Solomon Pell. It is worth noting the difference in Mr. Weller's manner when his son suggested " dispensation " instead of " dispensary." He was not in the least convinced, but he was not angry, saying that Sam could have it his own way, but that personally he called it a dispensary, and what was more it was always so described " at the places vere they gives you physic for nothin' in your own bottles." On any question of language Mr. Weller was decidedly sensitive, though he allowed his son some latitude. It is alarming to think what would have befallen Mr. Pell, if he had dared to say that " circumscribed " was as good a word as " circum-wented." He would have been blasted on the spot. To Sam his father indulgently admitted that it might have the advantage in tenderness, but that was for the sake of peace and quiet. Can it be doubted that he was of the same opinion still ?

That little argument about the dispensary is as good an illustration as need be of the relations between Sam and his father. They are charming and touching, only to be approached by those between the attractive little minx, Miss Bella Wilfer and her poor little down-trodden " Pa " in *Our Mutual Friend*. Mr. Weller never wholly gives up his parental authority and that sense of superior wisdom that width and age must confer. At the same time he recognises in his son certain intellectual qualities, in particular a power of bold decision and a fluency of utterance, which he cannot himself claim. He is not afraid to reproach Sam for having been bamboozled by Job Trotter and so having tarnished the family escutcheon in the matter of gammon, a reproof which Sam receives with a very proper humility. At the same time he realises that he himself shows some weakness in respect to the red-nosed man. Discipline must be maintained, and he makes the best of a bad job by pointing out that Sam is not a married man and that when he is he will understand much that is now hidden from him. But when Sam makes his tremendous declaration that if he owned the Marquis of Granby he would poison Mr. Stiggins's rum and water, Mr. Weller gives up the struggle and admits that here is a grandeur of conception that is beyond him. He " bestows upon his son a look of deep unspeakable admiration."

In many ways Mr. Weller appears wonderfully docile. In the matter of his wife's will, for instance, he submits to a most undutiful speech by Sam who, having first called him a lunatic, accuses him of preaching—a most offensive word—on subjects that he does not understand. Mr. Weller is as philosophical as he had been when Mrs. Weller broke his pipe. "Wery good, Sammy," he replies mildly, "I'm quite agreeable to anythin' as vill hexpedite business." At the same time he will not yield beyond a certain point. On that point he is adamant : " Nobody but Pell as a legal adwiser."

On that occasion Sam said that he did not want any one else, and so there was no further argument, but generally speaking, save only on the admissibility of an alibi, Mr. Weller, having made his protest and asserted his authority, surrenders in the end. This is noticeable in the discussion as to the Valentine. He objects violently at first to the whole project but allows himself to be mollified. He gives way over " circumwented," he admits against his better literary judgment the too abrupt conclusion, and finally, having declaimed against the lowness of poetry and even hinted that some of

Sam's prose is too poetical, he cannot prevent the ending with a verse.

Mr. Weller is like a good many other elderly fathers who have grown-up sons. In general they regard themselves as holding the reins of government and have no intention of giving them up, but when it comes to any particular instance they realise that their sons have superior qualities, and by allowing those qualities free exercise they will save themselves a good deal of trouble. Nevertheless they will not fully delegate their powers and put in a face-saving suggestion now and then, which rather confuses matters than otherwise. Mr. Weller takes Sam with him for the interview with Mr. Pickwick on the subject of his eleven.hundred pounds. He has sternly declared beforehand that he is going to do the talking, and then, finding it beyond his capacity, turns upon Sam and accuses him of unfilial conduct in not helping him out. Sam thereupon begins to unfold the plan and Mr. Weller is appeased and says, " I didn't mean to speak harsh to you, Sammy ; " but soon he thinks that Sam is not getting on fast enough and breaks in upon him with some impatience. It must fairly be owned that Sam has now and then a good deal to put up with.

On at least two occasions Sam, realising that there is to be no delegation of authority, takes the law into his own hands. The first is that of the meeting of the Brick Lane Branch of the United Grand Junction Ebenezer Temperance Association. Mr. Weller is engaged in dancing round Mr. Stiggins with pugilistic intent and Sam, having in vain remonstrated on the unwisdom of this conduct, seizes the old gentleman round the waist and hauls him out. He follows the same course at the Bank when Mr. Weller sturdily refuses to conduct his business under the letter " W " when it should have been " V." Sam drags him to the counter and holds him there till he has signed the required documents, nor is there any reason to believe that Mr. Weller resented such treatment or lost any of his monumental calm. Probably on considering the matter afterwards he knew his son had been right even as did Mr.

Pickwick, with whom Sam had sometimes, as in Dodson & Fogg's office, to adopt similar peremptory measures. Is it perhaps too fanciful to see in one respect a certain resemblance between Mr. Pickwick and Mr. Weller? Both had a grand and beautiful simplicity; neither had lost the insatiable curiosity of childhood nor its sense of pervading romance. Sam was the knowing one who recognised that the gentlemen behind the counter at the Bank were nothing more interesting than clerks. His father had the far more romantic notion that they were reduced counsels. When he was assured that they were not, his imagination took another leap and he asked one of the typical questions of an intelligent child, to which the most knowing of grown-ups can give no answer. " Wot are they all a eatin' ham sangwidges for ? "

There is one remark which it is only fair to Sam to make. He has many superb scenes on his own account, whereas, except for a single brief one, we never see Mr. Weller unless his son is there skilfully to play up to him and lead him on. There is, however, one important exception, namely the account of Mrs. Weller's death. Dickens was only too good at death-bed scenes, and they were metaphorically conducted in the full blaze of the footlights with the theatre orchestra playing slow music. But Mrs. Weller's death mercifully takes place off the stage and by a rare piece of art it is left to her husband to describe it. This he does so simply and movingly and yet so utterly in character that this short passage of little more than a page is, I vow, worth all the Little Nells and Little Pauls, the Little Jos and Little Johnnys in the world. Sam plays his part of auditor and consoler to similar perfection, and in that scene, as I venture to think the greatest in all the book, there is not a pin to choose between them. And it is all the better because it ends by our laughing, with the tears still in our eyes, at Mr. Weller's final and complete revenge on the red-nosed man. That time Sam does not hold his father back.

Our true farewell to Mr. Weller and Sam comes with the last pages of Pickwick ; but since they reappeared for a space in *Master Humphrey's Clock*, and since many people who know them very well have yet never met them in their brief renascence a word or two of postscript may be added. *Master Humphrey's Clock*, which appeared in 1839, represented a design of Dickens whereby he should provide in weekly numbers various short stories, essays and papers. Other people were also to contribute —if there was room for them—but Dickens really conceived the project in Chesterton's words, " as a kind of vast multiplication of himself." Unfortunately he did not think of himself on this occasion as the writer of a serial story and that was the one form in which the public passionately wanted him. Master Humphrey was a kindly old recluse living in a suburb of London ; he had a small circle of friends, in the nature of a club, who posted their communications to it behind an old clock. Thence these papers were periodically extracted and read to the assembled company. As soon as the public discovered that there was to be no serial story the sales fell off alarmingly, and thereupon Dickens turned *The Old Curiosity Shop*, originally intended as a short story, into one of full length. All the cumbrous machinery of the club was quietly shed, even as it had been in *Pickwick*, and the clock ticked on merrily.

Before that, however, Mr. Pickwick had been invited to join the club and had duly weighed in with his story. When he comes to pay a visit to Master Humphrey he is accompanied not only by the faithful Sam but also by his father, who has constituted himself an additional bodyguard and carries a lantern to light Mr. Pickwick on his way. The restoration to life is not a success, and I fancy Dickens himself was conscious of it. Indeed, if it be not profane to say so, any clever writer, who knew the right catch-words, could have done the thing nearly as well as Dickens did it himself. Mr. Weller, who according to Mr. Pickwick has grown rather more opinionated and talkative, declaims against the railway as " unconstitootional and an inwader of privileges." He narrates his terrifying experience in having been locked into a railway carriage with a widow who screamed in all the tunnels. He returns to the law of probate with the story of Bill Blinder, the ostler, who chalks his will inside the lid of a corn-chest ; but somehow it will not do ; the first fine rapture has gone and neither author nor readers can whip themselves into the right mood.

There is perhaps one exception in Mr. Weller's pride in his grandson. " Samivel Veller, sir," he says, " has conferred upon me the ancient title o' grandfather vich has long laid doormouse, and wos s'posed to be nearly hextinct in our family." He tells Sam to relate an anecdote of young Tony and when Sam bashfully refuses, he tells it himself. It appears that the young Tony smokes a pipe and plays with a quart pot, utterly refusing a mere pint, and says, " Now I'm grandfather." There is here something of the old pleasant, and touching quality, but even here—perhaps it is our fault—Dickens seems no longer to be bubbling with fresh and beautiful invention ; he is, rather wearily, imitating himself. We feel as we do in seeing a friend off at a station. We have said our good-byes, and then as the train still lingers we linger with it, but the culminating moment of emotion has gone. Our friend has no more to say to us, and must fall back on commonplaces as to past delights enjoyed together. We are all wretched and embarrassed and wish the parting well over.

I have re-opened *Master Humphrey's Clock* to write my postscript. I now mean to shut it once and for all, and I solemnly beg those who have never read it not to make the experiment. If any one insists, then let him forget it as soon as possible, even as we try to forget the sight of some beloved old home that has changed hands and is now disfigured by other people's furniture. Mr. Weller still lives at an excellent public house near Shooter's Hill, where he is, very properly, reverenced as an oracle. There let him dwell for ever, one of the great, static, ageless figures of literature !

Portrait of a Dog of Character

WHEN he first appeared, scarcely a foot long, his brow furrowed with loose wrinkles, as if he bore all the cares of the world upon him, Rufus looked like a bloodhound on an extremely reduced scale. Then he grew and grew longitudinally and emerged from the process as a dachshund of highly respectable pedigree and a pleasing brown colour. From his unpopularity with the other dogs in the village it is believed that they do not recognise him as a fellow-dog and take him for some kind of rat.

He is above all a dog of character, perhaps, as we are sometimes tempted to think, too much character. He is also a dog of principle. His whole life is conducted on the grand principle of not doing what anybody else wants him to. As I write I can hear him whining because his mistress has gone out. I know, without troubling to look, that he is either sitting at the top of the stairs and refusing, despite all commands, entreaties or blandishments, to come down, or sitting at the bottom of the stairs and refusing to come up. If he is more obstinate and capricious in any one respect than in any other it is in this matter of sitting. He sometimes likes to sit on my lap, because it is the longest in the house ; it gives his own length ample scope and there is a comfortable resting place for his nose between my knees. If I invite him to come up he brusquely declines, but if I am reading a large book or a newspaper, which renders his presence inconvenient, he insists. He likes an arm-chair or the corner of a sofa, when somebody else proposes to sit there. On being turned out he gives the rival claimant a very ugly look, but if the chair is empty and he is urged, with much patting of the cushions, to take it, he remains firmly recumbent on the floor. He is as little amenable to a policy of appeasement as he is to one of force, having a capacity for making himself at any moment a heavy lump of immovable obduracy. He is at once a dictator and a passive resister. True when appeasement takes the form of open, unashamed bribery he occasionally condescends. The despairing formula, " See what I've got for you," is not without effect ; he knows the implied promise will be fulfilled, and, while doubtless feeling a contempt for those having so fatuous a sense of honour, is not above taking advantage of it.

If he can be induced to believe that he is doing what he wants and not what you want, there is hope. I discovered this by maddening experience when letting him out for his last little walk at night. On these occasions he plunges into the garden with a great show of energy and much barking at nothing in particular. Especially on moonlight nights he bays the moon in an impressive and formidable manner. At first I was so foolish that, after allowing him what I deemed a reasonable time, I used to whistle and call for him with rising impatience. This was fatal. He would draw so near that I could dimly detect a small black shadow on the grass and then with the obvious if unspoken words " Sold again," he would prance away into the night and soon his barks could be heard faint and far away, from the remotest point of the garden. Now I have learnt to remain unseen and whatever the provocation to give no sign. Thereupon he concludes that I am no sportsman and the game is not worth playing ; so after a few perfunctory or token barks he comes galloping in again and rushes upstairs to bed. The air of extreme complacency with which he does it is sometimes a little hard to bear, but there is so much to be thankful for that irritation would be absurd. After all, though he may not think so, I have, in however paltry and despicable a manner, won the game.

Once indoors it must be admitted that Rufus goes to bed in a sufficiently docile spirit. In fact, he sometimes puts himself to bed prematurely, I can only suppose because he is not expected to. He has, however, one caprice that must be regarded. Now and again, having tucked himself up under the blanket in his basket, he feels too hot, and so keeps his head covered while lowering his hinder end on to the floor, rather in the attitude of one saying his prayers before retiring, and thus presenting the singular appearance of half a dog. Should any kindly but misguided person try to help the other half in he is greeted with furious growls. These, being interpreted, mean that this is a matter which a gentleman must be allowed to decide for himself ; when he has cooled down he will put himself in again, but it must be at his own time. He is equally decided as to when he wants to get up and go for his early bark. He comes into my room with a smiling and benignant air, as of one greeting the morn, and generally at the moment when I am tying my shoe laces, a process he tries to accelerate by licking my hands. If, however, this early promise is not fulfilled and I am not ready as soon as I ought to be, he changes his mind and burrows his way under a neighbouring eiderdown, saying very clearly, " You've had your chance and have not taken it. Very well, I am perfectly comfortable and you can now wait till I choose to come."

Despite these constant assertions of his independence, Rufus is in some ways almost pathetically dependent on human society. He loves hunting for rabbits ; he has even once caught a very little one, when he was divided between pride

250

and shame, not being quite sure that he had done the right thing. Yet though he has his happy hunting ground, where he can pass many interesting hours, he needs a chaperon to take him there, somebody to whom he can return at intervals to report progress. An empty garden seems to induce an unbearable feeling of solitude. Similarly, at the sight of anybody with letters in his hand he makes an instant dash down the lane to the pillar box, leading the procession like a herald. Otherwise, he seldom ventures into the lane by himself, although, having feudal notions as to the magnificence of his family, he is convinced that the lane is part of its estate, and resents the presence of other people there.

He is essentially a one-man, or rather one-woman dog in his adoration of his mistress, but he has a strong family feeling. He likes it to be an united family ; he cannot bear any members of it to go away, and is apt to deplore their absence by whinings of vague discontent. In order to satisfy him that there is no help for it, he is held up to see through a glass in the hall door the departure of the car. This he finds so exquisitely painful that at the last moment he turns his head away and gazes with miserable eyes into the gloomy cavern of the hall. Yet, having got it over, he gallops *ventre à terre* for the kitchen where consolation for the parting is traditionally administered. His journeys in the car are enjoyed not so much for their own sake, since once safely in his haven he immediately goes to sleep, but because the family must be kept together, and he is one of the family. Should any one get out at a shop, he wakes up and looks out of the window in a state of acute anxiety. When the prodigal shopper returns Rufus greets him with profuse and comprehensive lickings and " goes mad dog " as far as the limits of the car will permit. It must be owned that his loyalty is beyond question.

He is a sportsman rather than a game-player, and if he is on the trail of a real or imaginary rabbit will treat a golf ball with disdain. Yet, although golf balls are but second best and he knows them to be forbidden, he cannot always resist them.

In themselves they are not exciting, but the carrying one off, when temptation has proved too strong, provides a delightful game, an intoxicating opportunity for the defiance of authority. The shouts of " Drop it " go straight to his head so that he races round and round in circles, mocking his pursuers. It is an alarming game to be sure, for it is apparent that the owner of the golf ball is really annoyed and not merely pretending, but a measure of terror is as the spice of life. There are, for example, few things more terrifying than a waste-paper basket advancing towards you in a slow and infinitely threatening manner, so that in the intervals of brave rushes and piercing yelps, you must now and then retreat behind the writing-table to a city of refuge.

An old lawn tennis ball provides healthy amusement, but it has not the golf ball's charm of being illicit. Rufus has not, I fear, the whole-souled enthusiasm of the true ball-player. There was once another dachshund, an occasional visitor to the house, who had the genuine passion. He remembered from previous visits the exact drawer in the drawing-room in which a ball was kept and the instant he arrived took up his position and gazed at it prayerfully, if need be for hours. He was the single-minded athlete whereas Rufus is by comparison the intellectual who does not disdain an occasional game for air and exercise. Indoors he prefers to any ball his large india-rubber biscuit. This is an heirloom in the house, bought years ago for Rufus's predecessors, but they never really cared for it. He has discovered its merits as productive of a tug-of-war game. The rules are simple. You take your biscuit and drop it with a loud thump on the floor at the feet of your proposed antagonist. He, if he agrees to play, takes hold of one side of the biscuit in his fingers. You take hold of the other in your mouth and then you pull, encouraging yourself by horrific growls. After a while you let go : the biscuit is then thrown for you to the further end of the room. You pursue it snarling, and bring it back. And so on for ever, or as long as the other party will play, but it is very odd how quickly people get tired of the most enchanting games. Sometimes you get so excited that you cannot help breaking out into a bark, but for some mysterious reason those who are amused at your growls cannot abide your barks : so you had better not.

This question of restraining your barks also arises when you do one of your two tricks, called " Sit up and ask for it." The sitting up is easy, but the asking for it by means of a sad little strangled noise between a grunt and a squeak is exceedingly difficult. Your throat works convulsively and sometimes no sound will come forth and at others it will turn into a bark, when you get no piece of cake and have to begin all over again. It is particularly annoying to be invited to take part in such tomfoolery when you are still half-asleep before a nice fire. Sometimes you positively decline to do so, at any rate until you are more awake, thinking that independence is preferable even to cake. The other trick of " Trust," though obviously silly and irritating, is quite simple. You stand rigidly over the reward where it lies on the floor and keep your eye on it, but some people do take an unkindly long time in saying " Paid for." That is putting too high a price on virtue's head. There is a third accomplishment called " Shake hands," but it is not an easy one for those having such long noses and such short legs. The two are apt to get confused and this trick is now almost obsolete.

People presumably get the kind of dog they deserve. I do not know how Rufus would have turned out if he had belonged to a family with stricter notions of discipline. There are those, and admittedly they are rewarded with adoration as deep as any, who do not believe in what they call spoiling, who repress any too demonstrative behaviour with a stern " Down," who disapprove of dogs in arm-chairs and indeed scarcely believe that the house is their proper sphere. Perhaps Rufus would have profited by a more Spartan upbringing, but I find it hard to believe that he would not generally have got his own way. It is a futile speculation, for he certainly gets it now. He has many seductive methods of signifying his wishes and can do much by a look into which he infuses considerable pathos. But he is not wholly dependent on these pleasing arts and has other methods in reserve. He has discovered that a restless roaming about the room with perpetual glances at the door is sooner or later successful. It may at first produce furious objurgations and cries of " Basket," even perhaps a slap, but much dripping wears away a stone ; people are always ready to buy peace and quiet at a price, and the door opens at last. The whine too is a most effective weapon. It begins plaintively and swells gradually into a low but penetrating moan which fills the house. It was unfortunately discovered early in his life that the singing of " Polly put the kettle on " caused him to respond with a melancholy song of his own. This was deemed an agreeable parlour trick and was encouraged accordingly. He has since turned the accomplishment to all too good account and has become a perfect Hound of the Baskervilles calling for his prey. It is not always certain what he wants ; sometimes his ululations seem to come only from a sudden conviction of the drabness of his life and the stupidity of everybody else ; but an invitation to come in and sit before the fire is often, though not always, grudgingly accepted by way of apology.

I suppose everybody has at some time or another had a disquieting experience in reading a novel. There is in it some character, of detestable weaknesses, in which the reader instantly recognises his own. He almost comes to believe that the author took him as his model. I confess that Rufus has sometimes in this way made me feel acutely uneasy, wondering whether I do not, like him, get my own way by a resolute helplessness and a persistent appeal to the better feelings of others. Is it not by these base means that I get parcels done up, buttons sewn on and even telephone messages sent for me ? If I do not positively whine I may employ subtler methods. My mind misgives me very much. Rufus knows that we shall always be fools and he will never be a gentleman. Here is a horrid similarity. He appears to me to have all my most unattractive characteristics. It is in such moments that he appears almost a tiresome little dog.

" Yet the worst of it is," as Sir Peter remarked of Lady Teazle, " I doubt I love her or I should never bear all this." Rufus contradicts all our humours and drives us sometimes to the point of frenzy and yet he is unquestionably lovable. He has on occasions the prettiest way with him. By a single adroit submission or a flattering lick he can make up for everything, and since he is not naturally yearning or senti-mental, there is a greater value in his rare caresses. After some prolonged whinings in the passage I have now let him into my room. I am writing, on a pad on my knee. He is clever enough to know that if he comes to sit there I cannot go on, but he protests that he wants to come. The outcome is certain ; the stronger will must prevail. In fact, he has now jumped up, and I have to stop.